D1176000

By Gavin Edwards

The Tao of Bill Murray

Can I Say: Living Large, Cheating Death,
and Drums Drums Drums
(by Travis Barker with Gavin Edwards)

Last Night at the Viper Room:
River Phoenix and the Hollywood He Left Behind

VJ: The Unplugged Adventures of MTV's First Wave
*(by Nina Blackwood, Mark Goodman, Alan Hunter,
and Martha Quinn, with Gavin Edwards)*

Is Tiny Dancer Really Elton's Little John?:
Music's Most Enduring Mysteries, Myths,
and Rumors Revealed

Deck the Halls with Buddy Holly:
And Other Misheard Christmas Lyrics

When a Man Loves a Walnut:
And Even More Misheard Lyrics

He's Got the Whole World in His Pants:
And More Misheard Lyrics

'Scuse Me While I Kiss This Guy:
And Other Misheard Lyrics

The Tao of Bill Murray

The Tao of Bill Murray

Real-Life Stories
of Joy, Enlightenment,
and Party Crashing

by Gavin Edwards

Illustrations by R. Sikoryak

CENTURY

1 3 5 7 9 10 8 6 4 2

Century
20 Vauxhall Bridge Road
London SW1V 2SA

Century is part of the Penguin Random House group of companies
whose addresses can be found at global.penguinrandomhouse.com.

Copyright © Gavin Edwards 2016

Gavin Edwards has asserted his right under the Copyright,
Designs and Patents Act, 1988, to be identified as
the author of this work.

First published in 2016 by Century

www.penguin.co.uk

A CIP catalogue record for this book is available
from the British Library.

ISBN 9781780894362

Typeset in 11/16pt New Baskerville ITC Std
Printed and bound in Great Britain by Clays Ltd, St Ives plc

Penguin Random House is committed to a sustainable future for
our business, our readers and our planet. This book is made
from Forest Stewardship Council® certified paper.

For Rob Sheffield,
the light that never goes out

Contents

Author's Note

Bill Murray has shown up everywhere, from the sideline of the 1986 NFC Championship Game, wearing an old-fashioned leather football helmet, to the Mediterranean island of Yeronisos, volunteering as a digger on a 2006 NYU archaeological expedition.

Because everything seems possible when it comes to Bill, the man has attracted more than the usual number of fabulists. For years now, inventing Bill myths has been one of the Internet's favorite games. (In case you were wondering, Bill isn't running for president and he doesn't actually have the contractual right to steal the master tapes of the Wu-Tang Clan album *Once Upon a Time in Shaolin* from Martin Shkreli.) But one of the beautiful things about Bill Murray is that there are more than enough staggering true anecdotes to fill a book. This book, for example.

While working on *The Tao of Bill Murray,* I conducted dozens of interviews with Bill's friends, collaborators, and acquaintances, and consulted countless published reports. If you want to know more about my sources for any particular story in the book, check out the section in the back that's cleverly titled "Sources."

Other writers have compared an encounter with Bill to a visit from an angel. While the man's temperament is more profane than sacred, I feel blessed that before I started writing this book, he answered some of my questions about his approach to existence. My conclusions, like any errors in the following pages, are my own; Bill gets the credit if you find inspiration in his extraordinary life.

The Tao of Bill Murray

Introduction

YOU ARE STANDING ON A CORNER IN NEW YORK City, waiting to cross the street. Lost in thought, you aren't paying much attention to the world around you. Suddenly a man puts his hands over your eyes and says, "Guess who?"

Nobody's played this game with you since elementary school. It would be alarming, except that the voice is familiar. You can't quite place the speaker, but you're pretty sure he's a friend.

You whip around and see, much to your surprise . . . international film star Bill Murray. He is taller than you expected and his shirt is wrinkled. You sputter, groping for words, unable to process the unlikelihood of this situation. Bill grins, leans in close, and quietly says, "No one will ever believe you."

Variations on this story began to circulate widely around 2010. Sometimes it happened in New York, sometimes in Austin, Texas, or Charleston, South Carolina. Sometimes

Bill wasn't blindfolding people with his fingers—instead, he was stealing a french fry off somebody's plate or grabbing a handful of popcorn from a stranger at a movie theater. But the punch line was always the same, underscoring that this encounter was an eruption of surrealism on an otherwise ordinary day, meant to be enjoyed for a few flickering moments: "No one will ever believe you."

For years, it was unclear whether this was something that Bill Murray actually did, as part of a personal campaign to make the world a better, odder place, or whether it was an urban legend that had grown large enough to have its own zip code. Asked point-blank about it in a magazine interview, Bill artfully managed not to unravel the mystery.

"I've heard about that from a lot of people," he said. "A lot of people. I don't know what to say. There's probably a really *appropriate* thing to say. Something exactly and just perfectly *right*." Bill considered the rhetorical tightrope he was walking, and then he smiled: "But, by God, it sounds crazy, doesn't it? Just so crazy and unlikely and unusual?"

In the seventies and eighties Bill starred in comedy blockbusters such as *Ghostbusters, Caddyshack,* and *Groundhog Day.* Just as his success as a wisecracking film star seemed to be dwindling, he reinvented himself with wry, world-weary performances in much-lauded movies like *Rushmore* and *Lost in Translation.* In recent years, however, his fame has seemed almost completely disconnected from his accomplishments as an actor: Bill Murray, according to popular belief, has become the man who will drop by your bachelor party to give a toast, come to your assistance when you're having engine trouble, or crash your party and then wash the dishes. One minute, you might be walking around your hometown with your fiancé, taking engagement photos—the next minute, Bill Murray could be standing in front of you with his shirt over his head, rubbing his belly. If Bill Murray makes a surprise appearance in your own life, you know that no one will ever believe you.

But they should. All those things have happened to actual human beings. There is photographic evidence of Bill doing karaoke with strangers and crashing kickball games. I've spoken with multiple people who had a real-life Bill encounter that ended with those infamous words, "No one will ever believe you." When my friend golfer Dan McLaughlin ran into Bill at the annual Pebble Beach golf tournament, he asked Bill point-blank if that phrase was something he said. "Oh yeah, all the time," Bill confirmed.

It turns out that while it's fun to live in a world where Bill Murray *might* cover the eyes of strangers and *maybe* find other ways to prank the world, it's even better to live in a world where he *really* does these things. The Navajo had Coyote. The Ashanti people of Ghana had Anansi. The Norse had Loki. They're all mythological figures that taught humanity how quick thinking could enliven and enrich the species. Also high on the honor roll: Hermes (ancient Greece), Reynard (France), Bugs Bunny (Looney Tunes). The twenty-first-century U.S.A. has Mr. William Murray, our modern-day trickster god. The fact that he occupies this place in our society means not just that he's willing to engage the universe with freewheeling tomfoolery—it tells us that as a culture, we *need* somebody to embody this spirit of all-American anarchy. If celebrities have taken the place of demigods, living out myths in the pages of tabloid magazines, then Bill Murray is our philosopher-clown.

A couple of years ago, I interviewed actress Melissa McCarthy at an Italian restaurant in Los Angeles. When she told me about her first encounter with Bill Murray—in the makeup trailer for the 2014 movie *St. Vincent*—she remembered, "He was really funny and so distracting that I couldn't even be nervous. He's the most present person I have ever met. He's not trying to alter himself for the situation—he's absolutely in his shoes. If I could do that ten percent more in my life, I'd be a better, cooler person."

I confided, "I feel like Bill Murray is secretly teaching us how to live."

"I have those theories myself," she said, her voice falling to a whisper. "You can't read him. It's all part of the magic."

One night after *St. Vincent* wrapped, McCarthy and her husband, Ben Falcone, had two choices for an evening: They could do practical household chores, or they could sit in their backyard "and stare at nothing and talk about nonsense." Consciously trying to model their lives on what Bill would do, they chose the backyard nonsense—and had a wonderful time. "Thank you, Bill Murray," she testified, "for making me choose randomly and not practically."

If you want to learn life lessons from Bill Murray, however, it helps first to know how he's led his own life.

. . .

William James Murray was born on September 21, 1950, in Evanston, Illinois, a suburb of Chicago; he grew up in nearby Wilmette. He was the fifth of nine children for Edward and Lucille Murray. Money was tight; the kids slept three to a room. "In a large family," Bill said years later, "you have to learn to get along." Coming before Billy, as he was known as a kid: Edward, Brian, Nancy, and Peggy. Coming after him: Laura, Andrew, John, and Joel. When you're the middle child in a large family, it's hard to get attention from your parents. Billy figured out early that a surefire way of doing that was to make his father laugh. One of his most vivid childhood memories is the time he stood on his chair at the dinner table, doing a Jimmy Cagney impression. When Billy fell off, he smacked his head painfully on the table leg. Through his tears, he saw his father laughing, and the pain seemed worth it.

"No drunken audience could ever compare to working our dinner table," Bill remembered. "If you got a laugh, it was like . . . whoa! It was like winning a National Merit Scholarship." Three of Bill's brothers went into show business, the most successful of them being Brian, who works under the name Brian Doyle-Murray. His older sister Nancy became a nun—they called her the "white sheep" of the Murray family—and still ended up as a performer, touring the world with a one-woman show about a fourteenth-century holy figure, *St. Catherine of Siena: A Woman for Our Times.*

Bill long believed that his sense of humor was shaped

by his father, who worked as a salesman for a lumber company: He was severe and dry but also funny, in the vein of Bob Newhart. Much later in life, Bill's siblings informed him that his antic humor actually channeled his mother. "She's completely out of control," he said. "I just never noticed it."

It wasn't long before Bill was acting for an audience other than the Murray family. At St. Joseph's grade school, he played the innkeeper in a Christmas pageant; attending Loyola Academy (the largest Jesuit high school in the United States), he appeared in *The Caine Mutiny* and then auditioned for a production of *The Music Man*—largely, he said, because there were girls there. He got a role as a dancer and discovered there were other perks to a life in show business: "Showfolk don't have school nights but rather nights when rehearsals end early and the time till eleven-thirty is filled riding in your co-trouper's daddy's Cadillac, drinking stolen gin out of eight-ounce 7-Up bottles." The 1960s were a thrilling and problematic time to be a teenager. Bill recalled, "I had the misfortune of reaching adolescence at a time when the world turned upside-down, and I somehow had to represent the changing society to my parents—with limited success. I was speaking for the entire culture, everyone from Tim Leary to the Airplane."

Bill was a huge sports fan: "It was where I was first able to put an enormous amount of enthusiasm and energy as a child." One seed of that passion was planted at a young age, when his brother Brian (older than Bill by five years) took him to Wrigley Field for the first time. As they approached their seats, Brian covered Bill's eyes—and when they got closer, Brian lifted his hands, letting Bill get the full impact of Wrigley, from the lush green grass to the ivy-covered walls. Young Bill thought it was the most beautiful place he had ever seen; after his eyes were unexpectedly covered, his perceptions of the world had permanently changed.

Like his older brothers, Bill worked as a caddie at the Indian Hill Club in the neighboring town of Winnetka, laying the foundation for a lifelong obsession with golf. The worst part of the job: his time as a "shag boy." In an era before driving ranges, Bill would go out on the greens while a golfer hit a bucket of balls at him. Bill's job would be to recover the balls, but if he didn't pay attention, one might hit him in the head. He learned a lot about adult behavior by paying attention to how the golfers treated him, on the spectrum from solicitous to rude. He's described the fundamental lessons of that first job as "show up, keep up, and shut up."

In the final days of 1967, Bill's father died from diabetes; he was forty-six, and Bill was just seventeen. After the funeral, all nine Murray children, plus their mother, Lucille, packed into a limousine, overwhelmed by grief. Punchy and exhausted, they started laughing hysterically, making fun of everyone else walking out of the church. "The driver didn't know what to make of it," Bill said. "It was like the left-field bleachers in Wrigley Field." Money was even tighter after Edward's death, so Lucille went to work, laboring in the mailroom of a medical-supply company, and Bill took on hours at a local pizza parlor to help support the family.

Bill was bright, but he had always been an indifferent student, more interested in playing sports and mouthing off than studying. Nevertheless, after he graduated, some of his friends went to Regis College in Denver, and Bill went along, registering as a premed major. "I was not really college material," Bill reminisced. "I didn't know how to study, but I liked the lifestyle. You could dress any way you wanted. I was wearing pajamas and a sport coat to school and pajamas and loafers to formal events." He described himself as "one of the first hip dressers," particularly liking the combination of a cowboy hat and a long army coat.

Bill's primary extracurricular activity, other than partying: He traveled around the country, dealing top-notch Jamaican marijuana by the kilo. This put money in his pocket; it also gave him an opportunity to be funny. He would come back to Denver and tell friends stories about the various characters he had met on his travels or about misadventures like getting busted and fingerprinted but being set free when the small-town cops lost the evidence.

He wasn't so lucky, however, on his twentieth birthday, when he was going through O'Hare Airport in Chicago. He had tried to get on a TWA flight; when he was denied for lack of ID, he snottily retorted, "That's too bad. I wanted to get on 'cause I got two bombs in my suitcase." Even in 1970, this got the attention of law enforcement. Bill walked away and tried to stash his suitcase in a locker but had no loose change—so when he was arrested, he still had the luggage. His suitcase was searched, and Bill didn't have any bombs—but he did have five bricks of weed, about eight and a half pounds, worth roughly twenty thousand dollars. "It was stupid, but I guess I was turning myself in," Bill said.

Bill did take pride in one cool-headed action during his bust: He ate a personal check that a customer had given him, protecting the guy from arrest. The incident made the *Chicago Tribune;* Bill was convicted but got probation (lucky at the time, inconceivable now). Soon after, he dropped out of school, where he hadn't been liking his fellow premed students anyway.

Bill moved back home and tried to figure out what he was going to do with his life. He spent a couple of years walking the streets after midnight, sleeping late, and drifting from one odd job to the next: landscaping, surveying, hauling concrete blocks. "There was no job that really held my interest," he said. "It was sort of a lonely thing, because I really wanted my mother's approval, but what she needed wasn't what I was delivering."

He began hanging around the legendary Second City theater in Chicago, where Brian had joined the comedy troupe, and eventually Bill summoned up the nerve to audition. After some false starts in the Second City improv workshops, he made it onto the main stage, joining the troupe the same week as John Candy and acting alongside John Belushi, Harold Ramis, and Gilda Radner. His mentor was the venerated acting coach Del Close, who taught him to be fearless about failing onstage: "You've gotta go out there and improvise and you've gotta be completely unafraid to die. You've got to be able to take a chance to die. And you have to die lots." Murray says that all his Second City training boils down to one simple acting lesson: "If you make the other actors look good, you'll look good."

Bill's self-penned biography for the Second City was an early draft of his smart-ass persona: "Bill Murray, the fifth of nine children, is currently casting to replace himself in his family. Bill has lots of personal problems, most typically with his employer at The Second City. He is interested in organic foods, ecology, and human relations, but just doesn't have the time. Basically insincere, he hopes his experience in theatre, movies, and television can perhaps get him work as a *Playgirl* centerfold."

Bill started off by replacing Brian (who had just left the troupe) in scripted sketches and flailing through bad improvisations but soon emerged as a Second City star, known for a wide range of characters, including proto-versions of Carl Spackler (the groundskeeper in *Caddyshack*) and Nick the Lounge Singer (later seen on *Saturday Night Live*). Bill seemed to be dangerous onstage—some evenings more literally than others, like the time he jumped into the crowd and physically assaulted a heckler. He also made a habit of not being at the theater fifteen minutes before curtain, or even at the moment the show started—the theater would leave the back door open and he would always show up in time for his first entrance.

"There's a charming assholeness to Bill, and it's how he really has gotten through life," remembered Betty Thomas, now a successful film director, then a fellow member of the Second City company. "That was how I thought of him, as this charming, always seducing, assholey kind of guy. But asshole in the sense of old-fashioned asshole. Like, a jerk willing to make a fool of himself—willing to do anything in order to get the girl. And there's something admirable about that, and there's something that makes you want to punch somebody like that."

In 1974, Belushi relocated to New York City, became a producer on *The National Lampoon Radio Hour,* and encouraged the Second City ensemble to follow him. Bill hadn't been close with Belushi, but when he moved east, Belushi hired him for the radio program and the theatrical *National Lampoon Show.* When that show went on tour, the two of them were roommates, hanging out and drinking Rolling Rock. Bill grabbed any acting work he could find, no matter how improbable; that included a gig as Johnny Storm, aka the Human Torch, on a *Fantastic Four* radio show that dramatized old Stan Lee scripts. In 1975, Bill auditioned for Dick Ebersol, Lorne Michaels, and a crew of writers, who were casting for a new late-night comedy program on NBC, *Saturday Night Live.* He was beat out for the final male spot in the cast by Dan Aykroyd (also a Second City alumnus). Michaels was leaning toward Bill, but Ebersol thought Aykroyd had greater range.

Instead, Bill ended up on the other show named *Saturday Night Live*—the one that forced Michaels's program to be known as just *Saturday Night* in its first season. The ABC program was called *Saturday Night Live with Howard Cosell,* and it featured the abrasive sportscaster Cosell as ringmaster of an old-fashioned variety show. "We were on with

the Chinese acrobats and elephants," Bill said. The program was a huge bomb and got canceled after eighteen episodes. Bill moved out to California to work with the pioneering video collective called TVTV—but returned to New York in January 1977, filling the hole in the cast of *Saturday Night Live* (the good one, which had been an immediate success) after Chevy Chase left in the middle of its second season.

Bill was initially reluctant to sign on with *SNL:* He had remained friendly with both Belushi and Aykroyd, and he had seen up close how sudden stardom fed their egos and their destructive tendencies. Bill concluded, "You've got to say okay, I have to cut these guys some slack for a year and a half until they calm down. You can't give them more than two years. Two years—then they've got a problem." Nevertheless, he signed on to the hottest show on television.

But as the junior member of the Not Ready for Prime Time Players, Bill found that he was getting few opportunities. The writers were coming up with sketches for the established actors, not the new guy, so Bill was spending his Saturday nights filling out the ensemble as the second cop or the second FBI man, trying to make an impression beyond "disgruntled guy with acne scars." During his sixth show, on March 19, 1977, Bill made an appeal to the audience. Wearing a red sweater and looking young and overwhelmed, he spoke directly into the camera: "I don't think I'm making it on the show," he said. "I'm a funny guy, but I haven't been so funny on the show." It was a scripted comedic bit rooted in truth: Bill even name-checked all eight of his siblings ("It's no concern of yours whether or not they *need* the money I make") and mentioned how his father had died when Bill was just seventeen. "People always said to me, 'Aw, you'll never grow up to be as funny as your dad.' And now he's not around to see me be not as funny as him."

After that sketch, Bill got more of the spotlight on *Saturday Night Live:* as the unctuous entertainer Nick the Lounge Singer (most famous for singing the *Star Wars* theme with lyrics: "Star Wars! Nothing but Star Wars!"), as *Family Feud* host Richard Dawson ("Hello, everybody. I hope you're as excited as I am pretending to be!"), as a showbiz correspondent on "Weekend Update" (his catchphrase: "I'm sorry, but that's the way I feel. Now, get outta here, I mean it"). A common thread through the roles was the characters' insincerity. Bill's work on *SNL* was an ongoing vivisection of phoniness, especially in show business. He was romantically involved with fellow cast member Gilda Radner, and their affection came through in the "nerds" sketches they did, where two teenage geeks transformed their confusing attraction for each other into awkward insults.

After starring in *The Blues Brothers,* Aykroyd and Belushi left *Saturday Night Live* before its fifth season, making Bill the biggest remaining star—and the biggest remaining ego. Tina Fey, who became an *SNL* star and head writer decades later, said that Michaels developed a philosophy of talent management from those early seasons: "He's told me that if you have one actor that's a problem, if that actor were not there, then one of the other existing actors would rise up and become that problem. Chevy and John Belushi were difficult—when they left, Bill Murray rose up and would yell at people." Michaels's conclusion, via Fey: "Talent is sometimes crazy and there's nothing you can do. If they're really talented, you let them be that way."

At the end of the fifth season, with their contracts expiring, the remaining cast (and Michaels) left the show en masse: They were burned out by the pace of live TV and eager to follow Aykroyd and Belushi to Hollywood. With his time at Second City and *SNL,* Bill had completed his apprenticeship. Nothing he did in show business would ever seem quite as hard. Bill reflected, "On a movie, they'll say, 'All right, we're only going to have three minutes to get this coat off and get you in the other shirt.' And I just start laughing. Three minutes? In three minutes I can take off a shirt, put on a wig, a hat, a fat stomach, an enormous raincoat, galoshes, soak my head, take a shower, and be covered with soap and walk out and talk in another language."

In 1981, Bill married his girlfriend Margaret "Mickey" Kelly: Despite her reluctance (she just wanted to go out for Mexican food), they drove through the desert from Los Angeles to Las Vegas and got hitched on Super Bowl Sunday at 4:30 A.M. They had started dating as teenagers in Wilmette and been in an on-and-off relationship for over a decade; Kelly had worked as a talent coordinator for *The Tonight Show* and *The Dick Cavett Show.* In 1982, they had their first son, Homer Banks Murray (named after Homer's, an ice cream store in Wilmette, and Cubs great Ernie Banks).

By the time he left *SNL*, Bill had already starred in a couple of movies, including the surprise summer-camp hit *Meatballs*. Ivan Reitman directed that movie, while Harold Ramis punched up the dialogue. Working with either or both of those men, Bill reeled off a string of hits in the early eighties, all of them now comedy classics: *Caddyshack, Stripes, Ghostbusters*. Bill developed an onscreen persona: the wiseass slacker who gets the girl. He also developed an offscreen persona: the actor who shows up late and throws away the script, only to improvise the best scene in the movie.

Reitman remembered, "He would do what was written—he wasn't arrogant about that. But even when he was happy with it, he always hated doing the same punch line more than once or twice, unless he knew it was so great you had to have it there, and then he would keep spinning it different ways to make it better." When he told Bill he needed a straight-up take where the actor believed in the truth of the words in the script, Bill would give it to him—and in return, Reitman would then give Bill a "free one," a take where he could do whatever he liked. "Often, those were kind of spectacular."

This period culminated in *Ghostbusters:* an action-comedy blockbuster about a team of paranormal investigators, cooked up by Dan Aykroyd. (Bill's part was originally intended for Belushi, who died in 1982.) Even before it was filmed, it was a hot property, with multiple studios competing for the distribution rights. Bill correctly predicted that it would be "bigger than *Tootsie* and smaller than *Star Wars.*" He got paid $3 million for *Ghostbusters,* plus points (a percentage of the take, which turned out to be quite valuable). At the same time, Bill was trying to set up an adaptation of W. Somerset Maugham's *The Razor's Edge* at Columbia; he wanted to tackle a role that demanded more of him than sarcasm and wisecracking. When Aykroyd found out, he said, "You tell 'em that they do your movie there and they'll have the GBs." Still impressed by Aykroyd's generosity years later, Bill joked, "Forty-five minutes later we had a caterer."

Bill did fine work in *The Razor's Edge,* demonstrating that he had aptitude as a dramatic actor, but the movie was flawed and got mixed reviews. *Ghostbusters,* however, sold enough tickets to be the second-highest-grossing film of 1984, saturated the airwaves with Ray Parker Jr.'s theme song, and inspired a legion of children to strap on proton packs that Halloween. Bill described *Ghostbusters* as "such a big phenomenon that I felt slightly radioactive."

As the biggest star in *Ghostbusters,* Bill could have followed it up by making any movie he desired. What he decided to do instead was move to France. "I knew that *Ghostbusters* was going to be the biggest thing that ever happened and that being in the United States, with that level of fame, would be destructive for me at that time," he recalled. "If I went to another country, I would be able to hold on to what I value in myself." So he transplanted his family to Paris; while living there, he and Kelly had another son, Luke François Murray.

In Paris, Bill attended the Sorbonne, where he studied French and philosophy. Among the philosophers he was exposed to there: George Gurdjieff, a Greco-Armenian-Russian guru who, before dying in France in 1949, founded the Institute for the Harmonious Development of Man. A central tenet of Gurdjieff's belief system was that most people, even as they lead their waking lives, are actually asleep on the inside. Taking the teaching to heart, Bill started waking people up.

Harold Ramis remembered, "Gurdjieff used to act really irrationally to his students, almost as if trying to teach them object lessons. There's a great story along those lines that Jim Belushi tells about Del Close, the improv teacher: Jim went up to Del once, when he was a young actor, and he said, 'Del, I want you to know that I really, really trust you.' And Del kneed him in the balls, really hard, and asked, 'You still trust me?' Bill was always teaching people lessons like that. If he perceived someone as being too self-important or corrupt in some way that he couldn't stomach, it was his job to straighten them out." Bill never met Gurdjieff, but the guru became as important a teacher for him as Del Close had been.

But mostly, Bill went to the movies. The Cinémathèque Française in Paris was having a retrospective on the history of film, so Bill would go see another black-and-white classic every day—maybe *A Romance of Happy Valley* (a silent 1919 D. W. Griffith film that had been thought lost for decades until a print was discovered in the Soviet Union). "No sound, Russian subtitles," Bill remembered. "I didn't know what they were saying and it destroyed me. How can somebody make *The Love Bug* after they saw this?"

Bill loved life in Paris. Every day at lunchtime, he would stop by a chocolatier: "I was always walking around with a hundred fifty grams of chocolate in my pocket, and offering a piece was a great way to start a conversation." But after six months, he returned to the States. The lure: Ivan Reitman was working on a movie about the Abstract Expressionist painter Mark Rothko and the battles over his estate after his 1970 suicide. Bill became fascinated by the genius of Rothko, but during script revisions, the movie turned into the vapid rom-com *Legal Eagles*. "I mean, really," said Bill, who, disgusted, dropped out of the film.

When Bill was in his mid-thirties, the Murrays settled in the Hudson Valley, just north of New York City. Bill appeared in a Bertolt Brecht play upstate, umpired Little League games, and spent time with his family. Otherwise, Bill worked when he felt like it and stayed out of Los Angeles as much as he could. As he once explained it, "The first day you check in to a hotel in L.A. there's a message under your door. The second day, there's eleven messages under your door. The third day, there's thirty, forty, fifty, sixty, seventy messages. And I realized that they just want fresh blood. They. Just. Want. Fresh. Blood. You gotta get the hell out of there."

In early 1986, Bill tried to sidestep the Hollywood machine. He wondered: Could actors, through improvisation, build a story that would end up working as a movie? So he assembled a repertory company, with performers including himself, his brother Brian, Dana Delany, Jami Gertz, Bud Cort, and O-Lan Jones. He flew them out to Chicago to learn improvisation from Del Close—and to attend a Bears game in subzero weather. Soon after, they worked for a few weeks in New York, improvising stories set in a small American hamlet. Brian usually played the mayor or a fire chief; Delany played his wife; Bill adopted the role of a drifter. Then Bill brought the actors out to Los Angeles, trying to interest director Sydney Pollack and screenwriter Steve Kloves in working with them. Kloves wrote thirty pages of a screenplay based on their improvisations and then incurred Bill's displeasure by shifting his attention to his directorial debut, *The Fabulous Baker Boys*. Bill quietly ended the experiment, taking the actors out to lunch and handing each of them an unexpected check for fifteen thousand dollars.

Even if he hadn't succeeded in founding a modern-day Mercury Theatre, Bill still had a lot of Hollywood clout, not least because the powerful Michael Ovitz of CAA was his agent. Over the next decade, Bill made the obligatory *Ghostbusters* sequel and a full range of high-concept comedies: great (*Groundhog Day*), painful (*Scrooged*), and in between (*What About Bob?*). He turned down lots of movies and was surprised to discover how many of them ended up getting made with other actors. He also directed a movie with writer Howard Franklin, *Quick Change*, only to decide that directing was too much work. "What kind of a world is this?" Bill demanded after discovering that the job required late nights in an editing room. "I should be eating veal in a nice restaurant."

For all of Bill's clout, he couldn't stop the world from changing around him. In 1988, his mother, Lucille, died—despite being a grown man, Bill found that he felt like an orphan. Ovitz, his Hollywood protector, retired from CAA to run Disney. And his marriage broke up; he and Kelly separated in 1994 and divorced two years later. "I went through a lot of pain in my divorce," he said. "It made me feel empathy for people I don't even like, because they're going through it." Bill had been having a long-term affair with costume designer Jennifer Butler; he married her in 1997.

Bill similarly lost his moorings in the movie world, even making one film where he costarred with an elephant. In most of Bill's early work, he was a wisenheimer mocking authority figures, whether it was the management of a summer camp or the top brass of the U.S. Army. Bill smirking at the camera communicated his contempt for both the people in charge of Ronald Reagan's America and the people behind the camera. He played out that attitude as far as it would take him, but eventually it wasn't clear what he actually believed in: *Scrooged* facilely suggested that the answer was "Christmas." *Groundhog Day* answered the question best with "enlightenment," but an answer that cosmic seemed beyond the scope of most of Bill's movies. And knowing the limitations of his career didn't mean Bill had solutions.

"People say, 'You can do anything you want,' " Bill complained. *"Well, what do I want to do?"*

Bill Murray had an excess of fame but a lack of purpose. One passion that endured, however, was his love of sports. During the 1994–95 basketball season, Bill even starred in a series of commercials in which he announced that he was quitting acting to join the NBA. He explained in a fake press conference that he had achieved everything possible in the field of show business. Asked if he had ever won an Oscar, he conceded he had not, and added, "But I have an Emmy for writing." (True—he got it at *Saturday Night Live.*) In other spots, Bill displayed the "no-look no-catch" and lay down on a public court to "reoxygenate." Bill accepted no payment for the ads but got total creative control over them. Best of all was the one where he dribbled a basketball down a city sidewalk, while declaring in a portentous voice-over, "I believe in the ball, and the ball is there for me"—but he couldn't find a court.

Bill couldn't actually ditch his career to join the Chicago Bulls, but after a few flops in a row, he thought, "Maybe I should strap on an automatic weapon and get serious about having a hit movie." Fortunately, at a moment when he had no plan, he found somebody else who had one for him: Wes Anderson had grown up watching Bill Murray movies and had written a script that showed how a smart-aleck young man could grow into a world-weary middle-aged man. Bill made that movie, *Rushmore,* and delivered a wry, truthful performance as love-smitten industrialist Herman Blume. That 1998 film redefined his career (with a greater emphasis on dramatic roles), kicked off a long-term collaboration with Anderson, and opened the door to working with a variety of other cool independent-minded directors: Sofia Coppola (*Lost in Translation*), Jim Jarmusch (*Broken Flowers*), Aaron Schneider (*Get Low*).

In this new stage of his career, Bill grew disenchanted with his representation: "You know, when you have an agent, the phone rings all the time, because there's someone there whose job it is to get so-and-so on the phone, and so they dial the number, and they'll let it ring seventy-five times." For a time he established a don't-call-me-I'll-call-you policy with his agents, and after about six months, he decided that he liked the lack of communication so much that he got rid of them altogether.

At the 2004 Golden Globes, where Bill won the award for best actor in a motion picture musical or comedy for his *Lost in Translation* work, his acceptance speech was also an announcement that he had changed the rules: "You can all relax—I fired my agents a couple of months ago. My trainer, my physical trainer, killed himself." (The crowd laughed, but this was also true.) "And I would thank the people at Universal and Focus, except there's so many people trying to take credit for this, I wouldn't know where to begin." Bill, unlike any other movie star of his stature, now had no agent, no manager, and no publicist. He came up with a new procedure if you were a filmmaker who wanted to pitch him a movie project and didn't already have a personal relationship with him: You could call a 1-800 number, leave a message and hope he listened to it. Maybe his lawyer would call you back. But even if you could find Bill and he agreed to be in your movie, he wouldn't sign a contract in advance.

Bill has said that the difference between an art movie and a commercial Hollywood enterprise is that on an art movie, he feels compelled to be punctual. "When I do schlock with other hacks, I come in late, in order to hold up hundreds of people for hours, days, and weeks. This is how one earns respect," he's observed, half-joking. But even on art films, he has never liked to be pinned down.

Sofia Coppola, for example, spent eight months pursuing Bill for *Lost in Translation*, ultimately reaching him through his friend Mitch Glazer: Bill agreed to the job. "They had been shooting for a week or so in Tokyo," Glazer remembered. "Sofia called me, I thought, to tell me how great things were. But she said, 'Um, have you heard from Bill?' And I said, 'Isn't he there?' She said, 'Well, no. He's supposed to show tomorrow and we haven't heard, and we've shot everything we could without him.'" Let the record show, however, that Bill did turn up, gave the performance of his life, and even helped move equipment from one location to the next.

Bill's inaccessibility has meant that he's missed out on starring roles in many great movies, including some that he might have wanted to be in if the filmmakers had been able to track him down: *Little Miss Sunshine* and *The Squid and the Whale* were written with him in mind, for example.

But he doesn't care. "I just really only want to work when I want to work. Life is really hard, and it's the only one you have. I mean, I like doing what I do, and I know I'm supposed to do it, but I don't have anything to bring to it if I don't live my life."

In that life, Bill had four children—all boys—with Jennifer Butler, bringing his grand total to six sons. Caleb James Murray was born in 1993 (when Bill was still married to Mickey Kelly); Jackson William Murray in 1995; Cooper Jones Murray in 1997; Lincoln Darius Murray in 2001. The family relocated to Charleston, South Carolina— Butler's choice, but a town that Bill came to appreciate. He became a patron of Charleston restaurants and bow-tie makers and even bought a piece of the local minor-league baseball team, the Charleston RiverDogs. Charleston residents traded stories about seeing him out on the town and spread rumors about Bill engaging in "reverse pickpocketing," where he reached into a stranger's pocket and left some money there.

Then, in 2008, his marriage to Butler fell apart in dramatic fashion. She filed for divorce, accusing him of "adultery, addiction to marijuana and alcohol, abusive behavior, physical abuse, sexual addictions, and frequent abandonment." Her filing said that "Defendant would often leave the state or country without telling Plaintiff," "Defendant travels overseas, where he engages in public and private altercations and sexual liaisons," and that in 2007, "the Defendant hit her in the face and then told her she was 'lucky he didn't kill her.'" How you feel about Bill as a human being will likely be colored by how accurate you feel these accusations are (and vice versa).

The divorce ended up with Butler getting two houses and $7 million (basically, the terms of their prenuptial agreement). She also got custody of their four sons, with Bill granted visitation rights. "That was the worst thing that ever happened to me in my entire life," Bill said of the divorce. "When you're really in love with someone and this happens—I never had anything like this happen. It's like your faith in people is destroyed because the person you trusted the most, you can no longer trust at all."

Shattered, Bill threw himself into his work. "I want to bounce off people that are positive and hope that'll make me more positive and give me momentum," he said. Bill found that he was the best version of himself when he was working: "The machine is working better. I have more will. I get a lot more done. All the parts of my life are better taken care of. By really getting into your work, the non-essential stuff drops away."

Without work, Bill discovered, he could drift aimlessly. "I do absolutely nothing," he said. "I go home and stay there. I wash and scrub up each day, and that's it. One month I actually grew a mustache, just so I could say that I'd done something. I am years behind on reading or seeing movies. I find myself watching sports on television or riding a stationary bicycle. Once I break into a sweat, I get off it."

Bill likes to compare acting and athletics. Both professions require grace under pressure, which comes from a strong internal sense of timing and balance. "Someone told me some secrets early on about living," Bill said. "You can do the very best you can when you're very, very relaxed. And that's sort of why I got into acting. I realized the more fun I had, the better I did."

Looking at his own work, Bill knows that he's improved as an actor: There's a lot of distance between *Meatballs* and *Olive Kitteridge* (the 2014 HBO miniseries that earned him an acting Emmy). "Sometimes it's hard to look at the old stuff," he told me. "But that stuff was kind of fiery, like an explosion of performance, especially in the early improvised ones. I used a lot of energy to get that out, but it was great fun. Now I'm more efficient doing it. It's hard—you're still exhausted when you're done, but you just track the energy differently. And hopefully there's more depth to everything. You're not in a hurry for it to move; you're comfortable watching it. When you watch a movie by a good filmmaker, you feel comfortable: This guy knows tempo, he knows pictures, he knows words, and we're not messing around here. You just sit back and watch. That's what you want to try to get to as an actor: You want to get so people feel comfortable watching you. The difference between liking someone and not liking them is whether you can actually stand watching them."

With over sixty-five years on this planet, Bill has developed strong opinions. He has a favorite car (Maserati), musical (*Oklahoma!*), and method of organizing the money in his wallet ("Fifties and tens—people like fifties; twenties are too big for most things and hundreds are hard to break"). That attention to detail is one of his strengths, as an artist and as a human being—he notices the small differences that make up our world. A Bill motto: "When you become an adult and get to pick your pleasures, they should be worth picking."

Bill Murray's goal for the twenty-first century seems to be remaining Bill Murray. He would like to live his life, be with the people he loves, and make great art. Although many people are rooting for him to win an Oscar, he's repeatedly vowed that it's not a priority for him; having come extremely close at the 2004 Academy Awards (his work in *Lost in Translation* won most of the preliminary prizes, but Sean Penn took home the best actor Oscar for *Mystic River*), he decided afterward that getting caught up in the hoopla hadn't been healthy and that winning would have derailed him for a couple of years. He'd also like to write a play, he told me: "I feel like my destiny is to do that, but I haven't gotten around to it."

And he's spent more time with his six sons than ever before. Four years after his divorce from Butler, he reflected, "As much as the divorce was very hard, the fallout of it has been really great. I ended up much closer to my guys than I ever would have been."

Bill's even considered the possibility of having a manager again: "Just to clear my head and have a plan." Or, on second thought: "Eh, it's not that attractive to have a plan."

Nobody, not even Bill Murray, fills every day by careening from one anecdote to the next. There are aspects of his existence—his home life with his family, for example—that are outside the scope of this book. One friend of his told me in an email that he thought Bill's defining characteristic was his intelligence rather than his zaniness and that he regarded Bill's antics as a protective layer to insulate his personal privacy: by having such a memorable public persona, Bill makes the separation from his private self more distinct.

Danny Rubin, the screenwriter of *Groundhog Day,* had his own theory: "I've always believed that the way he walks into a room and shakes things up had less to do with his desire to be the center of attention and was more to create a playful atmosphere in which to dwell."

Ivan Reitman, who has directed Bill in more movies than anybody except Wes Anderson, theorized, "I think he's way more serious than most people realize. He wants to be taken seriously. It's this weird dichotomy. He wants to have a serious philosophical, intellectual conversation, and at the same time, he never wants to feel that there was anything corny in it."

In researching this book, I sought the Bill Murray stories that have defined his public image, where he briefly warps reality and societal expectation. I found them by the score, but I also heard many stories about Bill that didn't make it into the book. I spoke with people who savored the moment when Bill came into their restaurant and looked at the menu, or who remembered how Bill once gave them excellent advice on how to get a better margarita in a bar without the proper ingredients (ask the bartender to add some orange juice), or who reminisced about the time they spotted Bill at a bluegrass festival on a Tuesday morning.

These encounters may have been mundane interactions for Bill, forgotten soon after, but they were treasured memories for the people they happened to. Even when he's engaged in everyday activities, Bill seems suffused with extra mischief, as if sparks were flying off his fingertips and igniting unseen possibilities.

"Thanks for coming to my party," Ayoka Lucas of Charleston, South Carolina, told Bill when he crashed her "hipster and hip-hop" dance party in 2013.

"Thanks for not inviting me!" he responded.

Bill isn't just being a clown. He has a tao, a way of being, a philosophy of life. He is extremely generous of spirit— but on his own terms. Reitman said, "He lives life to his standard, even though sometimes he's lazy and sometimes he's eccentric and he's frustrating to other creative people and, frankly, unfair, because everything has to go on his clock. But he's worth it."

"He's not a movie star by accident," Harold Ramis reflected, considering Bill's affinity for his arrogant weatherman character in *Groundhog Day*. "He understands vanity and self-centeredness."

Bill knows just how much clout his stardom has brought him and when he can use it for selfish purposes, like making other people wait for him. Describing the first time he saw a rough cut of an action scene in *Ghostbusters*, he said, "I knew then I was going to be rich and famous. Not only did I go back to work with a lot of attitude, I was late. I didn't care—I knew that we could be late every day for the rest of our lives."

Many movie stars have worked out the same equation and have a well-calibrated sense of just how much bad behavior they can get away with, enabled by studios and handlers. What makes Bill different is that he also figured out other ways to use his stature: not just for good deeds (although there are plenty of those too) but to transform the world, one chance encounter at a time. If making movies brings out the best aspects of Bill, as he believes, then his ongoing adventures with the public can be considered an effort to make real life more like the movies.

In September 2014, I got to spend some time with Bill at the Toronto Film Festival, where he was promoting the movie *St. Vincent* and being the center of a celebration the festival called "Bill Murray Day." I chatted with him at a party for the film's premiere; the next morning, when we sat down for an interview in a hotel suite, he eyed my shirt, which was different from the one I had on the night before. "You changed," he said, sounding genuinely surprised.

Bill talked about drinking shakes rich in chlorophyll, whether people were more likely to pick up bacon or dollar bills, and his late-in-life appreciation of the police. What I really wanted to discuss, however, were his public antics and why he engaged in them. What did he want people to take away from a meeting with him?

Initially, he demurred. Then he conceded that he was

actually "a little more selfish about it" and wasn't necessarily thinking about what he wanted other people to take away from an encounter with him. "My hope always is that it's going to wake me up," he said. "And if I see someone that's out cold on their feet, I go, okay, *I'm going to try to wake that person up.* It's what I'd want someone to do for me: Wake me the hell up."

Asked if there were periods of his life when he felt like he needed to be woken up, he nodded.

Well, every day, really. I'm only connected for seconds and minutes a day sometimes. And sometimes you go, "Holy cow, I've been asleep for two days. I've been doing things but I've just been out." I get a little better as time goes on, but it's amazing how it gets harder. The better you get at something, life just gives you a little more challenge.

No one has a really easy life. Everyone's life is difficult. People can be oblivious or seemingly having an easy go of it, but everyone's getting it. It's just this face we put on: that we're not all getting rained on, that we're not all getting hammered. I think my face looks like it's taken a few hits. I'm happy if it appears that I've come out of it unscathed.

Life is hard. If you can get something right for someone, that's great. If you can help someone in any way, that's cool. But you can't start thinking about numbers: if I can change just one person or I had three nice encounters. You can't think that way, because you're cer-

tainly going to have one where you go, "What did I just do?" You're a disappointment to yourself and others, imminently. Any second.

Bill almost said something else—but then he cut himself off and smiled. Just because he had figured out some secrets about the world, that didn't mean he needed to say them all out loud.

O

THE BILL.

The Ten Principles of Bill

"Tao" is Chinese for "the way," and Bill Murray has charted his own road map through the world.

Taoism is the philosophy that originated in China in the sixth century B.C., codified in Lao Tzu's collection of poetry *Tao Te Ching*. It was inspired by the life of Huang Di: a legendary emperor of China who, four and a half thousand years ago, was allegedly responsible for curing diseases, inventing military strategy, and using magic to domesticate wild animals. Similarly, the Tao of Bill Murray is based on close study of another great man: the star of *Groundhog Day* and the 2011 champion of the Pebble Beach Pro-Am golf tournament.

Bill's not big on explaining his philosophy—summarized here as ten principles—or on setting himself up as a guru. But just by paying attention, we can learn from Bill's example. Bill has said, "My legacy's gonna have to be something different from my work," and these encounters might be what he's remembered for. If you apply his philosophical tenets to your own life, you can find the previously untraveled path to a better version of yourself.

The First Principle
Objects are opportunities.

. . .

The Second Principle
Surprise is golden.
Randomness is lobster.

. . .

The Third Principle
Invite yourself to the party.

. . .

The Fourth Principle
Make sure everybody else
is invited to the party.

. . .

The Fifth Principle
Music makes the people
come together.

The Sixth Principle
Drop coin on the world.

. . .

The Seventh Principle
**Be persistent, be persistent,
be persistent.**

. . .

The Eighth Principle
**Know your pleasures
and their parameters.**

. . .

The Ninth Principle
Your spirit will follow your body.

. . .

The Tenth Principle
**While the earth spins,
make yourself useful.**

The First Principle
Objects are opportunities.

THE GREATEST MISADVENTURE EVER INVOLVING alcohol and a nontraditional motor vehicle belongs to country-music legend George Jones: When his wife hid his car keys so he wouldn't drive to the liquor store, he made the eight-mile trip on a John Deere lawnmower. Bill Murray, however, gave the singer a run for his money in August 2007, when he went to the Scandinavian Masters, a golf tournament in Sweden. Late enough on a Sunday night that it was actually Monday morning—around 3:30 A.M.—Murray was spotted in downtown Stockholm, driving a golf cart through the streets. This was a sufficiently unusual mode of transportation that he got stopped by the police on suspicion of drunken driving. (Even if he had wanted to outrun them, he was *in a golf cart.*)

Apparently the golf cart had been on display all week outside Bill's hotel—until Bill and some friends commandeered it for a party at the Café Opera nightclub, about a mile away.

The Café Opera manager, Daniel Bodahl, said Bill "was a very good guest."

The man in charge of the Scandinavian Masters, Fredrik Nilsmark, said, "I don't hold any grudge against Bill Murray for borrowing our cart for a while."

Detective-Inspector Christer Holmlund of the Stockholm police force said, "I have done this since '68 and I've never experienced anything like this."

Bill's explanation? He hadn't personally borrowed the golf cart, he claimed—he had started off as a passenger, being driven to a party. (Which sidestepped the question of whether the people driving him had permission to use that golf cart.) "I was taken to the party by people who did not feel they could drive the golf cart back," Bill said. "They said, 'We can't drive back—we'll lose our license.' I said, 'I won't lose my license.' That's what America used to be famous for: helping out, pitching in."

So he drove the golf cart through the streets of Stockholm sometime after 3:00 A.M. A "twilight drive," Bill joked—being so far north, Stockholm has incredibly long days during the summer. He had about six passengers crammed into the back of the cart and he was dropping them off at various destinations, like a bus driver. To complete the surreal scene, two drunk Swedish guys were hanging on to the very back of the cart, singing the 1970 Cat Stevens song "Father and Son."

The last two people on the cart wanted to be dropped

off at a 7-Eleven. "I didn't know they had 7-Elevens in Stockholm," Bill commented. In front of the 7-Eleven, the police spotted Bill behind the wheel of the golf cart and called him over, assuming that he must be drunk. Bill's explanation that he was a golfer proved insufficient.

Holmlund said that when the police officer smelled alcohol, Bill declined to take a Breathalyzer test, "citing American legislation."

Or as Bill told the story, he told the police officer, "I'm sorry, but where I come from, you have to act stupid or goofy or hit something or drive erratically or something—you're just assuming that I'm drunk because I'm driving a golf cart at three-thirty in the morning."

Holmlund agreed that Bill wasn't visibly drunk: "There were no obvious signs, like when someone is really tipsy."

The confrontation migrated to the police station. "They said, 'We're going to take your blood now,' and I said, 'What if I politely decline?'" Then, Bill said, "They introduced me to this guy, Gunther or somebody . . . who had a smile on his face, but not the smile you want to see." Bill submitted to Gunther and the police administered a blood test; Bill signed a document conceding that he had been driving under the influence and authorizing a police officer to plead guilty on his behalf if the matter ever came before a judge. Bill was then released and allowed to leave Sweden.

When the blood work ultimately came back, Bill's blood alcohol content was around 0.03 percent—way below the general American DUI standard of 0.08 percent but above the strict Swedish threshold of 0.02 percent. He had to pay a fine. "For having any amount of alcohol and having a golf cart, you have to pay something," Bill said. "It's just a courtesy, I guess."

. . .

Producer Joyce Sloane founded the Second City Touring Company, where the junior performers of Second City would take the group's Chicago-tested material on the road, with everyone piling into a van. She said that in the early seventies, after the tour hit Notre Dame, one of their performers disappeared for about a week—apparently, Bill Murray had discovered that Saint Mary's College, a women's-only college, was next door. Even when Bill stayed with the group, he was a force of chaos.

The troupe did a show at Wabash College in Crawfordsville, Indiana, which went extremely well: They were even invited to a reception at the president's home. But as the van pulled away and headed out of town, the entire cast had the giggles. Soon enough, Sloane figured out why: "Bill had taken it upon himself to take the Oriental rug from the president's home and put it in the back of the van."

. . .

Dan Patrick, revered sportscaster on ESPN and other venues, tells this story:

> We were doing a pub crawl in New York, an A-to-Z pub crawl. I run into Bill Murray at a place in the Village, and I said, "Billy, we're going to go on a pub crawl and do you want to go with us?"

He said, "Sure." So we're walking down the street, there's Antique Boutique, and he goes, "Hold on." He runs in and comes out with an orange tie.

I said, "What's this for?"

He says, "Didn't you say on SportsCenter *that the hardest thing about being the coach of Tennessee is trying to find those god-awful orange ties?" He said, "Put it on!"*

I put it on, we went on the A-to-Z pub crawl, we got to the letter L . . . and there's a street cleaner, the street sweeper; the machine is on. And Bill goes, "What are you thinking?"

I go, "I don't know. Am I thinking what you're thinking?"

He said, "Let's steal this thing."

I wasn't thinking that. I wasn't. I was thinking, let's get to the next bar. I didn't even know the thing was running, and Billy goes, "Let's get in it." So he starts to climb up in the street cleaner.

And this guy runs out and he's like, "What are you doing? I'll lose my job!"

And he sees it's Bill and I think Bill said, "Don't worry." He said, "Can I just take it down the street a little bit?" So we just inched along like a tank down the street.

. . .

Lorne Michaels, creator and executive producer of *Saturday Night Live,* analyzed Bill Murray's location in the comedy firmament: "So much of my generation's approach to comedy was a reaction against the neediness of performers. When Bill was onstage, he didn't much care whether they liked him. Because of that, he had enormous integrity."

Michaels discovered, however, that integrity wasn't the same thing as reliability. In the summer of 1979, Michaels needed to get his Volkswagen Super Beetle from Los Angeles to New York; the producer had left it behind when he relocated to Manhattan for *SNL*. Bill volunteered to drive the car across the country—and he did, but on his own timetable. "Remember, I was his boss," Michaels said. "Occasionally I would hear from Bill on the road. He'd be in Florida, and I'd say, 'But, Bill—is Florida on the way?' Or a week later, he'd be in Aspen and I'd say, 'But, Bill . . .' " Bill may not have treated the driving mission with the focus Michaels expected, but he did ultimately deliver the car, and with a bonus. The car arrived weeks late, and had accumulated hundreds of unexpected miles on the odometer—but Bill had installed a top-notch stereo.

★ ★ ★ ★ ★ ★ ★ ★ ★ ★ ★ ★ ★ ★ ★ ★ ★ ★ ★ ★ ★ ★

BILL MURRAY MEETS THE YOUTH OF AMERICA

This happened when I was in seventh grade at the St. Vincent Ferrer Catholic School in Delray Beach, Florida. It was 1985—the year after Ghostbusters. *Bill Murray was the biggest star on the planet. And his wife had an uncle who was a popular priest at our school: Father Williams.*

Well, Father Williams died and Bill Murray showed up at the funeral. He was actually a pallbearer. And he was late. The family was sitting in the back of the church—a limo pulled up and out comes Bill. His hair was all messed up. He was in a tux, but his shirt was hanging out and he's frantically tucking it in. He runs up to the door and then quietly walks in and makes it into the pew just in time.

Afterward, a crowd of people gathered around him. It was a somber time, but at the same time people wanted to talk to him. He quietly signed a few autographs and then remarked on how all the kids were handing him hymnals that were clearly marked DO NOT REMOVE FROM CHURCH. *My friend Mike got an autograph—and remember, we're in seventh grade—where Bill wrote, "Mike, drive carefully, Bill Murray."*

After a minute or two of signing, he thanked everyone and then said something about how this wasn't the reason we were there, but he did it in a very gracious way.

—Keith M. Jones

In 1985, Trine Licht was a young Danish woman living in New York City, delighted to have gotten a job as an assistant at Punch Productions, Dustin Hoffman's personal production company. She worked in the Directors' Guild building, on 57th Street, helping to find novels and screenplays that Hoffman might want to star in or direct. After she had been on the job for a few months, she had a surprise visitor in her office: Bill Murray poked his head in and said hello. (Hoffman and Murray were friendly, having recently played roommates in *Tootsie*.) Bill became a semi-regular visitor. Licht said, "He had an office down the hall but was not always there, only between shooting films. I think he read screenplays and novels there; maybe he did other things too. But he did occasionally ask, 'Have you read this' or 'Have you read that,' and he always looked like he was reading."

One summer day, Bill dropped by Licht's office, as was his custom—only this time, he asked, "Want some popcorn?"

When she said that she did, Bill disappeared. He was gone for long enough that Licht assumed he had forgotten about the popcorn. But when he came back, he didn't just have a bucket of popcorn: He pulled a cart full of warm popcorn into the office. Bill had gone down to the street, negotiated with a popcorn vendor, and bought his whole operation.

· · ·

Circa 2005, Joseph Davenport was standing outside a bar in Charleston, South Carolina, smoking a cigarette. Bill Murray walked by, plucked the cigarette out of his mouth, and took a drag. He then returned the cigarette to Davenport, saying, "No one will ever believe you."

Davenport said the experience is unlikely to be repeated anytime soon: "I don't smoke anymore."

The Second Principle
Surprise is golden.
Randomness is lobster.

I N THE 1970S, BEFORE BILL MURRAY MADE IT ONTO
Saturday Night Live, Ivan Reitman would sometimes
walk down the streets of New York City with him. Being
unknown to the vast majority of New Yorkers didn't inhibit
Bill—he took that as an opportunity to get their attention.
Sometimes Bill would shout at passersby in what he and
Reitman called the "honker" voice (which later became
the voice of Carl Spackler, Bill's character in *Caddyshack*).
As Bill crossed the street, he would accost somebody coming the other way: "Look out, there's a lobster loose!" The
next pedestrian would be greeted with "Hey, get some hot
butter—it's the only way to get 'em!"

"They would just start laughing," Reitman says. "They
didn't know who this crazy person was, but they knew he
was funny."

. . .

Bill Murray walks down a school hallway, in slow motion.
He's in the middle of a group of five guys, standing out

because he's taller than the rest—and because he's Bill Murray. He's wearing blue jeans and a dark shirt; in his left hand, he's holding his phone and some folded documents. When he looks right into the camera, you know he doesn't have time for you: He needs to keep walking.

How did this bizarrely compelling footage, less than a minute long, come to exist? In 2011, when Bill agreed to film a promo video for the Trident Academy in Mount Pleasant, South Carolina, "a national leader in the education of children with learning disabilities," he took it as seriously as he would a multimillion-dollar Hollywood movie. In other words, he showed up late and threw away the script once he arrived.

"He came in hot and a little grumpy," said David W. Smith, who was part of the four-man crew shooting the video. "He was about thirty minutes late, and he complained that there were too many lights. He had a script, but he sat down in the school library and ad-libbed the whole thing. He got all these teddy bears and had a conversation with them. We're looking at each other—this guy is off-his-face crazy—but there was a method to his madness."

Bill opened the video surrounded by a group of teddy bears, reading aloud to them from *A Picture Book of Davy Crockett.* "Let's just leave it right there, at that chapter," he told the bears. "Okay? We'll pick it up later." Bill delivered a sincere testimonial for the school: "Trident Academy is for smart kids who learn differently," he said. "It's been a very successful school, successful for my son, who came here, and upon arrival, his IQ just leapt." Bill also shot a lot of B-roll while engaging in various activities with students: playing basketball, writing cursive letters in pans filled with shaving cream, considering the wisdom of guzzling paint.

Bill loosened up after the first hour, Smith said: "As the shoot went on, he became more and more like the guy that everyone thinks they know, which I guess is who he actually is." When they finished shooting and broke for lunch, Bill could have gone home, but he stuck around for another hour. His lunch request was a tuna sandwich with no crusts. (While that's mildly eccentric, it's nothing compared to the sandwich that was his favorite circa 1984: peanut butter, lettuce, and mayonnaise on pumpernickel.)

Not wanting to spook their star, the guys working in the crew were reluctant to ask Bill for autographs or pictures. Finally, one of the kids who appeared alongside Bill in the video asked to take a photograph with him. Bill readily complied, saying, "Oh, I thought no one was going to ask." So as Bill was leaving, Smith asked him for a favor: Would he walk down a school hallway with the crew members so they could make a short film of it? Bill was confused, but he complied. When they reached the end of the hallway, the filmmakers stopped walking and their friend who was holding the camera stopped shooting. Bill kept walking, not stopping to say goodbye, heading to his car without breaking stride.

Smith played the footage in slow motion over an old Kinks song ("Powerman"), added some titles, and had a short Bill Murray film that looked like an outtake from a Wes Anderson movie. It was titled "New {fake} Trailer," and touted itself both as a trailer for the nonexistent film *Les Cinéastes* and as "a film about walking in slow motion."

Then Smith put the clip online. For the first year, it had maybe 150 views, which hugely confused him: Why wasn't it going viral? But one day, while Smith was in the shower, it did, for reasons he could never figure out—by the time Smith had gotten dressed, hundreds of thousands of people had discovered his little movie. Ultimately, about two million people watched a one-minute film of Bill Murray (and four other guys) walking down a hallway in slow motion. Smith had heard stories of Bill being difficult to work with on movie sets, so the lesson he learned from the "really nice guy" version of Bill who he spent the day with is that it's possible to remake yourself into a better person. The second lesson: "If Bill Murray is in it, people will watch anything."

TALES FROM THE GRAPE D'VINE

It's a hot summer day in 2002, and in Rockland County, New York, Joe Printz is settling into his new life as a wine-store owner. His shop, Grape D'Vine, has been open for just a few weeks—he has plenty of ambitions for the store, but he doesn't know if it's going to be financially viable. Then the phone rings: a new customer with a Yiddish accent who wants three cases of wine,

THE TEN PRINCIPLES OF BILL 57

most of them from obscure vineyards. He details his order, tells Printz his name is Murray, and leaves a 1-800 number to call when the wine arrives.

Printz dutifully tracks down all the wine. Once it arrives, he leaves a message on the 1-800 number—but doesn't hear back. He begins to worry.

"You're an idiot for not getting a deposit," his wife tells him. "You have no idea who this guy is."

Joe leaves another message on the 1-800 number, imploring Murray to come pick up his wine: "I don't know who you are, Murray, but I'm brand-new in the business. I can't afford to be holding on to nine hundred dollars of wine."

Joe hangs up, and almost immediately the phone rings. "Hi, it's Murray," the voice says, this time without the Yiddish accent. "I'll be there in five minutes."

"What, are you hovering over the store in a helicopter?" Joe asks.

Five minutes later, Bill Murray walks through the door of the Grape D'Vine: "Hi, I'm Murray."

Imagine a silver-haired Bill Murray posing for a sequence of four headshots, wearing no shirt but with a bright red kerchief tied rakishly around his neck. In the first photo, Bill gives the camera his best Clint Eastwood squint. In the second one, he holds out his hands and is captured mid-laugh, appealing to the better nature of the viewer. The third one: With his head at a forty-five-degree tilt, he rests his chin on his hand, looking like a beloved children's-book author. And, finally, he gazes off into the distance with his hands clasped together and his index fingers touching, suggesting that he's either about to make an important theological point or ready to show you his strategy for winning at laser tag.

Now imagine those four photos printed in a grid on a Christmas card with the message "Murray Christmas" underneath.

Now imagine that you are the legendary professional wrestler "Rowdy" Roddy Piper. You died in 2015, which is a downer, but for the purposes of this exercise, it is December 2013. You have never met Bill Murray. In your mail, you find the "Murray Christmas" card, which Bill apparently sent to you on a whim, and you are utterly confused.

. . .

Most people treat getting a phone call because of a misdialed number as an intrusion to be dispatched as quickly as possible. Bill Murray is not one of those people: For him, it's an opportunity to improvise, to create something unexpected, and to add a surreal jolt to a stranger's day. "Wrong numbers can be an adventure," he declares. What makes it interesting to Bill: His unwitting scene partner is a little vulnerable emotionally, having made a mistake and hoping that the resulting conversation isn't going to be uncomfortable. How good is Bill at keeping people on the phone when they really want to hang up and call somebody else? He once convinced a girl who called him because of a wrong number that she should go on a date with him. "It was a great date, and it was a great time," he says. "I should do that a little more often!"

. . .

Bill Murray used to frequent an Italian restaurant called Asti, in New York City's Greenwich Village. It featured signed photographs of Babe Ruth and Noël Coward on the walls and a grand piano in the center of the dining room. The waitstaff was composed of opera singers, and when not serving up plates of pasta and seafood, they would break into arias.

Asti closed at the end of 1999, but a decade later, Bill sat down to talk with a film critic who was a friend of a friend. She reminded him of the time Bill had gotten the diners to form a conga line and led them snaking through the restaurant, out the door onto 12th Street, and then back inside to their food.

Bill brightened. "Were you there the night we were with what's-his-name, Sergio Leone?" he asked. "And we tried to stick [him] with the bill?"

The story according to Bill: It was a group dinner with about fourteen people at the table, including Bill, his friend Tom Schiller (the director of many short films on *Saturday Night Live*), and Sergio Leone (the legendary Italian director of spaghetti westerns including *A Fistful of Dollars*). Schiller decided that it would be an excellent idea to stick Leone with the bill, and Bill enthusiastically seconded the motion.

"So we passed the word," Murray said. "If people just start getting up and disappearing from the table one by one—act like they were going to the restroom or something—we'd all meet outside." Bill relished the idea of leaving Leone, a burly icon of macho filmmaking, alone at a huge table.

"But he didn't get beat with it!" Bill reported. "He got out of it—he was like the third one from the end." Leone joined the crowd milling around on the sidewalk of 12th Street. Bill says, "So we didn't catch him with the bill, but it was such a novel idea to try and catch a real movie guy and stick him with the bill. We were just a bunch of wise guys."

ON THE DARK SIDE

Before *Scrooged* started filming, Bill Murray invited the movie's screenwriters, Michael O'Donoghue and Mitch Glazer, to go to a Mexican desert resort with him for a male-bonding vacation. Glazer remembers, "We did a lot of swimming and hiking, and Billy was really sweet to all the other guests, who loved meeting him. Unfortunately, there was this one Beverly Hills woman, a Rodeo Drive type who wore furs in the blazing sun, and she insisted on treating Billy like he was some ornament to her vacation."

Murray says, "She was overdressed, even around the pool, and overbearing. She kept ordering me to give her autographs, and she was on me like all day, like I was her personal trinket. The next day she was on me again and was holding out another sheaf for autographs. I said that I would sign them, but in return I would get to throw her in the pool. She laughed. 'Oh, sure you do,' she said. She thought I was kidding, and she pushed the papers on me. I walked her to the pool as I signed them, then I grabbed her, and she slipped to the deck, screaming. Then I rolled her into the pool—furs, designer clothes, and all. It was a beautiful picture."

Around 1988, Bill Murray picked up a phrasebook by Todd and Erika Geers called *Making Out in Japanese,* which finished with a couple of chapters of colloquial phrases for lovers, such as "You have a beautiful body" and "I don't want to get married yet."

"I thought it was so stupid—I don't know why I got it," Bill said. But in 2002, when he went to Tokyo to make *Lost in Translation,* he brought the book along and soon decided it was a treasure. "It made my life so much fun," he said. Bill selected bon mots from the book to use on the set—for example, he would solemnly tell a crew member a sentence that translated as "I really don't love you anymore, so I'm going to change my phone number."

"He was saying a lot of these phrases in a really convincing way," director Sofia Coppola remembered.

Bill went out for a lot of sushi while shooting the film, and he would bring his paperback copy of *Making Out in Japanese* along. So his icebreaking conversational gambits with scowling sushi chefs would be: "Do your parents know about me?" Or "Do you have a curfew?" Or "Can we get in the backseat?"

Or best of all: "Do you mind if I use protection?"

"These guys all had big knives!" Bill remembered. But

they also had senses of humor, and they laughed at the large American who was asking inappropriate questions in butchered Japanese.

One phrase that proved particularly potent was *"Dare-ni mukatte mono itten-dayo?"* which translates as "Who do you think you're talking to?" It's a line generally delivered by someone with considerably more status or power, to give an unwitting antagonist one final chance to back down before getting stabbed or beaten up. If a yakuza (a Japanese gangster) said it to you, a better translation might be "Now you're going to die."

Lost in Translation was made on a low budget and often without permits—with a small crew, Coppola would get whatever shot she needed and then move on before the authorities could notice. So instead of hauling around trailers for makeup and costumes, the movie often rented a small hotel room where they could prepare the actors. Early one morning, Bill was getting ready in one of those hotel rooms. He had just acquired his first iPod, and with the earbuds in and the music cranked up, he was singing loudly to the Beatles, oblivious to his surroundings—or the fact that it was 5:30 A.M.

As Bill told it, "Some guy steps out of his hotel room in his robe and he comes down and he's shouting at me. And I had the headphones on and I just looked at him and said, *'Dare-ni mukatte mono itten-dayo?'* And this giant man just went completely white." The man ran down the hall, slammed his door, locked it, and didn't emerge again.

. . .

Remembering their time together on the *St. Vincent* set, Melissa McCarthy confided, "Bill literally throws banana peels in front of people." While many people use "literally" to mean "metaphorically," McCarthy was completely correct in her choice of words. Hanging outside a sound-stage during a break when the lights were getting reset, Bill Murray kept tossing banana peels in the path of passing crew members. "Not to make them slip," McCarthy clarified, "but for the look on their face when they're like, 'Is that really a *banana peel* in front of me?'"

. . .

When the estimable writer Peter Richmond spent three days in June 1990 hanging out with Bill Murray for an article—mostly at Wrigley Field, watching the Cubs play—Bill showed up bearing Polish sausages and explained that what he most enjoyed were baseball games with fielding errors, because it emphasized the human element in the game. (He didn't comment on whether that was the root of his affection for the Cubs.) Although Bill was mostly gracious about the parade of fans coming up to him at the ballpark and asking for autographs, he clearly wanted to be paying attention to the game. "You don't understand—there's a baseball game going on," he told many of them. Or, "Hey! There's a two-and-one count here!"

Bill's ten best interactions with human beings that weekend:

1. When one fan at Wrigley said, "Hey, Bill, I think it's great how you support Chicago sports," Bill replied, "I can't do anything else."

2. When slumping Cubs first baseman Mark Grace walked into the on-deck circle, Bill rose to yell, "I can swing that bat!" Grace, startled, looked to see who the crazy person was. When he saw it was Bill, he broke into a grin but gestured frantically for Bill to sit back down.

3. A drunk woman approached Bill and informed him that she worked for the Illinois secretary of state. Bill told her, "You look like the kind of person I could go on a kill spree with. Knock over a few gas stations, kill a few people."

4. Leaning out the window of a cab after the game, Bill shouted at a woman with sunglasses and a scarf over her hair, driving a Mercedes the color of pond scum. "Nice color!" he greeted her. "Hey, I'll bet ten dollars you just quit smoking and drinking." She didn't respond.

5. At dinner with a bunch of Cubs, Bill was interrupted by a kid seeking an autograph. Pretending to be furious, Bill hoisted the kid up in the air and threatened to shove his nose into the mashed potatoes on the table. Then he signed the autograph.

6. A woman at a bar commented on Bill's depressed affect. "I'm emotionally down because the Cubs lost," he told her. "If they'd won, I'd be out ripping the antennas off cars."

7. In the weight room before a game against the Expos, pitcher Rick Sutcliffe asked Bill where his seats were. The answer was: "Up among the weird and the damned."

8. When somebody a few rows away at Wrigley shouted out, "Dogs and cats, living together!" Bill quietly observed, "This *Ghostbusters* thing is not going to go away until somebody kills themselves with one of the toys."

9. A woman at Wrigley invited him to watch her team play softball. "Well, maybe I'll come by and insult you," Bill offered.

10. Bill's five-year-old son, Luke, sitting next to him at Wrigley, saw the parade of people walking up to Bill for autographs, so he gave a baseball to Bill and asked if he would sign it. Bill inscribed it "Dad" and handed it back to him.

Voice of Harold

"Any experience with Bill Murray is better than any other experience," Harold Ramis said, "because he does things no one you know would ever do."

Without Ramis, Bill said, his career would be "totally different."

Ramis first met Bill Murray in 1969, when Ramis was in the Second City comedy troupe with Bill's older brother Brian Doyle-Murray. Ramis said, "At that time, Bill had just finished high school and was operating the refreshment stand at a country club in Wilmette, Illinois, but in less than three years he had advanced to selling hot chestnuts in front of a supermarket in Chicago's Old Town."

Bill joined Second City and quickly became both the breakout star and the most difficult member of the troupe. Ramis was assigned the job of talking to Bill about his conflicts with other cast members.

"I heard there was some bad blood with other company members," Ramis said.

"Yeah," Murray agreed.

"Do you care?"

"No."

"Okay. Good talk."

Ramis turned into one of Bill's closest collaborators, punching up the script for *Meatballs*, costarring with him in

Stripes and *Ghostbusters,* and directing him (and writing for him) in *Caddyshack* and *Groundhog Day*. Ramis described Bill as "*All* the Marx Brothers rolled into one: He's got the wit of Groucho, the pantomimic brilliance and lasciviousness of Harpo, and the Everyman quality of Chico." Which didn't mean that it was easy working with him, Ramis said. "If there's no drama, he'll create one for you. He likes walking to the edge, and to get to the edge means pushing everyone else there. He has two modes: sleep and overstimulation."

Ramis professed that he couldn't believe some of the things Bill said or did, but he was fascinated watching them, as if he were witnessing a sociological experiment. "I've seen a total stranger come up to Bill on the street in New York: 'Bill, love you on *Saturday Night!*' He says, 'You motherfucker, I'm going to bite your nose!' He wrestles him to the ground—total stranger—and bites his nose. I guess you *can* do that."

Ramis acknowledged that Murray could fall into the role of the tortured artist. Sometimes, he said, "It's like working with Vincent van Gogh—on a bad day." Ramis's theory was that the root cause was Murray's acting style: "He hates the Strasberg Method and won't really prepare in the classical manner, so he is forced to rely pretty much on inspiration, wit, instinct, and impulse. When it works for him, it's truly magical. But there are times when he really has to dig for it, to mine his deepest energy reserves to come up with something good."

The apogee and perigee of their work together was *Groundhog Day*. Ramis said, "Bill pretty much gave his all, or at least most of his all." Although *Groundhog Day* is probably their greatest joint achievement, the shoot also permanently ruptured their relationship.

Bill was splitting up with his first wife (Mickey Kelly) at this time and was acting erratically. Apparently, he was offended that Ramis wasn't taking time to work on the script with him, sending screenwriter Danny Rubin in his stead, and so he lashed out. Ramis said, "At times, Bill was just really irrationally mean and unavailable; he was constantly late on set. What I'd want to say to him is what we tell our children: 'You don't have to throw tantrums to get what you want. Just say what you want.'"

Rubin said, "They were like two brothers who weren't getting along."

Bill went incommunicado from the movie's creators, not returning phone calls and dodging production assistants. It was suggested to Bill that everything might go more smoothly if he hired a personal assistant, so that he wouldn't constantly be bothered by details and logistics. He assented, but in a totally unhelpful way: He hired a profoundly deaf woman. She couldn't communicate orally, and nobody else working on the movie knew American Sign Language, including Bill. "That's anti-communication," Ramis said. "Let's *not* talk."

Hiring that assistant was widely regarded by the people who knew Bill as an elaborate way of giving the finger to Ramis, but Bill's gambits are often multidimensional: When he looked back at hiring her years later, he thought of it as an overambitious move born from optimism. "She was a bright person and witty, but she had never been away from her home before, and even though I tried to accommodate more than I understood when I first hired her, she was very young in her emotional self, and the emotional component of being away from her home was lacking. I tried my best, but I was working all day." She lasted on the job for only a few weeks. "It didn't go particularly well for me, but for a few weeks she really was a light and had a real spirit to her. She was like one of your own kids that never had a job, and then they get a job and realize that certain things are expected."

After *Groundhog Day* wrapped, Ramis and Bill didn't speak for twenty-one years, except briefly when crossing paths at a bar mitzvah or a wake. Ivan Reitman, who was friendly with the two men, tried to reconcile them, without success. "I couldn't tell you what the issue was with Harold," he said. "I've asked Bill about it. He never could articulate it to me."

Ramis said that because he never knew why Bill had frozen him out, it played into all his worst fears: "Did he think I was weak? Or untrue? Did I betray him in some way? With no clue or feedback from him, it's this kind of tantalizing mystery. And that may be the point."

Ramis died in 2014, due to complications from autoimmune inflammatory vasculitis. Before Ramis passed, Bill's brother Brian convinced Bill to visit their old friend one last time. He did; reportedly they discussed Chicago and the Cubs. "He earned his keep on this planet. God bless him," Bill said in a statement after Ramis died. And a week later, he interrupted his presenter patter at the Academy Awards to pay tribute to Ramis.

But decades before, Ramis and Bill visited the Indonesian island of Bali together, which spurred what Ramis said was one of his favorite Bill Murray stories. Ramis spent three weeks on the island, mostly in the tourist district on the south shore. "But Bill rode a motorcycle into the interior until the sun went down and got totally lost. He goes into a village store, where they are very surprised to see an American tourist, and starts talking to them in English, going, 'Wow! Nice hat! Hey, gimme that hat!' And he took the guy's hat and started imitating people—entertaining. Word gets around this hamlet that there's some crazy guy at the grocery, and he ended up doing a dumb show with the whole village sitting around laughing as he grabbed the women and tickled the kids. No worry about getting back to a hotel, no need for language, just his presence, and his charisma, and his courage. When you meet the hero, you sure know it."

Ramis summed up the difference between the two of them: "Bill loves to get lost, to throw the map out the window and drive till you have no idea where you are, just to experience something new." Ramis himself, on the other hand: "I'd be the one with the map. I'm the map guy. I'm the one saying to Bill, 'You know, we should get back now. They're going to be looking for us.'"

The Third Principle
Invite yourself to the party.

O N AUGUST 16, 1977, ELVIS PRESLEY DIED. IT WAS the summer after Bill Murray's first season on *Saturday Night Live;* Bill decided to go to the funeral, bearing witness to a landmark American event and making it that much more surreal just by being there.

> *I was the twenty-seventh person on standby. The last flight out of New York City to Memphis the night before the funeral. Miraculously, I got on the plane—standby, twenty-seven people, I was the twenty-seventh person that got on the plane. And I got to Memphis. I just took a cab to Graceland. I said, "Graceland," you know, which is kind of a funny thing to say when you get a taxi anywhere!*

Bill wasn't able to enter Graceland or to see the body of the King lying in state; the family had stopped letting people in, because the *National Enquirer* had offered a bounty for a picture of Elvis in his casket. (Despite photographers repeatedly getting their cameras confiscated, the *Enquirer* got its shot, taken by a cousin with a spy camera, and sold a record-breaking number of issues as a result. According to Bill, the Presley family disowned the cousin, but he was one of a half dozen relatives who took an illicit photo of Elvis in the casket—he just got the clearest picture.)

"The actual funeral was a spectacular thing," Bill says. He got a seat on the press bus that rode in front of the hearse—the last vehicle to travel from Graceland to Forest Hill Cemetery before the hearse slowly rolled down the same Memphis streets.

Hundreds of thousands of people waiting for the King to roll by . . . It looked like a collection of WPA photographs— people waiting in the shade underneath an aqueduct. It was about ninety degrees. Waiting in the shade for the King. And all the signs, like Dairy Queen, and all those kinds of places, their signs said, "God bless you, Elvis" and "The King lives." . . . When the hearse rolled out on the street, and it reached the speed it was going to go at, I burst into tears. It was like the long, slow walk. The speed of the car was only maybe six miles an hour—five, six miles an hour. It rolled out in traffic and straightened out and just moved like a swan gliding down the road. And it was just so poignant.

When Elvis's hearse arrived at the cemetery, so did a disorganized squadron of helicopters and a huge throng of grief-stricken fans. There was a riot at the back gate as the crowd tried to push their way into the graveyard.

> *I started running toward where I thought the riot was coming from—I wanted to see what was going on. On the way I encountered the hearse being led by twenty-four motorcycle cops. It was one of the most terrifying things I have ever seen . . . there was one man standing in the cemetery right where they were passing by, and there was not supposed to be anybody there. There's one guy, and it's me. And this cop gave me a look that said, "If you move, I will shoot you right through the heart."*

Getting a strange vibe, Bill turned around and saw that he was standing at the foot of the grave of Gladys Presley, Elvis's mother. (Her body has since been relocated to Graceland, where it is buried next to Elvis's.) He stood frozen as the hearse and the motorcade and the twenty-four policemen on motorcycles slowly rolled by him, and then he ran back to where he had been before, by a mausoleum.

> *They carried the casket out and it had like, I don't know, three hundred roses on top of it or something amazing— like two or three masses' worth of roses on top of the casket. They were going to put it in a mausoleum overnight—it turned out later that people tried to tunnel into it and all kinds of crazy things. But they were going to put it in this mausoleum building before they actually buried it at Graceland. Anyway, as they tried to carry it up the steps,*

they almost dropped it . . . I mean, it wasn't solid gold,
but it was some sort of incredible metal—bronze or
something—and he wasn't that light to begin with.

Bill was twenty-six when he attended Elvis's funeral. By age twenty-six, Elvis had recorded fifteen number-one singles and changed the world—but Elvis spent his final years a prisoner of his own success, locked away behind the gates of Graceland. As Bill's fame grew in the following years, he looked for the path that would let him engage with the world, not confine him to a golden box.

· · ·

Lake Winnipesaukee—the small-town New England setting of most of the action in *What About Bob?*—is a screenwriter's invention. There's no town by that name, although it is a real body of water in New Hampshire. The movie is set in August, but the production was shooting through the fall, so the cast and crew ended up spending most of autumn 1990 in Moneta, Virginia—a small town on Smith Mountain Lake, where the leaves wouldn't be turning gold and orange. The nearest city was the not-very-big Roanoke, Virginia, roughly an hour away.

"We were in the boondocks," Bill Murray recalled. "On this man-made lake with nothing to do, and I mean, the middle of nowhere—not even much television." Then Bill found out MC Hammer was coming to Roanoke.

Hammer was at the height of his career, touring behind the multi-platinum *Please Hammer, Don't Hurt 'Em* album, which was spinning off hit singles like "Pray," "Have

You Seen Her," and especially the inescapable "U Can't Touch This."

So Bill called up his then-agents to arrange for tickets, chartered a bus, and filled it with fifty-five members of the cast and crew of *What About Bob?* They cruised down the highway to Roanoke, with a boom box blasting music the whole way—"and I think some moonshine," Bill said. When the bus got to the venue, Hammer and his people were delighted to see Bill. Their tour had been playing what the business calls "tertiary markets": smaller cities that don't have the population for frequent superstar shows, and they were astonished that somebody famous had showed up.

They invited Bill backstage and asked, "How many are with you?"

"All of them," Bill replied, pointing to a line of people stretching off toward the horizon.

As it happened, they had fifty-five extra seats on the side of the stage, which the group claimed. Hammer invited Bill onto his stage—or, as Bill described it, "this incredible, elevated stage that was filled with dancers and all of these musicians who weren't playing their instruments." He then encouraged Bill to do the "Hammer dance," the routine to "U Can't Touch This," which required an extremely wide stance, followed by a lot of hopping, spinning, and sidestepping.

"I did the dance," Bill said proudly. "Surprisingly, I knew all the steps. But I learned why he wore those weird chef's pants." (Hammer was famous for wearing baggy harem pants that puffed around the waist like a chef's toque does over the head.) Exerting himself during Hammer Time, Bill split his pants right down the back. And since he had been on location for about a month, he had run out of clean underwear and was going commando. "I was working without a net," he said. He went to the side of the stage, where the movie's costumer, Jennifer Butler— years later, his second wife—had some giant safety pins handy. With his decency restored, Bill returned to the action and finished the "U Can't Touch This" routine.

After the show, Hammer told Bill that professional athletes would sometimes come onstage and not be able to finish the number. When Bill wondered if they also had issues with their pants, Hammer told him, "No, they didn't have the stamina."

. . .

"Ghostbusters" is not only the biggest single in Ray Parker Jr.'s back catalog, it's an enduring part of the repertoire of the Harvard University Band (which we would call a marching band, except they're not real big on the marching). So at a Harvard-Cornell football game in October 2011, with Harvard on its way to a 41–31 victory, the band played "Ghostbusters" in the third quarter.

"This guy in pink pants walked up and said, 'Hey, play that song again,'" remembered Rachel Hawkins, the undergraduate band manager. "He kind of appeared out of nowhere." The guy was Bill Murray—he had flown to Syracuse to attend the game with Jim Downey, Harvard class of 1974, a former star writer at *Saturday Night Live* (and the uncle of Robert Downey, Jr.). The band obligingly played the song again, directing it at Bill's section, and tried to pretend this was an ordinary occurrence.

After the game, Bill reemerged and pretended to conduct the Harvard band. Evenhandedly, he also spent time with Cornell's Big Red Band, "conducting" them by standing on a podium and waving a bright-red jacket around while the band played the Who's "Pinball Wizard": First Bill twirled the jacket like a stripper, then he wielded it like a matador. By the end, he was stomping his feet and punching the air, turning his two minutes with the band into his own brand of interpretive dance.

· · ·

A Halloween party in East Williamsburg, 2008: Host Dave Summers, a twenty-nine-year-old grad student, was dressed as a cloud, wearing sky-blue clothes covered with cotton balls. One guest was in a yellow duck costume; another was costumed as Carl Spackler, Bill Murray's *Caddyshack* character. Since it was the week before the presidential election, multiple women showed up as Sarah Palin.

The party went late enough that October 31 turned into November 1 and the beer kegs ran dry; nevertheless, a couple dozen people stayed in Summers's loft to dance. Around 3:30 A.M., a guest ran over to Summers to alert him: "The real Bill Murray just walked in the door."

Summers was skeptical but figured that either way he needed to make a beer run. When he returned from a local bodega, his shopping bag burst in the hallway, spilling bottles of Modelo Especial all over the floor. That was when he found out Bill had actually arrived—because Bill helped him pick up all the bottles (sticking one in his shirt pocket).

Soon Bill—who either wasn't in costume or was dressed as himself, depending on your philosophical bent—was drinking that beer, joking around with the decades-younger party guests, and, inspired by Summers's costume, expounding on the pleasures of sweet potato casserole topped with marshmallows.

Eventually Bill hit the dance floor and impressed the younger generation with some credible moves: "It wasn't like he was John Travolta or something, but it wasn't embarrassing," said one guest.

Apparently Bill had attended the Halloween concert by MGMT, then at the peak of their success, at the Music Hall of Williamsburg, and gone party-hopping with the band afterward. His presence felt validating to Summers—he was throwing a shindig cool enough to get Bill Murray to stay—and delivered the message that if you stay up late enough, magical things can happen.

"All parties are good," Bill has said. "Parties are only bad when a fight breaks out, when men fight over women or vice versa. Someone takes a fall, an ambulance comes, and the police arrive. If you can avoid those things, pretty much all behavior is acceptable."

The spell was broken at the Halloween party when a sanctimonious male guest marched up to Bill and told him, "I think you're making poor life choices." Bill politely thanked Summers and vanished into the night.

. . .

So we were walking in downtown Charleston, doing our engagement photos, and I don't know if you've ever been here, but Charleston is very historic. All throughout downtown, it has lots of people's doorsteps, which you just stand on. It was Masters Sunday—we were just walking doorstep to doorstep, sitting on people's front porches and taking pictures.

Two guys walked by and we didn't even notice them— but as our photographer was looking at us, taking a picture, we noticed a guy standing behind him, lifting up his shirt over his face and rubbing his belly. We had no clue who it was; it was just an older guy rubbing his belly. Okay, that's strange but kind of funny at the same time.

Our photographer noticed that we weren't looking at the camera. He turns around, the guy pulls down his shirt, and oh my God, it's Bill Murray. He was like, "Heeeey, have a great day."

I said, "Will you at least hop in our picture?"

He says, "Absolutely." He hopped in, took a picture, said congratulations, and walked on. It was so fast. I loved that it was so genuine—no security, just two guys walking around downtown. We didn't even see that picture until a month later; I forgot that it even happened because it was just like an interaction with a regular person.

—as told by Ashley Donald,
now married to Erik Rogers

. . .

Bill Murray is standing in the Wrigley Field stands before a Cubs playoff game. It's October 3, 1984, the second game of the National League Championship Series, Cubs versus the Padres, with Chicago having already won the first game. Bill's wearing an orange T-shirt with a plaid orange shirt over it and chatting with a camera crew from the local sports program *Time Out,* a roundtable discussion broadcast on WTTW. Explaining that he's getting ready to perform "The Star-Spangled Banner," Bill grabs the skin of his throat and wobbles it, saying, "I'm trying to get loose." Looking onto the field, he declares, "I feel good. I feel real strong." Asked why he'll be singing the anthem from the seats instead of on the field, or even on top of the dugout, Bill says, "I want to bring the game back to the people . . . I've talked about this with some of the other great entertainers who do the anthem, and they just say, 'You know what, Bill? If only one of us would have the guts.' And I said, 'I got the guts.' "

The public announcer asks the Chicago crowd to rise and join in the singing of the national anthem—with "popular recording star Bobby Vinton." Bill gazes out at the sixties crooner who sang such number-one singles as "Blue Velvet," "Roses Are Red (My Love)," and "There! I've Said It Again."

"God, it is Bobby Vinton," Bill concedes. Vinton, it turns out, is in fine voice at age forty-nine, his clear tenor ringing through Wrigley Field. "He did a good job," Bill admits begrudgingly. "I guess they wanted a Hollywood type to come in and do it." Undaunted by reality, Bill proclaims his willingness to sing the anthem when the Cubs reach the World Series. (Although the Cubs would win that day 4–2, taking a 2–0 lead in the series, they would then, in trademark Cubs style, drop three straight games in San Diego and lose the series 3–2.)

BILL MURRAY MEETS THE YOUTH OF AMERICA

E. J. Rumpke was the first man in his group of friends from Boston College to get married—so his bachelor party, on the Memorial Day weekend of 2014, served as an informal reunion. Twenty friends, scattered up and down the Eastern Seaboard, gathered in Charleston, South Carolina (a town chosen for no reason other than convenience). They convened in a private room on the second floor of the Oak Steakhouse.

One of Rumpke's buddies, Bo Mlnarik, went downstairs to use the bathroom and spotted Bill Murray dining with some friends. Via a discreet conversation with a waiter, Mlnarik offered to buy Bill and his table a round of drinks and asked if there was any chance Bill might come up to the bachelor party and say a few words. Bill politely declined, but soon everyone at the bachelor party was whispering and buzzing about the presence of Bill in the restaurant—except for Rumpke, because his friends were still hoping they could find a way to get Bill to show up and wanted it to be a surprise. "They wouldn't even let me go pee," Rumpke says. Eventually, he insisted on going to the bathroom and spotted Bill, which seemed like enough of a bonus experience for the night: "Shit, that's pretty cool."

Rumpke's buddies asked again if Bill might come upstairs—he declined again, but then, while Rumpke's group was settling up the tab, he decided to do it. So although some people later breathlessly described this evening as "Bill Murray crashing a bachelor party," Bill was actually invited to the party more than once. It's what he did with that invitation that made it memorable.

Bill entered the room to riotous joy from Rumpke's bachelor pals and quickly made himself at home. "What do you think?" he asked them about Rumpke's fiancée. "Thumbs up on her? I want to know if it's a hundred percent."

Bill then addressed the room: "I have a little experience with this. I say, you know how funerals are not for the dead, they're for the living? Bachelor parties are not for the groom, they're for the uncommitted."

("That is a great quote!" somebody hollered, playing either aphorism aficionado or Bill Murray hypeman.)

Bill continued, "Listen here, I'm going to give you all this advice, because it's too late for this guy. Besides, she's a hundred percent." He rolled his eyes, not unkindly.

"Here's what I recommend to you. If you have someone that you think is the one, don't just think in your ordinary mind, think okay, let's make a date, let's plan this and make a party and get married. Take that person, and travel around the world. Buy a plane ticket for the two of you to travel all around the world and go to places that are hard to go to and hard to get out of. And if when you come back to JFK, when you land in JFK, and you're still in love with that person, get married at the airport."

As the assembled bachelors cheered, Bill asked Rumpke his bride's name.

"Kelly," Rumpke told him.

"That sounds lucky," Bill joked.

"Let's pick him up over our shoulders!" Bill told Rumpke's friends. Bill led the way by hoisting Rumpke up in the air, to his shock and delight. Rumpke's friends, shouting with enthusiasm, rushed in to make sure Bill didn't drop the groom. As they lifted him higher, Bill let go. And then, before anyone could thank him or buy him a drink, he quietly slipped out the door.

In the summer of 1977, Bill Murray was driving a beat-up Nash Rambler across the country, heading back to New York City for his first full season on *Saturday Night Live* (he had made his debut halfway through the show's second season, after Chevy Chase left). His friend, artist and video producer Van Schley, had become owner of a minor-league baseball team in Texas, buying into the Lone Star League for the grand sum of five hundred dollars. So Murray visited the team in Texas City (a small town famous for lethal industrial explosions and not much else).

On a hot July day, Bill rolled up to Robinson Stadium in a limousine. A bunch of the team's players were outside the ballpark, about to walk to a nearby 7-Eleven to buy some orange juice. They didn't recognize Bill, but they wouldn't soon forget him, because when he stepped out of the limo, he was wearing an authentic New York Yankees cap—which he promptly threw on the ground.

"Fuck Billy Martin!" he shouted. (Martin was the pugnacious manager of the Yankees, who would end up getting hired and fired by team owner George Steinbrenner five times.) "I'm here to play baseball, and if anybody doesn't like it, I *will* fight him for his job!"

The dramatic entrance had the players worried—was this some stud from double-A or triple-A ball? Soon enough, they found out the truth, and Bill stayed in town for a week or two, hanging out with the Texas City Stars, taking batting practice with the team, and not taking anybody's job.

. . .

On a Sunday morning in October 2012, Bill Murray was supposed to be at an expensive photo shoot for the cover of *GQ*. He skipped it in favor of taking some of his sons and their friends to Roosevelt Island: the small chunk of land in New York City's East River, connected to Manhattan by an aerial tram. Bill had seen a PBS documentary about the building of a monument to Franklin D. Roosevelt's Four Freedoms. (In the 1941 State of the Union address, about a year before the United States entered World War II, FDR laid out four freedoms that everyone in the world should enjoy: freedom of speech, freedom of worship, freedom from want, freedom from fear). Having recently played Roosevelt in *Hyde Park on Hudson*, Bill felt a personal connection to the granite memorial. Although it wasn't yet open to the public, not being quite completed, he felt confident in his ability to gain access, just as he used to talk his way into movie premiere parties before he became a star. (The best one was probably the New York City fete for *Tommy* in 1975, held in the 57th Street subway station for some reason—it was wall-to-wall celebrities, plus Bill and his friends. Bill met Andy Warhol and embarrassed himself by saying "I love the soup can," receiving a blank stare in return.)

The memorial's construction crew recognized Bill and let him in without any hassle—a bit of a letdown for him, since half the fun for Bill is having the blarney (or, as he sometimes calls it, "the sand") that gets him through the gate. So afterward he wandered around Roosevelt Island, looking for another party to crash.

He found it in the form of some hipsters playing kickball. (Adults who play kickball are, pretty much by definition, hipsters.) Clad in a brown T-shirt, a knit cap, and bright blue shorts, Bill walked up and asked the referee if he could join the game. (Since the game had a referee, we may conclude that it was an absurdly well-regulated gang of hipsters.) The ref interrupted the action to ask the teams if the newcomer could join in. Everyone agreed without thinking about it much, although opinion was split on whether the new player was the father of one of the kickballers or just a random homeless dude. Bill's sons stood on the sidelines, watching Dad do his thing.

The second baseman on the opposing team described the action: "The man kicked the ball and ran pretty well to first base, trying to round to second, but one of my teammates chased him back to first, deciding not to attempt to peg the man. That was when everyone on my team realized who he was . . . BILL MURRAY DECIDED TO PLAY KICKBALL WITH US!"

Bill advanced to second base on a teammate's kick, and

then got doubled off on a line drive. As the second baseman told it, "As awesome as it was to be playing with the legend, I couldn't let him best me at my game and I touched him out by an inch to get the double play."

Bill stuck around through the end of the inning, posing for photos, giving high-fives to all the players, and even hugging one player's mom and hoisting her into the air. One player, Courtney Beard, walked up to him and asked, "Bill Murray, what are you doing here?"

He smiled, shook her hand, and said, "Oh, y'know, just wanted to kick the ball around."

The Fourth Principle
Make sure everybody else is invited to the party.

THE PREMIERE PARTY FOR *MOONRISE KINGDOM* was held on the beach in Cannes, and for most of the party, Bill Murray sequestered himself with the film's grown-up stars (Tilda Swinton, Jason Schwartzman) in a VIP area. Many of the movie's actors were the kids playing "Khaki Scouts," so they occupied themselves with an epic game of hide-and-seek, which ended when one of them successfully hid for over thirty minutes.

When Bill found out that thirteen-year-old Jared Gilman, the film's male romantic lead, wanted to dance, he started getting down with him (plus three other juvenile actors: Seamus Davey-Fitzpatrick, Charlie Kilgore, and Gabriel Rush). The other adults at the party pulled out their cellphones to document the boogie fever, but Bill shouted out, "We're just chilling! We're just chilling!" and got everyone to put them away.

The DJ played songs like the Pointer Sisters' "I'm So Excited." Whenever a woman stepped forward, wanting to dance with Bill, he would redirect her, partnering her up with one of his barely pubescent costars.

Once the dance floor had reached a sufficient boil, Bill decided that everyone needed to do a "Hava Nagila"–style dance—linking arms and joining in a circle. "Boy, girl, boy, girl," he instructed the partygoers. "Can you be a girl?" he asked one woman. Once the circle had reached over twenty people (including Swinton), he put it in motion, first spinning one way, then the other. The partygoers did high kicks ("Kick higher! You have to kick higher!" Bill exhorted them) and generally followed his lead: When Bill ran into the center of the circle, so did everyone else, in one happy, sweaty scrum.

At the end of the song, the participants gave each other high-fives. Bill had turned a starchy movie-business soirée into an actual party.

. . .

Garry Trudeau, creator of the *Doonesbury* comic strip, wanted Bill Murray to make a cameo in his TV series *Alpha House,* about a group of congressmen sharing a house in Washington, D.C.—Bill would play an indicted senator who had overslept and neglected to turn himself in to law enforcement. Trudeau had a way of circumventing Bill's 1-800 number: Trudeau's wife, Jane Pauley, had gotten to know Bill back when she was hosting NBC's *Today* show and he was a cast member of *Saturday Night Live.* The *SNL* staff used to stay up all night working on material and then raid the *Today* craft-services table in the early hours of the morning. Pauley and Bill had stayed friendly in the following decades, so she texted him to hand off the *Alpha House* script. Bill responded, "Well, I'm having a party. Come on over, I think you'll really enjoy it. It's tonight." Pauley begged off, saying she couldn't make it that night. "Don't worry," Bill responded. "It'll still be going in three days. Just get here before Monday!"

TALES FROM THE GRAPE D'VINE

On a snowy winter day, Bill Murray was hanging out at the Grape D'Vine wine shop with proprietor Joe Printz, who opened a bottle of Barolo (a red Italian wine) for the two of them to enjoy. People would walk into the shop to buy some wine—and freak out when they realized Bill was there. Surrounded by a small crowd, Bill stood up, handed his wineglass to a woman, and headed outside. In the street, he gathered up a handful of snow, made a snowball, and pegged a man walking away, halfway down the block. Irate, the man turned around and charged toward Bill—but when he saw who his attacker was, he broke into a big grin and instead made a snowball of his own. Everyone poured out of the store to follow Bill's lead. Soon, the street was filled with adults having a massive snowball fight.

In the final months of 1988, Kyra Bromley was living in Aspen, Colorado, working as a waitress so she could spend the season as a ski bum. Her housemate discovered that Jimmy Buffett was coming to town and playing a high-end private event at a local hotel, so they decided to sneak into the party. They dressed up fancy, went to the exit at the back of the hotel, and pulled the old trick of pretending they were talking to people and walking in backward.

When they got inside, Jimmy Buffett was in the middle of his set. "Bill Murray was there, and he was dancing with this woman who was one of the town eccentrics," Bromley remembers. "I don't know who she was—maybe she had piles of money—but she used to walk through the streets, talking to herself. And he was dancing with her, which I thought was hysterical."

At the end of the song, Bill headed over to the bar. Bromley walked up and warned him, "You're dancing with this local eccentric who talks to herself."

Bill laughed, completely nonjudgmental, and told Bromley it didn't bother him—that sort of thing happened to him all the time.

Bill then danced with Bromley for a song. "I remember thinking that he was chill," she says. "This was Aspen in 1988—celebrities were everywhere, and a lot of them were assholes. And a lot of them were not. Some of the ones you'd expect to be complete assholes were really nice. I expected him to be nice—and he was nice."

. . .

In the summer of 2006, twenty-year-old Massie Minor was sitting in a pickup truck outside the Cronig's grocery store on Lamberts Cove Road in West Tisbury, Massachusetts, on the island of Martha's Vineyard. He and his fifteen-year-old cousin gazed at the tableau before them: two women, with the hood open on their Jeep Wrangler, studying the engine, along with an unusual character. This man was wearing a straw cowboy hat, a Hawaiian shirt, orange cargo pants, and blue water shoes.

"That's Bill Murray," Minor's cousin said. Minor checked the guy out. It didn't seem possible: No actor would ever leave the house in an outfit like that. But the more he looked at him—Minor was blatantly staring at this point—the more it looked like Bill. Finally, Minor and his cousin summoned up their courage and walked over to introduce themselves.

It was Bill, orange cargo pants and all. The women had thought their car was low on oil, and they were right—but while they tried to figure out exactly where in the car they needed to put the oil, Bill had walked up, started flirting, and given them a confusing monologue about the multiple locations that allegedly needed oil.

As soon as Minor and his cousin got up to the Jeep and flanked Bill, he stood up straight, put one hand on each of their shoulders, and said, "This guy and this guy—they're the man." He nodded at them and walked into Cronig's. The grammar was a bit mangled, but that didn't reduce the pride Minor felt: He had gotten a personal endorsement from Mr. Bill Murray. Then he realized the situation Bill had left him in. The women—both in their mid-twenties, both way out of his league—were looking at him expectantly, waiting for him to solve their car problems.

BILL MURRAY MEETS THE YOUTH OF AMERICA

Actress Jami Gertz kicked off her career as part of the ensemble on the Sarah Jessica Parker–starring sitcom *Square Pegs*—which was smart enough and enough of a cult favorite that Bill Murray made a guest appearance as a substitute teacher in a 1983 episode. He affectionately nicknamed the teenage Gertz "Chicago," because she was from his hometown.

His response when Gertz, who had just gotten her driver's license, told him, "Mr. Murray, I know how to drive!"? He threw her the keys to a Mercedes convertible and said, "Let's go!"

"I got in the car, and we just started driving around," an adult Gertz said. "We went to In-N-Out Burger in Norwalk, California." Meanwhile, the *Square Pegs* production staff freaked out, worried that their talent had wandered off the lot and that Bill had absconded with a minor. Gertz said, "We came back to, like, 'Where the hell were you?'"

Bill, unabashed about contributing to the deliquency of a minor, explained, "She just learned how to drive!"

In her senior year of high school, Bill Murray's oldest sister, Nancy, decided that she wanted to be a nun. Nobody in the family supported her decision—all the nuns they knew were stiff disciplinarians, plus Nancy liked to go on dates—except Ed Murray, the family patriarch. Nevertheless, she packed up and moved into a Dominican convent in Michigan. Ultimately, she said, the Murrays came around to her choice, although they told her to cool it with the pious letters home: "Only stay if you remain our Nancy. We don't want a nun in the family we're embarrassed of."

That support, however, didn't stop Bill from razzing Sister Nancy when a bunch of the Murray brothers made a road trip to Michigan to visit her. Pulling up behind a building where the younger nuns lived, the Murrays parked beneath the bathroom windows. While the teenage nuns looked out the windows and giggled, Bill shouted up: "*Naaan-cy!* We have a bag packed! You can leave! Come on! We'll drive away! We'll take off! *Naaan-cy!*"

. . .

"Everyone had slept with everyone else," said writer Michael O'Donoghue of the *Saturday Night Live* cast and staff. "Everyone had had a fight with everyone else." They were young and it was the seventies: There was a complicated, interlocking web of romantic and sexual relationships. Laraine Newman, for example, was involved with Dan Aykroyd, who in turn was dating writer Rosie Shuster, who was still married to producer Lorne Michaels. Gilda Radner and Carrie Fisher had a dramatic confrontation over Paul Simon; Radner and Bill Murray had a tempestuous relationship of their own.

"I never enjoyed making anyone laugh more than her," Bill said of Radner. He remembered one sustained comedy jag where Radner was laughing so hard for so long, she thought she might die. "I used to be really funny, and in those days I used to have almost like a vengeful thing; I could just go for a long period of time and try to be funny. I don't do it like I used to. And I miss that. I'm still funny, but back then I would take something and not let go of it."

In 1980, Radner married guitarist G. E. Smith (who was not yet a musician on the show), and then a few years later she fell hard for actor Gene Wilder. After she and Smith split, she married Wilder in 1984. She contracted ovarian cancer; it went into remission, but then it recurred and she died in 1989, just forty-two years old.

"Gilda got married and went away," Bill said. "None of us saw her anymore." Except one last time in March 1987, when Laraine Newman turned thirty-five and had a party at her house in Los Angeles. It seemed like all the funniest people in the world were there: the original *Saturday Night Live* crew, members of Monty Python, and L.A. notables including Steve Martin and Sam Kinison. Bill was DJ for the night, playing Newman's 45s, and Radner showed up.

When Radner tried to head home, Bill didn't want her to leave. So he picked her up and carried her around the house so she could say goodbye to everybody. When he was exhausted, Aykroyd took a shift; then he handed Radner back to Bill. "We kept carrying her around, but like upside down, every which way—over your shoulder and under your arm, carrying her like luggage," Bill said. "And that went on for more than an hour."

Radner would say goodbye to the same people over and over—and because they were the funny people that they were, they would make their farewells into a top-notch performance, over and over. Even upside down, Radner laughed uncontrollably.

"It was just one of the best parties I've ever been to in my life. I'll always remember it," Bill said. "It was the last time I saw her."

It's Hard to Be a Saint in the City

What's it like trying to get Bill Murray to be in your movie? Ted Melfi had worked on the fringes of the film industry for a while and had written a well-regarded screenplay called *St. Vincent de Van Nuys,* about a cantankerous Vietnam War veteran who forges an unlikely alliance with the young boy next door. Jack Nicholson had flirted with making the movie, but when he passed, Melfi set his sights on Bill. His producer, Fred Roos, had also produced *Lost in Translation,* directed by Sofia Coppola (not to mention *The Godfather: Part II,* for which Roos won an Oscar).

"Good luck," Roos told Melfi. "To tell you the truth, Sofia and I didn't know he was going to come to Japan to do the movie until the day he showed up on the plane."

Melfi had the 1-800 phone number that Bill uses to screen his calls. He called up, listened to the generic voicemail greeting—unpersonalized by Bill—and left a message. Then he deleted it, because he was nervous and worried that he was babbling, and left another one. Over the next month, Melfi left a dozen messages, some serious, some funny, not knowing if Bill was listening to any of them.

Since Bill doesn't have a manager, an agent, or a publicist, Melfi eventually tracked down his attorney, David Nochimson. "What number are you calling?" Nochimson asked.

Melfi recited the 1-800 number.

"That's what I got," Nochimson said. (Bill's friends and professional associates have ways of getting in touch with him beyond the 1-800 number—but you don't stay close with Bill by providing them to anyone who calls you up.)

Finally, Nochimson called Melfi with good news: Bill wanted him to write a one-page letter pitching the movie. Melfi wrote it and sent it to a PO box in upstate New York.

Two weeks later, Nochimson called back: "Bill thought the letter was swell. Can you send him the script?" Melfi sent it to another PO box, this one in Martha's Vineyard.

Weeks passed. Bill called the assistant of producer Fred Roos and asked, "Is he ever going to send me that script?" Melfi sent another copy, this one to a PO box in South Carolina.

Two more weeks of silence, and then Melfi's cellphone rang while he was driving down the road in Los Angeles. "Ted Melfi? It's Bill Murray. Is now a good time?"

"Now is the *best* time," Melfi assured him, and pulled over.

"I don't Google people," Bill told him. "That's not my thing. Can you tell me who you are and what you do and why?" Melfi stammered his way through a twenty-minute monologue about hustling his way through his career as a commercial director.

"That all sounds good," Bill assured him. "I'd love to sit down with you for a coffee tomorrow."

Melfi assented: He was shooting a commercial that day, but he knew he could make time.

"In New York?" Bill added, and Melfi had to decline. "How about Friday, then?" Bill suggested.

Melfi eagerly agreed: Yes, he could be in New York on Friday.

"No, in Cannes." Bill was going to Cannes for the world premiere of *Moonrise Kingdom,* but it was physically impossible for Melfi to get there. "Cannes is going to be a *great* time," Bill promised, but there was no way for Melfi to do it. "Don't worry about it, we'll connect later. I'll call you in a couple of weeks."

Sensing that his opportunity was slipping away, Melfi said, "Bill, is there a better number for you, anything—"

"No, no, you've got the number." Bill hung up.

Three weeks went by. Melfi was convinced that he had blown his one chance to persuade Bill and was so stressed by the whole enterprise that he threw out his back and started walking with a cane. At 8:00 A.M. on Sunday morning of Memorial Day weekend, Melfi was lying in bed, immobilized, when he got a text from Bill: "Can you meet me at LAX in an hour?" Melfi eagerly agreed, strapped on a back brace, popped a Vicodin, and drove to the airport.

At the designated baggage-claim area, Melfi spotted a man in a rumpled black suit, holding a card with B. MURRAY printed on it. "I think I'm with you," Melfi told him.

"Yeah?" the guy replied.

Melfi thought, "Oh God, he doesn't know anything either."

Soon enough, however, Bill strolled toward them with a golf bag. "Ted? What's with the back?"

"I threw it out," Melfi told him.

"You gotta stretch," Bill counseled. "You want to talk about the script? Let's go for a drive."

The driver in the rumpled suit escorted them to a town car. First stop: In-N-Out Burger, where they picked up four grilled-cheese sandwiches and four orders of french fries. Melfi confessed to Bill that he was vegan. "That's an awful life," Bill said.

Bill had a dog-eared copy of the screenplay in his attaché case; he pulled it out and they discussed it for three hours, kicking around Bill's ideas and notes, as the town car headed south. They drove through the Pechanga Indian Reservation in Temecula, ending up at a modest ranch house owned by Bill, adjacent to a golf course. Bill gave Melfi a tour, showing off groves of trees: orange, tangelo, avocado.

Melfi excused himself to use the bathroom. "Don't forget to jiggle the handle," Bill told him. When Melfi finished, Bill said, "I think we're good. Let's make a movie. Do you want to do this with me?"

Melfi assured him that he would love to make this movie with him. But he had one favor to ask: "Could you tell someone other than me that this happened? Because I'm not sure they're going to believe you're doing the movie if you don't tell them."

After another two weeks, Bill called up his attorney and confirmed that he wanted to do the movie (which, with a shortened title of *St. Vincent*, came out in 2014). Melfi on his Bill Murray roller-coaster ride:

Bill is by far the free-est person I've ever met in my life. He lives in the moment more than anyone I've ever known. His whole life is in the moment. Bill doesn't care about what happened; he doesn't think about what's going to happen. He doesn't even book travel two ways. Bill buys one-way tickets and then decides when he wants to go home. Then he'll call and say, "Hey, I think I should go home," and we'll figure out how to get him home. There's no bullshit, no manipulation—it's so honest and so pure to have someone like that around. What you see is what you get: He throws people in the pool in private and he throws people in the pool in public.

Bill stayed at a friend's apartment in Williamsburg. And then he gave the production back all the money for hotels. He rode his ten-speed bike to the set every day: After a forty-minute ride, he'd show up a sweaty mess. He'd throw on a clean shirt and come to the set.

A lot of comedians come in and do their schtick. And Bill doesn't put his stink on something. When he's in a scene, nothing else exists. He brings everyone else there with him, and you have to be prepared for that ride. He'll do anything: He'll run, he'll jump, he'll scream. He's not a hijacker: He believes improv lives within the scene.

Bill has a lot of children, so he's a big texter. Sometimes he'll text one word and sometimes a long paragraph. I would get texts from him while he was shooting Monuments Men—he told me when he was meeting his makeup artist in London. They designed a whole look for his physical being: He looks like an old Brooklyn war vet. When he first came to a costume fitting, I said, "Oh my goodness, you have such great teeth."

He said, "Thank you—I just had them Waterpik'd."

I said, "Yeah, I think they're too great."

He goes, "Okay." And then a day later he had a special veneer shipped in from London.

There were times, depending on the scene, when Bill was so deep into Vin that you just didn't talk to him. That scene when he finds out his wife dies and he falls down? That's all Bill. I didn't ask him to fall down: I just said, I want you to go to the fridge, hear the message, and whatever happens to you, happens to you. It was the last shot of the day.

And then there were times when Vin was having a great time, like when he's at the racetrack. Bill stole a golf cart that day and rode around the actual track until security came and got him.

Sometimes it was challenging to get Bill to come to the set, not because he's a diva, but because you can't find him. He's not trying to slow things down, but he likes to wander. If he sees a scooter and a bike, he'll go look at it. We hired a PA [production assistant] just to follow him around, but he could lose her on command. One time we couldn't find him for the longest time—he was in an Army recruiting center with Naomi Watts, giving autographs and hugging our armed forces.

Another time, I couldn't find Bill, so I called his assistant Chris. Bill answered Chris's phone: "Hello?"

I knew it was Bill, but I said, "Hi, Chris, it's Ted—we're trying to find Bill."

"Oh, Bill? Yeah, he's getting a sandwich. He found a great sandwich shop. Would you like one?"

"No, I just want you to get him the message that we kinda need him because we're trying to make a movie."

"Okay, I'll tell Bill, no worries."

He had heard about the very best sandwich shop in the Bronx. And we were shooting only five or ten minutes away, so he drove there. He came back and said, "That's the best sandwich in the Bronx."

The Fifth Principle
Music makes the people come together.

BILL MURRAY IS THE PATRON SAINT OF KARAOKE. His appearances on *Saturday Night Live* as Nick the Lounge Singer demonstrated that singing ability is only tangentially related to being entertaining on the microphone. Bill proved that when you don't know the words, it's totally fine to make them up, as long as you do it with confidence ("Gimme those Star Wars! Don't let them end!"). Then in *Lost in Translation,* Bill showed that karaoke could be more than just a goof: It could express your innermost longings. When he sang Roxy Music's "More Than This," the song contained everything his character felt about Scarlett Johansson's character but could never say. Bill can use other people's songs to express both poles of karaoke: deeply felt emotion and complete insincerity.

So in early 2011, when a young man named Mike went out to sing karaoke at a hip New York City joint called Karaoke One 7 and spotted Bill Murray amid the candles and exposed brick, it was like having Albert Pujols show up at your company's softball game. Mike and his friends confirmed that it was, in fact, Bill—accompanied by a couple of women—and even invited them to join their group in a private karaoke room. The offer was politely declined, so Mike's crew headed into the room for some serious singing and drinking.

Fifteen minutes later, there was a knock on the door: Bill and his friends had decided to join them. In ordinary circumstances, Mike's group might have freaked out, but they were already pretty drunk, Mike said, "so the party just kept going." One of Bill's companions was the Dutch actress Carice van Houten, whose memorable work as the fire priestess Melisandre on the TV show *Game of Thrones* had not yet aired. To Mike and his friends, she was just a cute girl from Amsterdam with a good voice, who liked to sing songs in French. Bill ordered everyone a round of Chartreuse, the bright-green liqueur made by French monks, but declined to tell them what it was: Mike gulped his down, and only then found out he was supposed to be sipping it.

Mike's high point was duetting with Bill on a cover of Elvis Presley's 1961 hit "(Marie's the Name) His Latest Flame." "Random, I know, but so was the night," he said. "We were all drinking and dancing and screaming our asses off."

Bill and his friends stayed for about four hours, and then vanished into the night, leaving Mike and his friends with only one regret: They had neglected to dial up the theme from *Ghostbusters*.

. . .

Bill Murray had a long association with David Letterman's various talk shows, beginning with the premiere episode of *Late Night with David Letterman* on February 1, 1982. But on the evening of that first episode, minutes before Bill was supposed to walk into the studio, with the cameras already rolling, he was nowhere to be found.

"We basically put out an internal APB," said Sandra Furton, who along with Cathy Vasapoli was one of the show's talent coordinators. "Everyone looked in all the doorways, looked through all the rooms. The show was starting, and we found out that he had left the building." Just in time, Bill returned to 30 Rockefeller Plaza, through an entrance that he knew from his days on *Saturday Night Live.*

When Furton and Vasapoli asked Bill where he had gone, he said casually, "I had to go home and feed my cat."

Bill used his interview segment to show off the widest mood swings possible, from declaring, "I swear, Letterman, if it's the last thing I'm gonna do, I'm gonna make every second of your life from this moment on a living hell," to weeping at a video of a baby panda. He was also the first musical guest ever on the show, concluding his segment by declaring his love for aerobics and singing an enthusiastic but ungainly version of Olivia Newton-John's "Physical."

"We learned the song," bandleader Paul Shaffer said, "and then got ready for anything to happen."

"That first show might have been just a touch too unstructured," Letterman confessed two years later. "When we asked Bill to be on our first show, he said he'd like to do something different: Could he come up to the office and talk with the writers and see what they could come up with together? I said, 'Great.' So he arrived one afternoon when [head writer] Merrill [Markoe] and I were out shooting a remote and brought six half-gallon bottles of whatever tequila was on sale, and he and the entire staff proceeded to get shit-faced all afternoon. When I got back, the place was a shambles; everyone was dangerously drunk; all the lamps were hidden, because Bill had convinced them that the fluorescent lights were draining their vitamin E; nothing had been written; and the only explanation I could get out of anyone was 'Bill was here.' And when we did go on the air, Bill didn't want to do any of the things we had finally gotten around to preparing. Instead, he had a sudden urge to sing 'Let's get physical' and do aerobics. So he did. And it was very funny."

. . .

Early in the 1980s, after Bill Murray had finished making *Stripes* but before he signed on to *Ghostbusters,* he had an epiphany: He wanted to make a movie with Clint Eastwood. He'd seen some of his films and was particularly impressed by 1974's *Thunderbolt and Lightfoot,* which costarred Jeff Bridges. "I don't want to be Clint Eastwood," Bill thought. "He's got that covered. But look at the other guy in his movie . . . the second banana gets amazing focus." Bill admired how Eastwood went out of his way to let the spotlight shine on his costars, even if they didn't have his acting ability or his charisma. "He gives them a moment, he gives them their shot. Whether they do it or not is up to them."

Bill thought, "Man, I could kill one of these movies. I could be great in one of these. There's lots of fun action stuff to do, there's some funny repartee, you get some jokes. The sidekick gets all the funny stuff; Clint gets to go, 'Hmm.' And then you get killed! So that Clint can avenge you! And you have a *fantastic* death scene."

So Bill phoned up Eastwood to express his admiration and tell him that he wanted the sidekick gig. The laconic response: "Well, would you be interested in doing another service comedy?" Eastwood was developing a movie about the final days of World War II and had a role for Bill as a fast-talking supply sergeant, responsible for moving millions of pieces of machinery around. Bill declined, saying that after making *Stripes,* he didn't want to become the military-comedy guy. "It probably wouldn't have happened," he conceded of the hypothetical pigeonholing, "but I didn't want to do two in a row. I just wanted to stay a little loose." Ruefully, Bill said, "I wish I had done it. It would have been fun."

Bill did get to impersonate Eastwood in *Groundhog Day:* In a throwaway scene in the middle, he goes on a date to see the movie *Heidi II,* having told a Punxsutawney girl that they were going to a costume party. She shows up in a French maid outfit, while he has the hat, spurs, and poncho that Eastwood would wear in a spaghetti western—and he insists on being called "Bronco." According to director Harold Ramis, the Eastwood tribute came directly from the mind of Bill.

Three decades after Bill Murray first called Clint Eastwood, they finally collaborated: They got onstage at a private party at the Pebble Beach golf tournament and sang a cover of the 1972 number-one single by the Looking Glass, "Brandy (You're a Fine Girl)." The song was written by Elliot Lurie, who went on to serve as music supervisor on dozens of movies, including Bill's 1996 elephant comedy, *Larger Than Life*. It's a memorable slice of cheese—in other words, exactly the sort of material that Bill is expert at dispatching in his Nick the Lounge Singer guise. He rolled up his sleeves and tackled the song, giving it the aural equivalent of a head-noogie.

Eastwood was somewhat more diffident, croaking out a line here and there. And when the duo harmonized, the results were a bit gruesome. But Eastwood was obviously enjoying himself. Just as Bill knew that it would have been fun to be in a Clint Eastwood movie, Eastwood was discovering that it would have been a blast to be in a Bill Murray movie.

ON THE DARK SIDE

In the mid-seventies, Ivan Reitman was not yet the revered director of comedy classics such as *Stripes* and *Ghostbusters*. But he was a producer of a hit Broadway musical: *The Magic Show*, starring illusionist Doug Henning. So Reitman cold-called the offices of the *National Lampoon* and got a meeting with the magazine's staff, trying to pitch them on the idea of doing movies. They didn't want to do that (yet), but they were interested in putting together a sketch-comedy revue that would play in Manhattan and asked if Reitman would produce it.

That became *The National Lampoon Show*, which, before *Saturday Night Live* launched, employed Bill Murray, his brother Brian Doyle-Murray, John Belushi, Gilda Radner, and Harold Ramis. "I saw this remarkable group of comedians who were just as confident, just as funny, just as arrogant as they were at the height of their careers," Reitman says.

The first time Reitman went to a rehearsal, he sat in the back and watched them work. Belushi was nominally the director, although the cast made most decisions collectively. When they started arguing about a sequence in one of the sketches, Reitman voiced his opinion, figuring that as producer of the show, he had a valid opinion. "Hey, wouldn't it be better if—" Reitman said, but that was as far as he got. "They all stopped and looked at me, and it was the scariest thing you ever saw."

Reitman remembers, "Bill walks up to me really slowly, puts his hand very lovingly on my shoulders, and walks me over to where my coat and scarf were hung on the side—it was wintertime. He takes the scarf and starts wrapping it around my neck really dangerously, and I was thinking, 'Wow, this could go anywhere.' Then he said, 'Hey, man, it was really nice having you here,' and he pushed me out the door. I said, 'Oh my God, this is going to be hard.'"

Hyde Park on Hudson was set entirely in the Hudson Valley, close to Bill Murray's home in New York State, but for budgetary reasons filmed entirely in England. Staying in London, Bill had some opportunities to seek out adventure, like the night he went to a Japanese restaurant and the owner told him, "Duck-a-Dunn! He in town!" By which she meant that soul legends "Duck" Dunn and Steve Cropper were playing a gig. And although she had no way of knowing it, Bill was friendly with the musicians: Not only were they the core of Otis Redding's backing band and the Stax Records house band, but they were some of the ringers employed by his pals John Belushi and Dan Aykroyd when they recorded as the Blues Brothers.

"So I ended up stuffing all these crazy Japanese women into a car and rolling up to the gig," Bill said. "Steve and Duck killed it—they were unbelievable. For the encore I went out and banged the tambourine." Word got out that Bill had joined the band for "Soul Man": "I went to work the next day and people said, 'Bill, were you onstage last night? Weren't you supposed to be learning your lines?'"

. . .

Andrew Groothuis is a history teacher in Florida, but back in 2011 he was working as a personal assistant to one of the actors in the Wes Anderson movie *Moonrise Kingdom.* They headed to Newport, Rhode Island, for five days of filming. "I'd been working the business for seven or eight years, so I didn't get starstruck," he remembers, "but I was superexcited because I'd never met Bill before. There were two or three people who could get me to go to a movie theater, and he was one of them."

He didn't want to approach Bill on the set. One of Bill's sons, Cooper, was in the troop of "Khaki Scouts" who form an important part of the movie, so Bill was spending most of his off-camera time hanging out with the kids and enter-

taining them; Groothuis thought it would be rude to inter-
rupt. They were staying at the same hotel, however—the
Vanderbilt Hotel, a converted mansion—so he held out
hope that they'd cross paths. The movie was shooting before the Newport tourist season started, so it felt as if the
moviemakers had taken over the hotel—except during
those times when everyone was on set, when its empty hall-
ways made people feel as if they had wandered into *The
Shining*.

One day after another passed, and Groothuis still
hadn't had his Bill moment. Late on the fourth night, after
his employer went to sleep, Groothuis ended up in the
hotel bar: just him and the bartender. The concierge—
a guy sitting at a table in the lobby—promised to let him
know if he spotted Bill, but Groothuis wasn't feeling optimistic. So he asked the bartender, "You mind if I screw
around on the piano?" She granted permission with a
nod, and Groothuis started noodling on the bar's neglected piano.

"Within ten seconds," Groothuis says, "in walks Bill
from a billiards room in the back that I didn't even know
was there. He had heard the piano." You can't rely on Bill
Murray to throw the party for you: Get the party started,
and maybe Bill Murray will show up.

Bill, accompanied by two middle-aged women, got the
bartender to make appletinis for everybody and started
singing along with Groothuis: everything from Billy Joel to
Bruce Springsteen to "Build Me Up Buttercup." Groothuis played every song he could think of that related to

Bill's career, and Bill gamely sang them all: "More Than This" from *Lost in Translation,* "Do Wah Diddy Diddy" from *Stripes,* the theme from *Star Wars* as done on *Saturday Night Live.* Bill remembered the words to all of them.

Groothuis, a true Bill Murray fan, launched into the CIT theme from *Meatballs*—"We are the CITs, so pity us"—and Bill just laughed.

"I'm not going to make you do that one," Groothuis said.

"No, no, I can do it!" Bill insisted.

Groothuis says he's not the greatest piano player—the theme from *Ghostbusters* was beyond his abilities—but he was able to fake his way through most of Bill's requests, such as Springsteen's "My Hometown."

"I was having a one-on-one with Nick the Lounge Singer," Groothuis said. "He was standing right behind me, just yelping the way he yelps, singing the way he sings. I must have been drunk, because all we were doing was drinking appletinis, but I remember everything. I can't even say it was a dream come true, because I never imagined it could happen."

They played music and sang for approximately five hours. Around 4:00 A.M., the concierge abandoned his post and came in to do a song. At 5:00 A.M., Bill said he needed to stop because he had to catch his plane. The two women took their leave, and Groothuis headed back to his own room, accompanied by Bill, who wanted to compare accommodations. When Bill saw that Groothuis's room was nicer than his own, he feigned anger: "Holy shit, I am so furious right now!"

Before he left for the airport, Bill told Groothuis, "Listen, I don't remember names but I'm good with faces. You ever see me anywhere, you come and say hello."

CUBS

BILL MURRAY

The Friendly Confines

In the opening weeks of the 1987 baseball season, longtime Cubs announcer Harry Caray was sidelined while he was recovering from a stroke. He was replaced by an all-star array of substitutes, including Bob Costas, George Will, and George Wendt. Nobody, however, seized the opportunity like longtime Cubs fan Bill Murray, who got behind the microphone on April 17 for a home game against the Montreal Expos.

Bill realized before he walked into the booth that, although he was going to be partnered with the professional Steve Stone, he was not actually a sportscaster himself. "I made the decision to do it as a *fan*," he said years later, "calling it like a person would sitting in front of his TV." That let him spin the broadcast on its axis, talking back to the screen in real time a full year before *Mystery Science Theater 3000* went on the air. It didn't hurt that Bill found Caray's personal refrigerator under the desk, crammed full of beer.

Bill on the air, describing the prospects for the game: "T. S. Eliot, the poet, once said 'April is the cruelest month.' But I don't think even that great man would have anticipated that the Cubs would lose their first four at home. I'm here today to turn this around, and I think with the help of the overrated and *not such a big deal after all* Montreal Expos, the Cubs will triumph today."

On the game starting late because the umpires were still getting dressed: "What is it that umpires do when they dress? I mean, how many problems can they have? It's basically the one color that they're wearing, right? It's not like they're holding up different sport coats in front of the mirror and saying, 'Well, Jocko, what do you think of this look?'"

On the Canadian national anthem: "Frankly, I love the 'O Canada' national anthem, 'cause there's only like ten words to it, and I wish they'd let me sing it. It's one of the goofiest national anthems I've ever heard. It makes the national anthem of the United States sound like Beethoven's Ninth. It's just ridiculous. They've only got five words in the song and they just keep saying them over and over again. I hope you Canadian folks call up and say something to whoever's in charge in your country about that theme song of yours."

On Montreal's first batter: "Starting for the Expos in left field, Casey Candaele. He's no good."

On the fans in the Wrigley Field bleachers: "These are people who take bad falls down the stairs and don't really know."

On the fans yelling to him in the booth: "Nice to see the gang from Joliet maximum security prison here."

On Montreal shortstop Tom Foley: "Is this that terrible Foley up again? Hey, Foley! Foley! Strike out, Foley! I hate everything you stand for!"

On cutting off beer sales after the eighth inning: "Anybody who can't get drunk at the ball game before the eighth inning doesn't belong here."

On Montreal pitcher Floyd Youmans, ejected for arguing

with an umpire: "You hate to see that sort of thing happen, especially when we're hitting him so well."

On Cubs pitcher Rick Sutcliffe, and why Bill was pleased he was pitching well: "Frankly, he owes me money."

The Cubs ended up winning, 7–0. "That was the peak of my performing career," Bill said years later of his day in the booth. "That was the peak—what I was born for."

One moment in the game had surprisingly long-lasting effects. In the bottom of the fourth inning, Rick Sutcliffe hit an RBI single to right field, driving in catcher Jody Davis for a 3–0 Cubs lead. The six-foot-seven Sutcliffe, known as "The Red Baron" because of his ginger hair, was a star pitcher who had won the Cy Young Award with the Cubs in 1984; he would end up spending eight seasons with the team (about half of his storied career). Like most major-league pitchers, he wasn't much of a threat at bat or on the bases.

After Sutcliffe's hit, Montreal pitcher Floyd Youmans got ejected, so up in the broadcast booth, Bill and Steve Stone had to kill time while Expos relief pitcher Andy McGaffigan warmed up. That was when Bill blurted out, "I bet you a case of beer Sutcliffe steals second." Stone was skeptical. Discussing Bill's proposition, he pointed out that Sutcliffe was nursing a bad hamstring and that even in full health, he wasn't the speediest guy around. In fact, Stone pointed out, in ten full seasons of professional baseball, Sutcliffe had never even attempted a stolen base.

"But I'll take the bet," Stone said, "because I'd like to win a case of beer from you."

As McGaffigan continued to loosen up, a fan who was listening to the broadcast shouted the news of the bet to Sutcliffe: "Hey, Sut, Murray just bet Steve Stone a case of beer you'll steal second!"

"Screw it," Sutcliffe thought. "*I'm going.*"

Sutcliffe almost got picked off right away, but then the Expos' manager Buck Rodgers shouted at first baseman Wallace Johnson, "Play behind him, he ain't frickin' goin' anywhere!" (Johnson wasn't the team's regular first baseman, but he had come in as a replacement for Andres Galarraga.)

Sutcliffe took off running—he said that McGaffigan saw him break for second but pitched the ball to batter Chico Walker anyway. "I'm going, 'Ah, he got me,'" Sutcliffe said. "Well, the dummy goes to home so now I've got to get going again. But there's still a play. That's how slow I am." Sutcliffe slid into second base: safe!

Up in the booth, Bill lost his mind. The impossible had happened, all because an All-Star pitcher shared his sense of the absurd. Sutcliffe nodded in Bill's direction; after that day, Sutcliffe and Bill were fast friends. As the pitcher put it, "I throw a shutout, I steal a base, and we were locked for life."

Two years later, Sutcliffe and the Cubs headed to Shea Stadium for two games against the New York Mets. Sutcliffe got a phone call from Bill, who was about to fly from Los Angeles to New York: Could he hook him up with two tickets? The answer was yes, but Sutcliffe didn't believe it when Bill told him that he loved Shea—he argued that the stadium was a dump.

Bill disagreed: "Down the left-field line they have the best

Cajun french fries I've ever had. And down the right-field line they have the coldest Heineken you've ever tasted."

Sutcliffe told Bill to knock it off: Around the seventh-inning stretch, he joked, he'd get hungry and he didn't want to be thinking about the culinary delights he was missing.

The game the following evening didn't go well. Mets pitcher Sid Fernandez was throwing smoke, the Cubs were losing, their spot in the pennant race was in jeopardy, and manager Don Zimmer, cranky and pop-eyed at the best of times, was getting angrier and angrier.

In the seventh inning, the Cubs could hear the Shea crowd excited about something, but the team had no idea what—until Bill's head popped into the dugout, wearing a bucket hat like the one he sported in *Caddyshack*. "Hey, Sut!" Bill shouted. "Here are those fries and Heineken that you wanted!"

Zimmer didn't even look up, but he was furious that anyone would think of intruding on the dugout during the game. As Sutcliffe described it, his "head was about to pop off his shoulders."

Reading the situation, Bill said, "All right, you can't drink the Heineken, so I will. But, here, have some of these fries. Give 'em to Zimmer. Maybe they'll loosen his ass up."

At this point, Zimmer jerked his head up to see who the intruder was—and to chew his head off. But when he saw it was Bill, he started laughing and said, "Well, what are you waiting for? Go get some of those fries. It ain't going to hurt anything at this point." Sutcliffe collected the Cajun fries and distributed them to the Cubs squad.

The Sixth Principle
Drop coin on the world.

WHEN BILL MURRAY INSISTS ON PICKING UP A check, there's a phrase he likes to say, something he learned from Dan Aykroyd: "You don't pull coin in my town." Since Bill is a guy who treats the whole globe like his hometown, his generosity can manifest itself in unexpected ways. For example, in 1994, at the two-day International Conference on Sturgeon Biodiversity and Conservation, hosted by the American Museum of Natural History in New York City, there were two hundred scientists in attendance, plus surprise guest Bill Murray. Bill even got up to speak before a room filled with PhDs: "Some of you are saying, 'What is he doing here?'" he acknowledged. He justified his presence by explaining that since he lived on the Hudson River, home to sturgeon, he was concerned about the travails of the endangered bottom feeders.

Not that Bill pretended to more expertise than he actually had. He said he had looked up "sturgeon" in his dictionary, published in 1954—"when men were men, women were chicks or babes, and sturgeon were sturgeon."

Bill worked the crowd like Nick the Lounge Singer asking if anyone in the audience was on their honeymoon: "How many of you are marine biologists? How many are ichthyologists? How many are systematists?" Before he left, he crumpled up a check and threw it into the lap of Kathryn Birstein, the wife of Dr. Vadim Birstein, a Russian-American molecular geneticist. At the time, Dr. Birstein was developing a method of using DNA analysis to identify the origins of caviar (sturgeon eggs), hoping that would help squelch the illegal importation of the caviar of endangered species.

When the Birsteins unfolded Bill's wadded-up gift, they discovered it was a signed blank check.

★ ★ ★ ★ ★ ★ ★ ★ ★ ★ ★ ★   ★ ★ ★ ★ ★ ★ ★ ★ ★ ★ ★

BILL MURRAY MEETS THE YOUTH OF AMERICA

In 2007, a high-school golf coach named Dave Lobeck approached Bill Murray and asked him to say a few words to his team, the Providence Pioneers. "You're stuck with Dave," Bill said into the camera, rolling his eyes. "He's really your problem. None of us are going to lift a hand, a finger, to stop you." When Bill was done fomenting violent revolution, Lobeck told him that the team had a record of eighteen wins and four losses and had a big match the following day against Bedford, Indiana. A look of disdain clouded Bill's face. "They should have burned that city down," he said into the camera, in one of the more unconventional pep talks ever. "Take some responsibility and eliminate those Bedford creeps. We all hate them. Everyone's on your side."

Stephen Tobolowsky, storied character actor, played Ned Ryerson, the obnoxious insurance salesman constantly trying to chat up Bill Murray's weatherman character, in *Groundhog Day*. Tobolowsky remembered his first day of shooting on location in Woodstock, Illinois, with Bill and director Harold Ramis:

> *I went down to the street and saw Harold and Bill having a little chat. I wandered up to them and Harold started to introduce me to Bill, who, standing at six-three, six-four, is quite an imposing figure. Bill cut Harold off from his polite preamble. He turned to me and said, "So, whaddya gonna do? Is it funny?" I went through a couple of lines of Ned, complete with my hand gestures and sound effects. Bill just stared at me and then held up his hand and said, "Okay, okay, you can stop. That's funny."*
>
> *Bill looked around, and there were about five hundred townfolk gathered to watch the shooting at dawn. Then he said, "You know what we need right now?"*
>
> *I said, "No."*
>
> *Bill fixed his eyes on the horizon and in a completely deadpan tone said, "Danishes. We need a lot of Dan-*

ishes. Come with me." Bill took off running, with me trailing behind. He ran into a local bakery, pulled out a wad of cash from his pocket, and said, "I need every Danish you have in this place."

Bill and I left with boxes of bear claws and dough-nuts. Bill started tossing them at random to the towns-folk. Everybody was laughing and cheering. Bill was like a lightning rod. I don't think in a universe of possibili-ties Bill could have done any one thing that could have united the town any more and put them on our side.

. . .

When Bill Murray was a caddie, he and his brothers some-times carried the clubs of Wallace Patterson, an older gen-tleman who was sweet-tempered but almost totally blind. He'd pay them for a complete trip around the course but only play four holes. The Murrays would narrate his shot for him, and inevitably they'd improve it: No matter how badly Mr. Patterson shanked a ball, they'd tell him that it was straight and true down the fairway. "Nice shot, Mr. Pat-terson," Bill would say, to which the reply was always, "Yes, I thought I'd caught that one pretty well." Eventually this bit of caddie salesmanship reached its zenith: Mr. Patter-son was informed that he'd managed a hole in one on the ninth hole. There was much rejoicing and the club gave the blind golfer a trophy.

So naturally, after a respectable interval, the Murrays did it again. Another trophy was handed over to Mr. Pat-terson.

Then they did it a third time. The club gave Mr. Patterson one more trophy for his mantel, but this time, management figured out what was going on and told Bill and his brothers to quit it.

TALES FROM THE GRAPE D'VINE

One winter, Bill Murray bought a large quantity of wine from Joe Printz to distribute as New Year's presents for local merchants and tradesmen. When he got to the bank, he went up to the drive-through window, got the attention of the teller, and stepped out of the car. He stuck two bottles of Veuve Clicquot champagne into a nearby snowbank and mouthed "Happy New Year." Then he got back into his car and drove away.

In the fall of 2008, Jenny Lewis, best known as a singer for the indie rock band Rilo Kiley, played the Austin City Limits festival. In the middle of her set, she realized that Bill Murray was standing on the side, watching her perform. Despite this distraction, she finished her show successfully.

The evening got weirder from there: "Everyone in my band took mushrooms that night except for me," she said. The presidential election was in full swing, so the group's plan was to ingest mushrooms and then watch Barack Obama and John McCain in rhetorical combat. "Me, I'm sort of tapped out on psychedelics," she remembered. "So everyone disappeared, and I found myself in a golf cart with Bill Murray." Before rejoining her bandmates, she and Bill drove out into the festival's midway, where he found a food stand selling barbecue sandwiches: "He bought every last one. So I rolled up to the tour bus with Bill Murray and a ton of barbecue sandwiches, and I think they probably thought they were hallucinating. And then we watched the debate, and eventually Bill Murray just disappeared into the ether. He's like Santa, in a way."

The Seventh Principle
Be persistent, be persistent, be persistent.

MITCH GLAZER, HOLLYWOOD WRITER AND producer, is home with his lovely and talented wife, actress Kelly Lynch. The phone rings, and Glazer hears Bill Murray on the other line, speaking in the voice of Carl Spackler, his groundskeeper character in *Caddyshack:* "Kelly's having sex with Patrick Swayze right now. They're doing it. He's throwing her against the rocks." Glazer knows that can mean only one thing: *Road House* is on TV again.

Road House was a likable B action movie, starring Patrick Swayze in the improbable role of a superstar bouncer (or "cooler") brought in from New York to keep things under control at a Missouri nightclub. After its modestly successful 1989 release, it became a cult favorite, mostly because of frequent showings on basic cable. Bill didn't appear in the film, but Lynch did, as the local physician Elizabeth Clay, aka "Doc," the movie's love interest. She and Swayze shared a particularly athletic, implausible love scene, with Lynch upright against a rock wall.

Glazer has been Bill's friend and collaborator for decades: they were introduced to each other by John Belushi in 1977, when Bill first joined the *Saturday Night Live* cast. So when Lynch married Glazer, she got pulled into the vortex of "the Murricane." She says, "Every time *Road House* is on and he or one of his idiot brothers are watching TV—and they're *always* watching TV—one of them calls my husband." More precisely, they call during her sex scene with Swayze and then provide play-by-play commentary for the action. Bill has kept this joke rolling for years, once even making the phone call from Russia.

Glazer sighs. "No matter what time, two in the morning, it's 'Patrick Swayze's fucking your wife right now. . . . He's pushing her up against the wall.' It was kind of funny, the first dozen or so times."

"I dread it," Lynch confesses. "God help me when AMC's doing their *Road House* marathon, because I know the phone is just going to *keep* ringing."

SIGN YOUR NAME

Over the years, many people have asked Bill Murray for an autograph. The experience rarely goes as they expected. A few examples:

At the John Deere Classic Pro-Am golf tournament in 2015, Bill signed a man's forehead—with the name "Miley Cyrus."

Circa 1986, Bill was having dinner at the Friars Club when he was approached by a young boy, maybe six, asking for an autograph. The resulting message: "Sidney, run away from home tonight.—Bill Murray."

In July 1988, waitress Becca Daniel Noyes was serving Bill at Walker Brothers, a pancake house in Wilmette, Illinois. When she nervously asked for an autograph, Bill signed his name with the message "Merry Christmas."

Around 2002, Peter Chatzky's grade-school kids, Jake and Julia, spotted Bill at a hotel pool in Naples, Florida. They ended up with autographed cocktail napkins. Jake, a skinny boy, got "Maybe lose a little weight, bud," signed, "Jim Belushi." Julia's napkin read "Looking good, princess. Call me," signed, "Rob Lowe."

Bill Murray has pursued his passions across the years with an unusual level of commitment—and there's nothing he's more passionate about than his golf game.

Date: May 26, 1990.

Location: Garrison Golf Club in upstate New York.

The foursome: Bill Murray, his brother Brian, journalist David Earl, and *Golf* magazine editor George Peper.

Bill's mood: Inscrutable.

Bill's self-described golf history after his youthful caddying: "From about seventeen to thirty, I played cooler golf—didn't improve much. That's when you fill up a cooler, load it on a cart, and play until the cooler's empty."

Bill's commentary on a bad shot: "That won't play. Even an alcoholic gypsy knows that."

Bill's approach to lost balls: Scrupulously honest.

Bill's worst shot: Over the road, onto the second-floor balcony of a house, narrowly missing a Labrador.

Bill's exhortation to himself when not playing well: "Oh, you pig. Come back, you chopper."

Bill's clothes: Baggy and ill-fitting.

Bill's best autograph of the day, signed for a mother asking for a memento for her two sons (Ed, twelve, and Steve, nine): "To Steve, Stay the hell out of Ed's way! Bill Murray."

The contents of Bill's golf bag: Eccentric. And heavy. The clubs included six wedges. (Two or three would be typical.)

Bill's explanation for his club selection: "I just throw them in there."

Bill's undistinguished final score: 98. (Not the worst in the foursome: Brian shot 100.)

Bill's flirtatious banter with a clubhouse waitress: "You got the looks and the figure. Now you gotta get the conscience to go with it."

. . .

Questlove of the Roots (and *The Tonight Show*), possibly the greatest drummer of his generation, had heard stories of Bill Murray at Williamsburg keg parties or of him stealing popcorn from people at a movie theater. That didn't prepare him for the reality of Bill crashing into his world: "Bill Murray strangely followed my DJ tours, like three of them in three random spots in Brooklyn. I didn't believe it was actually Bill Murray. He was the last guy to leave, every time. That was the strange part. It was a party of one thousand people, and when it came down to 7:00 A.M., he was still there."

ON THE DARK SIDE

With a *New York Times* reporter in the passenger seat, Bill Murray drove a black Mercedes station wagon through New York City in 1999. Behind the wheel, Bill drove aggressively and kept up a running monologue about the traffic around him. Five comments on a trip from Hudson Street (in Tribeca) to the corner of East 76th Street and Madison Avenue (on the Upper East Side):

1. (at a slow car) "Go, go, go! You damn screwball! Get your dad's driver's license and get out of the way!"

2. (at a car that cut Bill off) "He's a twit! We should drive with our brights on and scare him."

3. (at a pedestrian) "I'm sorry, but if you stand in the street, you're from some other city than New York."

4. (at a bus) "I'm comin' in, fat boy."

5. (at a car that wouldn't let Bill merge out of the bus lane) "They could ticket me for this. This guy's not going to let me in. Maybe he's a jerk or maybe he thinks I'm doing the wrong thing. They're both correct."

Bill Murray has been a Chicago Cubs fan for over fifty years, devoutly rooting for the team through decades of futility and blown opportunities. Late in the 2007 baseball season, Bill went to Florida to watch his Cubs take on the Florida Marlins, and with every game crucial as the Cubs tried to lock down a playoff spot, Bill made it clear he would do whatever it took to help the team. He met with Marlins manager Fredi Gonzalez (who many years earlier had managed a minor-league team that Bill owned a piece of). Afterward, Murray reported, "I don't want to say that money changed hands, but don't expect Fredi to be driving the same automobile tomorrow."

"There is no time for being cautiously optimistic," said Bill, who predicted that 2007 would be the year the Cubs finally won the World Series (spoiler alert: It wasn't). "I think the Marlins have been very brave and noble, and when they lose today, they're going to die with respect. They'll be humiliated today, but they'll have earned everlasting honor."

Bill did what he could to keep the team loose: during batting practice, he chatted with second baseman Mark DeRosa about Gregorian chants. (Bill, who was raised Catholic and has a sister who is a nun, has said that he misses the Latin version of Mass.)

And Bill approached slugger Aramis Ramirez with some added motivation. "I'm going to be in the hospital— I'm very sick," the completely healthy Bill told Ramirez. "Could you hit two home runs for me today?"

Poetry in Motion

Bill Murray is a poetry fan. In his youth, he even wrote some verse himself, although he's been wise enough not to share it with the world. "Everything rhymed," he once said of those youthful efforts, a sentence halfway between a brag and a confession.

As an adult, Bill has become a public supporter of the Poets House, an independent library in Manhattan devoted entirely to poetry, with over sixty thousand volumes in its collection. "I think there's really an alignment between comedy and poetry, and you see that in the way that Bill operates," says Lee Briccetti, the executive director of Poets House. "There needs to be a precision in the way you handle the language. Bill's a master of linguistic control and pacing."

At the Poets House annual blowout event—a walk across the Brooklyn Bridge, with pauses to read poems at various locations, and food and poetry reading afterward (or as Bill puts it, "even more blah-blah-blah")—Bill has read poems by Sarah Manguso ("What We Miss"), Cole Porter (the lyrics to "Brush Up Your Shakespeare"), and Wallace Stevens ("The Planet on the Table" and "A Rabbit as King of the Ghosts"). As one would hope, Bill is a thoughtful, empathetic reader who steps up to the microphone looking rumpled and professorial. Usually, that is: In 2013, Bill came straight from the set of *St. Vincent*, forgetting to take off the facial makeup that gave him two

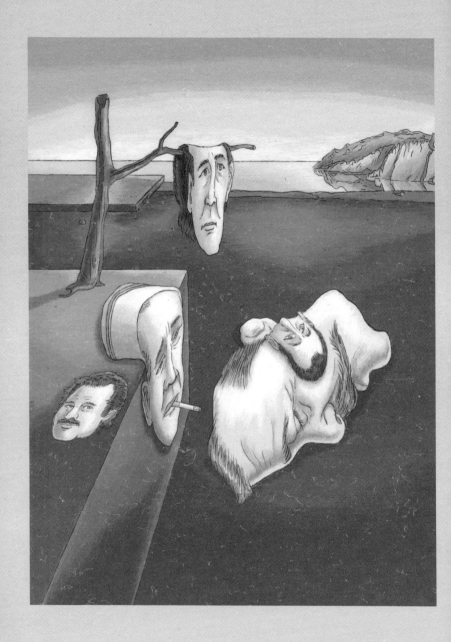

black eyes. One of his sons had to tell him that he "was scaring the straight people in the room."

Bill's been doing the Brooklyn Bridge walk for twenty years now. Originally, he showed up because of his friendship with the Poets House vice president Frank Platt—a dapper gentleman of a certain age who was Bill's next-door neighbor—but he kept coming back.

Every year, after the throng makes its way across the Brooklyn Bridge, somebody reads Walt Whitman's poem "Crossing Brooklyn Ferry." Bill's first time, the orator was Galway Kinnell, a Pulitzer Prize–winning poet who was greatly inspired by Whitman. Afterward, Bill spoke with Kinnell and told him how much he had enjoyed his performance.

"I really like what you do too, Robin," Kinnell replied.

"I guess I should call you W. B. Yeats," Bill shot back.

At a Poets House reading and party, poet Gerald Stern ("a big deal in our world," testifies Briccetti) read his poem "Stern Country," and told the story behind it: In a restaurant in Prague, having dinner with a group that included author Mary Morris, Stern talked about having a big mouth and poor impulse control, which he eventually demonstrated by biting Morris's shoulder.

Then, knowing Bill was present, Stern laid into the actor and his movie *Groundhog Day,* saying that he knew the town Punxsutawney and the titular groundhog much better than Bill did. At the end of Stern's reading, Bill rushed up to the aged poet and bit *his* shoulder. The result, according to Stern: "All the women there said, 'Why couldn't he have bitten *my* shoulder?'"

When Oprah Winfrey's magazine *O* asked Bill to share some of his favorite poetry with their readers, he didn't just select four excellent and surprising poems, including Naomi Shihab Nye's "Famous," Galway Kinnell's "Oatmeal," and Thomas Lux's "I Love You Sweetheart." He invited an *O* editor over to his hotel room at the Carlyle, read them out loud to her, and offered commentary over martinis he poured himself. Then, after his choices were published, he went on Jimmy Kimmel's show and read one—"What the Mirror Said" by Lucille Clifton, the award-winning African American poet often compared to Emily Dickinson. The audience snickered at his straight-faced recitation of "listen, / you a wonder. / you a city / of a woman." Although he must have been aware of the comedic potential in reciting verse in a patois not his own, Bill didn't mug for laughs: he radiated with a genuine love of the poem.

Bill also recites French verse to impress Andie MacDowell in *Groundhog Day* (Jacques Brel lyrics, it turns out), but his very best encounter with the poetic world came on May 1, 2009, when the Poets House was preparing to move from its old location in SoHo to a brand-new building in the Battery Park district. Bill showed up at the construction site, wearing a black fleece jacket and a white hard hat, and read poems to about two dozen construction workers, who seemed baffled but generally willing to roll with this unusual day on the job.

After Bill finished "Another Reason Why I Don't Keep a Gun in the House," by Billy Collins, and got silent stares in return, he warned the construction workers, "They get worse. Okay? So if you want to lie down or get sick, take a sick day, do it now."

He introduced "Poet's Work" by Lorine Niedecker: "Okay, this is for the shorter-attention-span crowd." After reading the poem—all of nineteen words—Bill said, "Got that done. We're getting paid by the poem here. It's piecework." Bill licked his fingers, shuffled his handful of papers, and announced to the construction workers, "Now we have an opportunity for one of you to step forward and do some of your own original poetry." He was joking, but there was a hopeful glint in his eyes—maybe this would actually happen? "Come on, don't be shy," he said, but there was just uncomfortable laughter.

Shifting gears, Bill declared, "Now I'm going to read a corny one for you. What's this gal's name again? Oh yeah, Emily Dickinson." Bill read from "I dwell in Possibility," a short poem that compares physical buildings with the architecture of the mind and includes the line "The Gambrels of the Sky." As some of the workers likely knew, a gambrel is a roof in two tiers: an upper half with a gentle slope and a bottom half with a steep angle. They listened raptly to the words that bridged the world of poetry and the world of building houses and applauded at the end.

Bill smiled. "Yeah, I've been waiting for applause, fellas. What's the deal? You think I'm getting paid for this?" He concluded, "Thank you for building this and putting yourselves into it, the way the poets put themselves into their words and the way all New Yorkers put themselves into what they really, really gravitate to—what really makes them a man or a woman." Bill was speaking conversationally, but it felt like he was uttering a secular prayer, a saint of New York City granting benediction to a new sacred space. "I know you feel it when you come here," he said. "I know I feel it when I come down here. The fact that it's going to be here is a pretty nice piece of bliss. It's a little bit of balm—it's the hope that comes out at the end of Pandora's box. So thank you very much. You've got about three more minutes before this break is over—smoke 'em if you got 'em."

The Eighth Principle
Know your pleasures and their parameters.

HOW IVAN REITMAN WANTED BILL MURRAY TO spend the summer of 1978: starring in a low-budget comedy called *Meatballs*. "I refused to hire anybody else," Reitman says. "Week after week, I said, 'I think I can get him.' I pleaded with him for about a month to be in the picture."

How Bill Murray wanted to spend the summer of 1978, his time off after his first full season on *Saturday Night Live:* playing golf and baseball. As it happened, Lorne Michaels, *SNL* impresario, wanted the cast to film "How I Spent My Summer Vacation" segments for use when the show returned in the fall.

Bill's friend Van Schley had bought the Grays Harbor Loggers, an independent baseball team in Washington State. So with a film crew tagging along, including writer Don Novello (also famous for his appearances on *SNL* as Father Guido Sarducci), Bill went out to the Pacific Northwest and was assigned Loggers uniform number 17.

Bill even got into a game against the Victoria Mussels as a pinch hitter. The Mussels pitcher, Paul Kirsch, was kind enough to groove him a pitch—a fastball down the middle—but Bill made good contact, smacking a single to left field. "Bill was really nice about it," Kirsch remembered. "After the game he came up and said, 'That meant the world to me.'" The Loggers beat the Mussels 7–4; 141 fans bought tickets to the game.

Bill hung around the team for a couple of weeks, often coaching first base. He filmed a bunch of bits for his *SNL* segment, including a speech to the crowd that riffed on Lou Gehrig's famous farewell address: "I consider myself the luckiest man in the world. No, in the universe. Well, maybe not the whole universe, but certainly the United States."

He noticed that nobody in the stands at Olympic Stadium was drinking beer—the city council of Hoquiam, Washington, wouldn't allow alcohol to be sold at the games—so one night he brought a keg to the game, along with a bunch of plastic cups. Bill then walked around, handing out cups of beer to fans—which prompted the Hoquiam police to arrest him. (They let him go when one of the team's owners convinced them that booking him would result in negative publicity across the United States.)

Bill went on a road trip to Walla Walla with the team and got into another game as a pinch hitter—this time, he struck out on three pitches, giving him a lifetime batting average in professional baseball of .500. "He threw three sinkers," Bill said. "I don't know a TV actor who can hit a decent sinker." Then he flew off to Canada, making it to the summer camp where Reitman was filming *Meatballs* on the second day of the production. "We closed the deal the day before," Reitman says.

"From the minute he stepped into the camp and we started filming with him," Reitman recalls, "I said, 'Thank God I waited for him.'" During the shoot, Reitman would periodically remind Bill that they might have a hit on their hands, which would make it a worthwhile use of his summer. Bill's response was always "I just wanted to play baseball."

. . .

David Gault remembers:

In 1983, I was about to decide whether I should ask my first—and only—wife if she would marry me. As part of the screening process, I suggested that we take a road trip from San Francisco to Telluride, Colorado. She's a fabulous skier, and a fabulous drinker. I was twenty-nine, so it was the peak of my burning-the-candle-at-both-ends years. We got to Telluride, and we were staying in a ramshackle house. The whole thing was heated by a wood stove, and there was cold leaking through the windows.

My friend who was hosting us had a roommate, Ming, who had been a friend of Bill Murray's in Chicago. Ming was crazy, but in a good way. He groomed the slopes, driving Sno-Cats—his specialty was taking them to altitudes and angles where no other drivers would go. His antics weren't an act—he got his fun from being over the edge, which I respected, as long as he could do it and survive.

Murray came to town and checked in with Ming—we were there, so he knew my face. The trip progressed, and one night we were all getting hammered in a bar called the Last Dollar Saloon. Murray was surrounded by fans, and I was keeping my distance, because I didn't want to get into that kind of relationship with him.

On my lapel, I was wearing a pin that had a piece of acid blotter shellacked on it. This particular piece of blotter had Disney characters on it, so I had Goofy on it. I was sitting one table over from Murray, and I realized he should really have the pin. The noise was deafening—it was around midnight, and the bar was at fever pitch—so I tapped him on the shoulder. He looked over, and I handed him the pin. I shouted an explanation: "Here's the patron saint of comedy."

He looked at it, said, "All right," and put it on. About a half hour later, we were all out on the street. I said, "You know what that is, right?"

"Oh yeah."

He was pretty hammered. He went into this second-hand store next door to the bar. Why it was open that time of night, I have no idea. Bill decided it was time to take a nap, so he showed really good hobo instincts: He found a bunch of used rugs, lay down, rolled himself up like a silkworm, and passed out.

Three or four months later, I was back in San Francisco, watching The Tonight Show, *and Bill was a*

guest. Carson asked, "What's that on your jacket?"—
and Bill was wearing the pin I had given him.

Bill just smiled and said, "It's Goofy." That made my
year.

BILL MURRAY MEETS THE YOUTH OF AMERICA

AT A LOSS FOR WORDS: a short play for two characters.
Time: September 2014.
Place: A Brooklyn sidewalk, outside the Theater for a New Audience, where JORDAN DANN (a New York City educator and
   theater artist) is waiting to see *The Valley of Astonishment,* a
   play by Peter Brook. She spots BILL MURRAY, also standing in
   the crowd, wearing a plaid shirt and a fisherman's vest,
   dressed unconventionally but looking younger than expected. When he walks by, she blurts out his name.

JORDAN: "Excuse me, Mr. Murray!"
BILL: "Yes?"
JORDAN: "I just, I just—I just think you're the best!"
Bill puts his arm around her shoulders and gives her a deadpan
   look.
BILL: "Well, kid, then you've got to get out more."

In 1994, Bill Murray was asked to play at the Greater Milwaukee Open Pro-Am, a golf tournament so small-time
that they had lost their sponsors and their course and were
holding the event on a local municipal course, Brown

Deer Park. He was sufficiently charmed by the invitation that he showed up at the end of a road trip in his RV, wearing a khaki work outfit and a pink baseball cap. "He was a sucker for kids," said his caddie for the day, Jerry Huffman. "He posed for dozens of pictures and signed hundreds of autographs." Huffman was so pleased that Murray had made the trip to Wisconsin, he gave him a baseball bat signed by Hank Aaron—which became a treasured possession of Bill's, always in the RV, he said, in case he needed to brandish a weapon on the road.

One local talked up the virtues of the ribs tent, saying that Bill couldn't miss them and that he was going to make sure Bill went home with some. Bill managed to eat one spare rib before leaving and was suitably impressed. And then he drove home to New York in his RV, with his golf clubs and his baseball bat.

A month later Bill got to play golf again. He headed out with some friends to his preferred local golf course, the Sleepy Hollow Country Club in Briarcliff Manor, New York. When he arrived, he handed off his clubs to a caddie, asking him to check the bag because he thought he might have left a wet towel in there.

As Bill collected a scorecard and some tees, he saw a tableau of horror on his left: a shocked crowd, a swarm of insects, and a horrified caddie removing fistfuls of Milwaukee ribs, covered in Saran wrap and emitting an unearthly odor. The caddie tossed the ribs onto the grass, trying to stay as far away from them as possible.

"This is where club membership becomes so important," Bill said. "As a guest, I'd have been forced to disavow ownership of the bag until down the fairway and out of sight of the clubhouse. This would save my member sponsor from shame. But as a proud member, I was able to march to my caddie and crisply announce, 'The sun's coming out. We won't be needing those today.' "

. . .

Dan Beers and Peter Karinen wanted to make a short film called *Fact Checkers Unit*, in which they would play hypervigilant magazine fact checkers, responsible for confirming the most picayune of details before they saw print. It proved to be a sufficiently entertaining premise that they turned it into a series, with cameos from stars such as Moby and James Franco, but they dreamed of having Bill Murray appear in the first installment. The overzealous fact checkers, vetting the factoid that Bill liked warm milk before he went to bed, would break into his home—where Bill would find them, befriend them, and play checkers, drink martinis, and watch *M*A*S*H* with them before falling asleep.

Beers had worked for Wes Anderson for five years, so he knew Bill well enough to send him a fax—which Bill didn't read. But when Beers ran into him at a Brooklyn bar, Bill asked what it had been about. Beers pitched the project, and Bill responded, "All right, I'll do it. Sounds cute. How's March?"

Bill had one demand for donating his time to a twelve-thousand-dollar Sundance entry: He wanted a gun. Told that wouldn't happen, he scaled down his compensation to a knife. "A really big knife," he specified. "Something I can strap onto my leg." So after Bill finished his day of shooting—during which he also helped the crew schlep equipment—he was presented with a gift-wrapped hunting knife with a twelve-inch blade. "Thanks for this," Bill said, accepting the knife, and moments later he was gone.

. . .

Bill Murray, co-owner and "czar" of the St. Paul Saints, a minor-league baseball team, spent the summer of 1996 showing up at random intervals at Midway Stadium in St. Paul, Minnesota, cheering on Saints players such as Darryl Strawberry (playing in minor-league purgatory after multiple drug busts) and entertaining the crowd.

Five highlights from that summer:

1. Before a game, our protagonist was introduced over the PA system as "the Ayatollah of hilarity, Bill Murray." He wound up and threw the baseball—not to the catcher, but over the grandstand and right out of the park, almost giving a concussion to somebody in the press box. He embraced the catcher and then the umpires working the game—kissing the umps on the lips. Throwing the ball out of the park would become Murray's go-to move whenever he had to throw a first pitch.

2. Signing an autograph for a fan, he mused, "You know, I was reading the Gettysburg Address the other day, and that guy was really onto something."

3. Standing next to the dugout during a game, Bill was shouted at by a fan, a man in his twenties: "Hey, Bill! It's

my mom's birthday today. Will you come up and sing her 'Happy Birthday'?"

Bill thought about it and then told the young man, "I'd rather shove a piece of cake in her mouth." Warming to the idea, he said, "Where is she? Get a piece of cake, and you can get a picture of her nose in the frosting. And then I'll buy her a bratwurst."

4. His comment for a six-year-old girl wearing a hat shaped like a pickle: "Are you Faith Daniels of CBS News? I love your show."

5. In the Midway parking lot, a man asked Bill to sign a pennant. "I hate insincerity," Bill told him as he autographed it. "And I don't mean that."

TALES FROM THE GRAPE D'VINE

Joe Printz fondly remembers a line that Bill Murray said in appreciation of a particularly good wine (although he emphasizes that it was a joke, not a reflection of Bill's actual behavior): "This wine makes me want to drive."

Pam Tietze, an artist and eyewear designer, met Bill in Austin, Texas, in March 2015.

I was at some kind of fancy VIP event, and nothing was really happening—and then Bill Murray and his crew arrived. He definitely had a crew, like ten people. They sat in a booth and immediately the room had this change of energy: Everyone was aware he was there but pretending not to be. Everyone was standing around, trying to have natural conversations, but everyone's conversation was "Oh my God, it's Bill Murray." He looked very casual, a little disheveled. Someone tried to take a photo of him, and one of his people came over and told them not to. Someone went around and told everyone, "Don't take photos." He had this air of not wanting to be bothered. All this food that wasn't available at the party magically appeared at his table—what the hell?

I was definitely one of those people who did want to engage with him. I was sitting at a table with my friends, talking about Bill Murray with my friends, wearing these glasses that have prisms for lenses—they're trippy and weird, and I'm thinking that he'd like them. Finally his table started to get up—everyone was watching them move. He walked up to me and handed me a drink and said, "Here, you should have this drink, because you're tall." By the way, I'm five-four.

I took the drink, but I didn't know what to say. Everyone was noticing us—just the fact that he spoke words. I started drinking: I think it was a vodka soda. And then he walked away and everyone was freaking out: "That's his drink!" "I want to drink his drink—don't drink it all!" I was feeling special, and then I turned around and he was coming back to me.

I was sitting in a chair and he was standing over me. He said, "I really want to kiss you."

I don't remember what I said: something like "Huh. Okay." There were some consenting words. He very slowly tipped over—it was the slowest thing ever—and we started kissing. At this point, people were screaming. This was definitely not how we thought things were going to go—and I say "we" as a collective group. I was outside my body—I was so confused, I didn't even know if I was kissing or my mouth was moving. I thought it was going to be a peck, but it lasted for what seemed like a pretty good amount of time—because I wasn't going to pull away! It kept going and going. It was a movie-like kiss, very slow and gentle. At some point, tongue happened. I was like, "I don't even know what's happening with my mouth."

Then, as slowly as he arrived, he pulled away and said something like "Yeah, that's what I thought."

He pulled my trippy glasses off my head and said, "What the fuck is this?"

I really couldn't speak—at that moment, I didn't know how to say things. He put the glasses on and he walked off. The thing about these glasses is that they give you kaleidoscopic vision; they distort your vision quite a bit. And somehow he walked effortlessly out the door in a straight line.

Everyone was just screaming and grabbing me and giving me high-fives. Then somebody from his entourage ran back in and said, "I can get those glasses back for you if you want." She took my phone number—I wanted Bill to call me—but I told her that I didn't need the glasses back.

It's a crazy story relative to my life, but I'm sure he's done a lot of much crazier shit. The rest of the night, people were staring at me like I was Bill Murray—people attached a lot of meaning to it, like I had been blessed or anointed.

INTERLUDE
Every Grain of Sand

"I know a lot about golf," Bill Murray has said—and that might be an understatement. "I was a caddie for seven years, an assistant greenskeeper for two years, and I ran a hot-dog stand on a golf course for one year." As one of the stars of *Caddyshack*, everyone's favorite golf comedy, Bill uttered many of its best lines, becoming the patron saint for a generation of golfers. Particularly beloved is the monologue where his character, greenskeeper Carl Spackler, narrates his own triumphs: "This crowd has gone deathly silent. Cinderella story. Outta nowhere. A former greenskeeper, now, about to become the Masters champion. It looks like a mirac—it's in the hole! It's in the hole!"

Golf is important enough to Bill that when he wrote an autobiography (called *Cinderella Story*, of course), he told the story of his life in golf—and it revealed more about his philosophy and his approach to the world than a book with a wider remit might have.

Since 1992, Bill's favorite golf tournament has been the AT&T Pebble Beach National Pro-Am, held on the coast of northern California; he's attended it almost every year, with a few exceptions for film obligations. It was traditionally one of the looser events on the PGA calendar—started by Bing Crosby in 1937, it was known as the Crosby Clambake until 1985. In case you're not a golf fan, here are some basics:

"Pro-Am" is short for "professional-amateur," meaning that pro golfers are paired with enthusiastic amateurs (including celebrities such as Bill). The partnership competes on the basis of their combined score. The tournament lasts for seventy-two holes (eighteen holes of golf a day for four days); after two days comes "the cut," when the bottom half of the field is excused from the rest of the competition.

Early on, a tournament staffer told Bill to stay within the ropes that separated the players from the galleries of fans who came to watch them: "It's your safety that's our concern."

"An assassin? If he wants me, he'll get me," Bill replied.

The staffer explained that the issue was crowd control. Bill mused, "Crowd control is my business. I have a highly developed sense of a crowd, and whether or not they need attention."

Bill has always given plenty of attention to the crowds at Pebble Beach, not just signing autographs but trading jokes, swapping clothes, handing out drinks, teasing kids, flirting, and sometimes even hoisting elderly women into sand bunkers. Bill has said, "Inside the ropes it's safe, but the gallery is where the fun is. Like the zoo. The closer you get to the bars, the more interesting the animals. It's hard to be sure which side of the rope holds the animals, but fair to say there is wildlife on both sides."

Bill loves the give and take: Once, when he was strolling across a fairway at the Pebble Beach golf course for a practice round, a construction worker helping build a mansion adjacent to the golf course spotted him and shouted, "How's it going, Bill?"

Bill shouted back, "A lot better, now that I'm off the medication."

While Bill's efforts to tweak the routines and traditions of golf have made him the biggest draw on the Pebble Beach course, he hasn't always been warmly regarded by golf traditionalists. "He's only making an ass of himself," actor James Garner complained in his autobiography. "I'm glad I was never paired with him, because I would have refused to play."

"He's the anti-Christ here," CBS color commentator Gary McCord said in 1996.

Bill, on the other hand, believes, "The best thing I do all year is Pebble Beach. There's eighteen greens and eighteen tees. That's like thirty-six shows—and that's just the formal rooms." Every hole is not just a chance to play golf, which he loves, it's an opportunity to improvise a moment that makes the world a better, more Bill-like place, whether network cameras are on him or not. Bill's turned the tournament into his greatest stage. Just consider the evidence across the decades.

1992: His first year at Pebble Beach, after one sorry practice round, Bill Murray claimed to be completely overwhelmed and filled with hate. "Is there a cut I can miss right now?" he asked a *Chicago Tribune* reporter. "Maybe I can go back home before there's trouble."

Bill confessed, "I've always been afraid to play here. Now I know why. What I should do is go back to the hotel room and find some religious literature."

He attempted to blame his poor play that day on having

missed breakfast: "I would think that after traveling thirty-five hundred miles from the East Coast, they'd have a doughnut and coffee for me here. Or at least a Pebble Beach cantaloupe. Nothing. They have nothing for me. And by the time the cart comes around after fifteen holes, the choices are Drambuie or Diet Coke. Nice. I hate everything about this place and I hope the organizers read what I'm saying so they never invite me back."

In a television interview, Bill said that he didn't have a caddie; when a local Monterey kid called Bill at his hotel and volunteered, Bill took him on. (The kid ended up not working out, so Bill made a call to Andrew Whitacre, a friend of a friend, who went on to caddie for him over the next couple of decades. Bill eventually described him as "the perfect caddie: scratch handicap, former psychology major, and no outstanding warrants.")

"That first year, when we got on the course, it was like the Pied Piper," Whitacre said. "The fans just came to him. The fans would yell something at him, and he'd yell something right back. They hadn't been getting that. From that point on, it was on."

Before he hit his first shot, Bill told the crowd he was going to take ten minutes to finish his beer and his Polish sausage. Bill played one round in an oversize Tam o' Shanter hat (a souvenir from the Super Bowl in Minneapolis). He also had a wad of cash sticking out of his shirt collar. "Don't ask," he said. "It's a side bet."

Later in the tournament, Murray gazed out at the Pacific Ocean. "God, there's a lot of water," he observed. "And that's just the top."

1993: Bill Murray was playing in a group adjacent to Dan Quayle, the former vice president famous for misspelling "potato." He threatened to shout out "P-O-T-A-T-O" at Quayle but settled for violating golf decorum by yelling, "Hurry up!"

On the eighteenth hole of Bill's third round, he spotted Kitty Ragsdale in the gallery, a self-described "little old lady" from a posh neighborhood in Monterey, California. Without warning, Bill lifted the eighty-year-old Ragsdale up on his shoulders and spun around, dancing with her in a nearby bunker until both crashed into the sand, Ragsdale's skirts flying. Not every Bill improvisation delights the participants: "I was so embarrassed," Ragsdale said. "I just hope my underwear was clean." Murray gallantly presented Ragsdale with a rose—the same rose that had fallen off her hat. Then he sank a fifty-foot putt.

1994: Deane Beman, the commissioner of the staid PGA, which oversaw the Pebble Beach tournament, sent a message to Bill Murray before the tournament started, asking him to tone down his antics. He also amplified the criticism in public, saying, "The Bill Murray thing was inappropriate and detrimental and will not be tolerated in the future. It goes beyond entertainment and into a circus atmosphere."

In return, Bill called the PGA Tour "a Nazi state" and asked for Beman's resignation, saying the commissioner was "just another screwhead too big for his britches." Bill didn't slow down on the course: On his opening round, he tipped over a woman sitting in a chair and then literally pulled her leg, leading her through some stretching exercises.

Later, Bill asked the gallery, "Is this the best foursome of the day or what?"

"Palmer's was better," a gentleman in the crowd shot back (referring to golf legend and drink eponym Arnold Palmer).

"Shut up, Gramps," Bill replied.

But although the crowds loved Bill's craziness, by the end of the tournament, he was still chafing at the criticism from Beman. "He's trying to ban us from the tournament because it's too much fun," he said.

Lining up his final putt of the weekend, Murray narrated the moment in the voice of Carl Spackler: "Probably his last putt at the AT&T."

1995: Beman retired as commissioner, either because he wanted to play on the senior golf tour or because most Americans supported Bill Murray. Tim Finchem replaced Beman and encouraged Bill to play Pebble Beach again. Bill cautiously returned with the slogan "It's all about golf."

Bill said, "I figured, well, I'll try again. But if it can't be fun, then I've got a lot of books to read, some cleaning around my house to do." Bill wore a straw hat like folksy golf superstar Sam Snead; he also kissed babies, dried his ball on a bystander's shirt, and dragged a fan who asked for an autograph into the wet grass.

Asked about his rumpled gray cotton shorts (which *Sports Illustrated* said "appeared to have been very carefully slept in"), Bill explained, "I just signed a very lucrative deal with Goodwill Industries."

Bill also played great golf. He came close to scoring a hole in one on the seventh hole, landing his shot just four feet from the cup. "It's a net hole in one," Bill told the crowd. "I'm buying." He helped his team by twenty-five shots, the best in the tournament.

At the end of the second day, a fan in the gallery shouted, "You made the cut! What's next?"

Bill's answer: "The Senate."

1996: A local spectator let Bill Murray drink some of her champagne and told him that her house was near the tee. "That house?" Bill asked. "Somebody give me a golf ball." Bill heaved the golf ball at her house—where it bounced off one of her picture windows.

The Pro-Am tournament was scrubbed because rain had rendered most of the course unplayable, so to fill CBS's airtime, the organizers improvised a celebrity shoot-out contest. Bill, partnered with singer Glen Campbell, played the final round wearing denim overalls. And although Bill teed off on the fourteenth hole with a novelty exploding golfball, they won the whole tournament. At the awards ceremony, AT&T Pro-Am chairman Bob Allen presented Bill with the championship purse and said, "I can't believe I'm giving a check to someone dressed like you."

Bill responded, "I can't believe I'm taking a check from someone like you."

1997: Bill Murray was strolling down the fairway when a female fan shouted out, "Bill, you're better looking than Kevin Costner."

Bill gazed upward, judging the wisdom of this comment. "You have a point," he said.

Bill was in a foursome with Chicago Cubs first baseman Mark Grace, who landed a shot in the bunker. "Not bad for a Cub," heckled somebody in the crowd.

"Who said that?" demanded a mock-furious Bill. "The man with the square head?"

Bill left the gallery with this wisdom: "I'm an athlete this week. Red wine only."

1999: Partnered with singer Huey Lewis, Bill Murray played the Celebrity Challenge: a five-hole charity match held the day before the actual Pro-Am tournament. The Celebrity Challenge is even looser than the regular tournament and helps celebrities get into a relaxed frame of mind. As Bill was lining up a pitch shot near the eighteenth hole, announcer Bob Murphy told a crowd of thousands, "Murray has promised not to throw any old ladies into the bunker again."

Bill promptly went to the crowd and took the hand of Fran East, a gray-haired woman from Fairfield, California. They ran toward the bunker, and as they reached the lip, Bill let go of East's hand, letting her roll into the bunker. "He didn't really throw me in the trap," East said. "He kind of more flipped me in by the wrist. I remember thinking that the sand was going to be soft. It wasn't, but I was laughing the whole time. I had sand everywhere on me, from head to toe."

Bill followed East into the sand, climbed on top of her, and pounded the sand—one, two, three—declaring a victory in their improvised wrestling match.

He then escorted East back to her spot in the gallery, making sure she was fine. "Don't let the celebrity go to your head now, Fran," he cautioned her.

Bill and Lewis won the Celebrity Challenge.

2001: Bill Murray encouraged the other members of his foursome (Grace, plus pro golfers Ed Fryatt and Scott Simpson) to join him in a piggyback race from one hole to the next.

2002: During the third round of the Pro-Am, Bill Murray spotted eleven-year-old Sarah Petersen of Pleasanton, California, in the crowd; the girl had gotten separated from her family. "Give her to me—I'll take care of her," Bill told security. He then climbed up a tree with young Sarah and pretended to auction her off to the crowd.

When Sarah was reunited with her parents, she said, "Mommy, I climbed a tree with Bill Murray!"

2003: Bill Murray and his partner, country singer Clay Walker, won the Celebrity Challenge.

During the main event, Bill was partnered once again with pro Scott Simpson. Playing in the second round, Simpson stood over a short putt, essential to make if they wanted to stay in contention. Bill shouted, "Scott, that kid just called from the hospital. He said he wanted you to make this putt for him."

Simpson dutifully made the putt. Bill then said, "Ah, the kid's an orderly. He's not sick or anything. He's on a work-release program from prison."

Bill had an eventful tournament: He gave a scalp massage to a fan at the fifteenth tee. He instigated a banana-throwing war among his Saturday foursome (Bill, Simpson, pro Paul Stankowski, actor Andy Garcia). He borrowed a blue scarf from a female fan, cinched it around his waist, and played for the rest of the day with the fashion accessory. He actively recruited followers: "Stick with us," he told two women. "We'll find some beer and wine." When he saw some fans wearing rubber masks of American presidents, he yelled, "I loved you in *Point Break*!" At the tenth tee, he abruptly pointed at a white-haired woman in the gallery. "You!" Bill called. "I need you in my posse!"

2005: Bill Murray and his partner, actor Chris O'Donnell, won the Celebrity Challenge. Bill donated his check—fourteen thousand dollars—to the cash-strapped library system of nearby Salinas.

Some fans showed up with a replica of the gopher from *Caddyshack*, which danced to the movie's theme song, Kenny Loggins's "I'm Alright." "Make it stop!" Bill said, and then knocked the gopher down with his putter. Bill later handed the mechanical gopher to a fan with the instructions: "I want you to raise him as a Hindu."

2006: Partnered with Andy Garcia, Bill Murray hit a ninety-yard shot on the eighteenth fairway to win the Celebrity Challenge (his fourth victory in that event). "I knew it as soon as I hit it," Murray claimed. "I hit ten of 'em this morning. I made ten of 'em, so I was hoping I had another one in me."

During the Pro-Am, Bill was killing time between the eleventh hole and the twelfth tee, waiting for other groups to play through. He wandered over to a house adjoining the course, where a catered party was in full swing, and returned with a Bloody Mary. He drank half of it before handing it off to a fan at the thirteenth tee, saying, "Do me a favor and polish that off, willya?"

2007: Bill Murray played Thursday's round in a woman's straw hat with plastic flowers on the brim. The millinery choice was a tribute to his friend Helen Westland, a Pebble Beach local and golf devotee; she had died five months earlier.

Some women in a gallery near the fifth tee were Hula-Hooping to kill time while waiting between shots. Bill spotted them and borrowed a Hula-Hoop. After a few false starts, he found his groove and got the hoop orbiting around his midriff—all while singing the Beach Boys' "California Girls."

Later, as Bill walked up a fairway to his ball, a fan told him, "Kevin Costner made it from here."

"Kevin Costner made *Waterworld*," Bill shot back.

2009: Bill Murray wore a kimono at the Celebrity Challenge. He missed a three-foot putt that let the team of Michael Bolton and Kevin James win the match. "It was no good at all," Bill told the crowd. "It's great to be here, but basically . . . well, I feel like a loser."

2011: A boy wearing a San Francisco Giants shirt asked Bill Murray for an autograph. Inspecting the shirt, Bill asked the kid, "Are you willing to at least look at some Chicago Cubs literature?"

"I have an uncle who lives near Chicago," the boy volunteered.

"Wouldn't you rather spend time with him than your mother?" Bill asked.

"Sure," the boy said.

Bill signed an autograph for him. "See?" Bill said. "Was that so hard?"

Pro golfer D.A. Points, who had long hoped to play with Bill, discovered that Bill would be his partner by checking his voicemail and discovering this message: "Hi, D.A., this is Bill Murray. I got your number from the police department."

They played a round behind pro golfer John Daly, whose golf bag sported a video screen that rotated commercials for a Chevrolet dealership and his own line of golf gloves. Bill's comment on the screen: "It would be nice to play some black-and-white movies, maybe some Kurosawa films, get some culture out here."

Bill was placed in a foursome with Harris Barton, formerly an offensive tackle for the San Francisco 49ers. Bill explained, "I said, 'I want someone with character, who can cheat without getting caught. Give me an offensive lineman.'"

Bill appropriated a cooler of beer and redistributed the beer to his gallery. He played his round on Saturday in a giant red Elmer Fudd cap. And he acquired a glazed doughnut from a fan. Then he flirted shamelessly with an attractive female spectator, asking if she'd like to lick his fingers clean.

While Points lined up a tricky putt, Murray waved the remainder of that doughnut in Points's field of vision and yelled, "Make it and you get a bite." Points did and ran over to Murray to collect his bite.

When Points made a gorgeous twenty-eight-foot putt, Bill started giggling uncontrollably. He later said, "Once knuckle-head here made that eagle and then the birdie, I was just laughing hysterically. I could not even speak. It's like when I see real art, I laugh. When I saw, like, the *Pietà* or a Rembrandt, I laugh, because it's so—it's just this combination of this beau-tiful thing, it's alive, yet it's not."

Points was a middle-of-the-pack pro: He said Bill's antics loosened him up and let him play the best golf of his life (he even set a short-lived course record by shooting a 63 in the first round). Together, he and Bill brought out the best in each other, and they went into the final hole with a decisive lead. Victory was theirs, barring disaster, and Bill realized he didn't know how to handle it: "I felt like my mind had left my body. Walking up the eighteenth fairway, I didn't know what to do. It was like, 'Holy cow, now what? I guess I have to die now.'"

Lining up his final putt, Bill fell back on the play-by-play commentary of his *Caddyshack* character Carl Spackler: "Tears in his eyes, a putt to make the cut, the sea otters and the har-bor seals paddling in attention, waiting for this young strong boy to hopefully make a dream come true, seal the deal, as it were...." Chattering kept him focused: His ball headed for the hole like it was going home. Bill Murray had won the Pebble Beach Pro-Am.

Bill was genuinely choked up by his victory. "I don't want

much, but I've always wanted to win this," he said. "It's one of the greatest things you can do in this world."

Afterward, Bill said, "I'm thinking of turning pro. I probably won't." Asked if he had a special place where he might put the Waterford Crystal trophy in his home, he said, "Well, I've got a garage." Discussing past tournament victories, he said, "I've won all kinds of things, but nothing I could cash in at a pawn shop. I mean, we were the low gross at the Boys and Girls Club tournament on Monday. I got pro-shop credit, you know what I'm saying? I got a vest that's marked down."

And how did Bill say he would celebrate? "Usually, I choose red wine. But tonight I may just be going from table to table, finishing other people's glasses."

The Ninth Principle
Your spirit will follow your body.

THERE ARE MANY WAYS TO BE A SPONTANEOUS free spirit. One of them is to act before you think: Throw your body into the moment and let your mind catch up. With practice, your body and your mind will fly through the air together and you will learn to live in the present tense.

On a spring day in 1977, Bill Murray was reaching the end of his second season as a cast member of *Saturday Night Live*. He went out to lunch at an old-fashioned bar and grill surrounded by wood and brass railings, near the *SNL* offices at Rockefeller Center. When he finished lunch, he tried to get the attention of his waitress, but she was about eight feet away and had her back to the table.

"Miss?" Bill called. She didn't hear him. So he tried harder.

Bill stood up at his table, took a few steps in the direction of the waitress, and then leaped through the air in an ungainly trajectory, crashing to the ground at her feet. She stared at him with horror.

Bill smiled. "Uh, may we have the check, please?"

. . .

Nine young women and Bill Murray. Split into two teams, they're running up and down a hardwood court in Cambridge, Massachusetts, playing basketball. The women are all Harvard undergraduates, in excellent physical condition. Bill is wearing a form-fitting sweatshirt that looks elegant but shows off his gut. How did this happen?

It was the fault of the Hasty Pudding Society at Harvard. The Pudding is famous for two things: putting on undergraduate theatrical revues where men dress up in drag and handing out awards to cool celebrities. Every year, they name two famous people as "Man of the Year" and "Woman of the Year" and throw a big party for each of them on campus (often with a parade). Some of the past honorees include Mamie Eisenhower (1953), Bob Hope (1967), and Johnny Carson (1977). In 1985, Bill Murray got the nod. (And on the distaff side, Cher.)

"He was exactly what we were hoping for," says Michael K. Allio, Harvard class of 1986, who was the Hasty Pudding Society's director of publicity when Bill came to Harvard. "Our press release said that we were honoring him for his 'unprincipled irreverence'—he delivered two hundred percent."

Speaking to the press about Harvard, for example, Bill said, "All we knew of it in the Midwest was that you could get in if your father gave money to it."

For his day in Cambridge, Massachusetts, Bill had one crucial request: He wanted to play in a private basketball game with the Harvard women's JV team. The Pudding delivered, and Bill played for a while, mostly keeping up with the young athletes. "The basketball game went on for longer than it looked like it could," Allio says.

On the evening of February 19, 1985, before the drag theatrical *Witch and Famous* (the Pudding's 137th annual show, set in colonial Salem), Bill came onstage as the band played the theme from *Ghostbusters*. Bill accepted an award from Alek Keshishian, then a Harvard undergrad but later famous as the director of the Madonna documentary *Truth or Dare*. The traditional Man of the Year hardware: a small golden pudding pot. "It looks like it's good for a small casserole," Bill said.

After the show, there was a party. Allio says that his enduring image of Bill's visit was seeing him on the dance floor, wearing sunglasses at night, getting down to "I Can't Wait" by Nu Shooz. "He was the Pied Piper on the dance floor," Allio says. "He was dancing with the undergrad girls—first five girls, then ten, then fifteen, then twenty-five, all dancing with Bill."

TALES FROM THE GRAPE D'VINE

"One day in May, it was raining cats and dogs," Joe Printz remembers. "It was raining really really hard. Nobody was even driving,

> but this son of a gun rides over on a scooter: Are you out of your mind?" Soaking wet, Bill Murray came in from an apocalyptic rainstorm, wearing jeans, a slicker, and Evel Knievel's helmet. For real. "He had just bought it at auction," Printz says. "It was the helmet that Evel Knievel had jumped over Snake River in."

May 14, 1991: Bill Murray appeared on *Late Night with David Letterman* and did a rehearsed bit where an audience member (actually Joe Furey, a writer on the show) heckled him—one of many scripted bits Bill did on the show over the years, ranging from bursting out of a cake to making his entrance in a Peter Pan costume, suspended over the stage by wires.

The setup: When Furey expressed an excessive amount of enthusiasm for the Finger Lakes (a region in upstate New York), Bill advised him, "If you get a chance, sir, while you're here, check out the rest of the world."

"Screw you!" Furey shouted, soon followed by "Hey, Murray, you suck!"

Bill stood up, ready but relaxed, like an athlete about to enter the game. "I suck? Who told you I suck?" Bill asked.

When Furey moved on to heckling Letterman, Bill said, "Hey, pal. Say what you want to me, but you leave David alone."

"Why don't you come up here and make me?" Furey challenged him.

Bill marched into the audience, grabbed Furey by the shirt, and shoved him out the stage doors, to wild cheers.

During rehearsal, Furey said, the confrontation got even more physical as Bill threw himself into the moment: "He grabs me. We're fighting and punching. He's kicking me and throwing me out of the doors. Then he literally slipped and fell right on top of me. Then he got up, helped me up, and said, 'By the way, I'm Bill.' "

. . .

Circa 2010, John Knizeski was doing construction work in Snedens Landing, New York: "Actually, we were doing de-molition of Orson Welles's old house," he says. It was near where Bill was living, so the crew would sometimes see him out and about, walking his dog. "A tiny little dog," John says, measuring out a space with his hands roughly the size and shape of a car battery. Some of the guys on the demolition crew spotted Bill and started shouting out to him: "Hey, Bill Murray! Come on over, Bill!" Instead of coming over, Bill mimed that the tiny dog was pulling him uncontrollably. He feigned being out of breath and exhausted by the immense power of his miniature canine, and waved helplessly as it pulled him out of sight.

. . .

Before Naomi Watts worked with Bill Murray on *St. Vincent*—she played Daka, a pregnant Russian prostitute, and Bill played a cranky veteran who was her long-term customer (and possibly the father of her child)—they had met at a party and gotten along well. He had even prank-called her voicemail. But she was nervous enough about working with him that she decided she would stay in character for the duration of the shoot: That way, if things didn't go well with Bill, he would be rejecting Daka, not her.

Compounding the stress: Their first scene together was going to be an athletic sex scene. "I pretty much had to straddle him right away," Watts said. "I thought, well, let's dive in deep and keep going with that." Sex scenes in movies are usually awkward to film: Even if the costars are attracted to each other, it's hard to feel erotic with a crew of teamsters standing around. Directors often schedule them early in a shoot, both to get them out of the way and to sidestep any problems that might come if the performers in question end up disliking each other.

So director Ted Melfi made shooting Watts on top of Bill the first order of business. She dutifully ground her body against his, her prosthetic belly bouncing, her ears turning red because the whole situation was embarrassing. Finally, Melfi called, "Cut!"

Bill looked up at Watts and said, "So, are you seeing anyone?"

★ ★

BILL MURRAY MEETS THE YOUTH OF AMERICA

Bill Murray lived for many years in Rockland County, New York, an idyllic stretch of small towns on the west side of the Hudson River. Flying into the New York City airports, airplane passengers would sometimes spot his house's most distinctive feature:

a large swimming pool with a Chicago Cubs logo on the bottom. Rockland County hasn't been Bill's primary residence for a while now, but people there still consider him one of their own and cheerfully share stories about Bill's Halloween parties, or how he helped them with packages outside the post office, or how they saw him get snubbed by a clueless Columbia graduate student on a shuttle bus into New York.

Local Diana Green, for example, used to see Bill at Little League games. Bill, who was very involved with his sons' athletics, once acted as umpire in a game where her son Dakota was the catcher. Bill kept up a steady stream of chatter and banter behind Dakota, distracting him sufficiently that Dakota didn't pay attention to an incoming fastball and missed it entirely. The pitch landed squarely on his forehead, and even though Dakota had his catcher's mask on, it bowled him over and knocked him out.

When young Dakota regained consciousness, he opened his eyes to the surreal sight of Bill Murray standing over him and advising, "I think you're going to want to lay there for a while."

Sigourney Weaver on Bill Murray's technique with women and children: "The way to a woman's heart is to make her laugh, and Bill makes you laugh when you least expect it. He'll go up to a strange woman, grab her, and behind heavy breathing, say, 'I want to know what makes you tick, baby.' It's such a shock to see someone break the conventions that they just end up laughing, because there's nothing malicious about him. He's pure fun. He's the same with kids, even little babies. He walks up to them and yells, 'How are ya, big guy?' He talks to them as if they were adults. At first they look at him in horror; then they get broken down and start laughing."

So how did Bill introduce himself to Weaver? They met for the first time on the *Ghostbusters* shoot, outside the New York Public Library on 42nd Street. Bill walked up to Weaver, said "Hi, Sue" (her given name is Susan Alexandra Weaver), hoisted her over his shoulder, and carried her down the street.

. . .

"The motto of the city of Chicago is 'I will,'" Bill Murray said. And so, on August 15, 2008, he donned a yellow jumpsuit, goggles, and a cap that strapped around his chin, and headed up two and a half miles in a plane with the Golden Knights, the U.S. Army's parachute team. His mission: at age fifty-seven, to skydive onto the shore of Lake Michigan to kick off the fiftieth Chicago Air & Water Show, a wildly popular festival that draws millions of people. He had agreed to do it when he felt miserable about his divorce proceedings. "They asked me on a day I didn't care," Bill said. "I didn't even care if there was a parachute. Of course, by the time I got there I had had a few good days and I thought, 'What am I doing?'"

Bill was terrified. One of the biggest surprises for him was how cold the plane was at an altitude of 13,500 feet: about twenty degrees Fahrenheit. "We circled around for a long time because they were being very cautious. They didn't want to lose me. That would have been noticed."

While he was waiting to jump, Bill got up and walked from the back of the plane to the front and discovered that he felt worse. One of the Golden Knights told him, "Well, you just walked eighty feet uphill at 13,500 feet.

There's no oxygen in here." They busted out a can of oxygen and passed it around.

"It was a fight to the finish for who was going to hold on to that oxygen can," Bill said. "It's like, 'Don't bogart that joint.' I couldn't believe it. I thought, 'You guys are supposed to be the pros. Can I have this thing?'"

Freezing and oxygen-starved, Bill began to think that, in a life full of random adventures, this jump was the stupidest thing he had ever done. "All of a sudden I really, really didn't want to go." But go he did, jumping out of the plane with Staff Sergeant Joe Jones strapped to his back and a bunch of other Golden Knights falling beside him, some with cameras, some trailing pink smoke so that the spectators could spot them.

Bill described the experience: "The physical sensation overwhelms your body. Overwhelms your mind. You can't think anymore. You're just in a washing machine of air." He tried to move his arms and his hands, with limited success. Bill realized that he was being filmed, so even hurtling toward the ground at high speed, he thought, "Oh, I'm supposed to be funny now." Never missing an opportunity, he played air guitar for the cameras.

Then Jones opened up the parachute. "It's not that *ka-kunk* thing you see in the movies," Bill said. "It's just that the people you're talking to or looking at just sort of drop through the bottom of the floor. Then it became extremely peaceful and really dreamy. I was like, 'Hey, there's Wrigley Field, can we go over there?'"

While the earth spins, make yourself useful.

I N OCTOBER 2006, BILL MURRAY PARTICIPATED IN a celebrity tournament at the legendary St. Andrews Links golf course, playing alongside Michael Douglas, Hugh Grant, and Dennis Hopper. One night after he was done with golf, Bill went drinking at the trendy Ma Bells bar and chatted up Lykke Stavnef, a twenty-two-year-old Norwegian blonde who was in Scotland to study social anthropology.

When last call came, Stavnef invited Bill to accompany her and her friend Marie Bergene to a party they knew about. To her surprise, he accepted the invitation. "You know, Scotland closes kind of early," Bill said later. "It was just a whole bunch of people saying, 'Oh, we're going to the next thing.'" They walked through the cobblestone streets of St. Andrews and ended up at a party in a Georgian townhouse, filled with Scandinavian exchange students. "Nobody could believe it when I arrived at the party with Bill Murray," Stavnef said.

She worried that there were no clean glasses at the party, but Bill was happy to drink vodka from a coffee cup. Then he went one step further: He walked over to the sink, rolled up the sleeves of his plaid shirt, and started washing dishes. As Bill told the story, "The party was way ahead of us, and there was no way to catch up. So I looked around and it was like a college dorm, not a dorm but a house. And, like a college house, it was kind of a mess. And I realized, *Well, I gotta do something;* I can't stand still, because everyone's way ahead of us. So I just started washing the dishes. And it was great fun because we got to wash the dishes and you could talk a little bit and keep washing the dishes."

Bill diligently scraped dried pasta off a dish, joking with an economics student that maybe they should just reheat it. As word spread that Bill was at the party, more people showed up, many of them young Scandinavians. The booze was quickly depleted, but Bill stayed for a while anyway: The party had acquired its own momentum.

"You can't just walk in and walk out," Bill said of the party. "That feels strange. But if you walk into someone's house, do all the dishes and leave, then you feel like you've made a contribution."

· · ·

Entitlement on display in New York City: a luxury car in a traffic jam, honking at everybody else. In the mid-1970s, Bill Murray regularly took action whenever he saw a rich jerk leaning on the horn. Bill would walk right into the traffic jam and try to make a path: "Whack! Just jump into it," he remembered. Bill would push pedestrians out of the way and slap the hoods of less expensive automobiles, shouting, "Can we get this car out of the way here? There's a Cadillac that needs to get through!"

ON THE DARK SIDE

In 2011, Green Bay Packers fan Matt Katrosar flew to Chicago to visit his friends and attend the NFC championship game: The Packers were playing the Bears for a spot in the Super Bowl. Committing to his out-of-town fandom, Katrosar wore a Green Bay jersey—specifically, a throwback jersey for Hall of Fame linebacker Ray Nitschke, who played for the Packers from 1958 to 1972. He was a dot of green in a vast crowd of blue.

The temperature was twenty degrees Fahrenheit, but Katrosar was warmed by the Packers' opening up a lead in the first half. When he was cheering a Green Bay play in the second quarter, he was suddenly shoved from behind by a Bears fan. An annoyed Katrosar turned around to see who had pushed him—and discovered that it was Bill Murray, who was wearing a bright orange hood and equally bright orange gloves.

Katrosar asked Bill if he could take a picture with him. Bill declined, but gave an explanation as to why. "Nitschke is a pussy," he told Katrosar.

Roughly seventy thousand fans showed up for the Grateful Dead's final concert at Soldier Field in Chicago on July 5, 2015, including celebrity Deadheads such as Bill Walton,

Chloë Sevigny, George R. R. Martin, Al Franken, Perry Far-
rell, John Mayer, and Katy Perry. It wasn't surprising that
Bill Murray was there too—but nobody expected him to
stick around after the show, helping the stadium cleaning
crew pick up the heaps of trash at the end of the night.

· · ·

The South by Southwest music festival takes over Austin
every year, with thousands of performers and tens of thousands of industry folk and music fans descending on the
boho Texas city. In 2010, one of the throng was Bill Murray, who wandered around town, drinking and catching
shows. "You go at it hard down there," Bill said of South by
Southwest. "Fun, but, man, you need to sleep for days afterward."

One afternoon, Bill ended up at the Shangri-La, a hipster dive bar on the east side of Austin that had been open
for a year. Bill had a few shots at the bar and got into a
conversation with off-duty bartender Trevor Rathbone—
when he started to get mobbed, he went down the street to
the "Mess With Texas" showcase. A few hours later Bill returned. This time he had brought along a friend: GZA
from the Wu-Tang Clan (also his acting partner seven
years earlier in a *Coffee and Cigarettes* scene), who imbibed
so much with Bill that he was visibly drunk when he performed later that night.

"Shots was goin' down, down, down," GZA said.

Shangri-La proprietor Tyler Van Aken was upstairs on
the patio, tending bar, when he got a text from a staffer
inside: "Bill is back looking for Trevor."

Van Aken texted back: "See if Bill will get behind the bar."

The request was unusual, so naturally Bill was up for it. Thirty seconds later, Van Aken received the reply: "Bill is bartending!"

Van Aken told a friend to watch the patio bar and ran downstairs so he could bear witness to the insanity.

"All of a sudden, Bill Murray's standing next to me behind my bar," said bartender Jesse Cates. "I found myself bartending with a Ghostbuster. It was pretty flipping sweet."

The crowd swarmed the bar, requesting drinks from Bill. He would lean in, listen carefully to the order, and then grab whatever bottle was handy and pour whatever he felt like. There were a bunch of bottles of Hornitos tequila next to Bill, so mostly he poured shots of tequila. You ordered a gin and tonic? Bill gave you a shot of tequila. A martini? Bill gave you a shot of tequila. A beer? Bill gave you a shot of tequila.

If people tried to pay him, Bill wouldn't say anything: He would just stick out his hand and accept their money. Somebody would press a twenty-dollar bill into it, and Bill would just hand it off to another bartender. If they had been expecting change, it wasn't forthcoming. Van Aken laughs at the memory: "Bill Murray's obviously not going to open the drawer and give you change! Why are you even trying to pay him?"

Bill was straight-faced the entire time, but he appeared to be in his element. "I think he had fun, or else he wouldn't have been doing it for fully thirty minutes," Van Aken said. "And he wouldn't have been pouring shots of booze into some kid's mouth."

After half an hour, the performance was over, and Bill was slipping out the side door. Van Aken made sure to catch him before he left: He wanted to thank him. "I just said, 'Sir, I really can't tell you what you did meant to me. Me and my dad built that bar.'"

Bill stopped, looked at Van Aken, and said, "Tell your dad I said hello." And then he walked away.

. . .

Michael Ovitz, talent agent supreme, was relaxing in his fancy Brentwood mansion when the doorbell rang unexpectedly: pizza delivery. Or, more precisely, Bill Murray was standing outside holding a pizza, claiming to be the pizza delivery man.

For many years, Ovitz was the most brilliant, ruthless representative in Hollywood. And until he left CAA (the Creative Artists Agency) in 1995 to run Disney, he was Bill's agent. But even the most powerful man in Hollywood couldn't reliably track down Bill Murray. Sometimes CAA wouldn't hear from Bill for weeks—and then he would call, saying that he was standing in front of the Taj Mahal. Ovitz didn't believe him until Bill put his Indian taxi driver on the phone to confirm his location.

So when Bill showed up with a pizza, as he did periodically, Ovitz said, "We'd let him in, he'd actually have a pizza, we'd eat it, and then he'd disappear again. It was like that for years."

BILL MURRAY MEETS THE YOUTH OF AMERICA

Bill Murray bought a house from my friend Jonathan's family—I think he bought it for his wife's parents. He showed up at the house—it was a large family, with eight kids, and he spent the entire time joking around with them and some other kids who showed up, including my family. In the backyard, there was a long stretch of grass, a ramp, and a swimming pool. Bill challenged the kids to ride a bike as fast as they could off the little ramp, into the pool. I think he offered five bucks to anyone who would do it and promised that if they did, he would too. So my friend's brother, Mike, went to do that—and just as he got to the ramp, Bill yelled something at him. Mike missed the ramp and did a somersault right into the pool. So then Bill said there was no way he was doing it.

Bill stayed and goofed around for a long time—he was at home making jokes with a whole group of kids. Before he left, he told Mike to stay out of jail.

—Keith M. Jones

In 2016, when David Granger was retiring after two decades as editor-in-chief of *Esquire,* he and writer Scott Raab had an "exit interview" with Bill Murray—in other words, a four-hour expense-account lunch at an Albanian steakhouse in New York City. Bill talked about getting fired from a job at a grocery store when he was nineteen (apparently he made an accidental double-entendre about sausage), extolled the virtues of Adele, and discussed whether he would prefer a championship for the Chicago Cubs or for Xavier University, where his son Luke was an assistant coach on the basketball team. His verdict: "I have several sons, but I only have one ball club."

Bill believed in this strongly enough that he challenged Granger to a bet: "We both have to take no work from anyone for a period of three months, not even talk to anyone until the end of the summer. And then at the end of the summer, if neither of us has an idea that's good enough to do—our own self-generated one—then we'll take the first piece-of-shit job that comes. And the guy who takes the first piece-of-shit job has to pay the other guy the five hundred bucks."

Bill concluded, "That's a great bet, and I get the summer off again."

. . .

Tia Carrera is a metal trio based in Austin, Texas, heavy on the improvisation, heavy on the heaviness (and with no connection to Tia Carrere, the Hawaiian-born actress and singer most famous for her role as Cassandra, the love interest in *Wayne's World*). In March 2012, Tia Carrera were playing a late-night showcase at South by Southwest. Around 2:30 A.M., they had finished their set and were loading their gear into their van.

Suddenly a head poked into the van: Bill Murray's head, in fact. "What are you doing?" he asked. Guitarist Jason Morales explained the just-finished-a-gig situation. Bill didn't miss a beat: He helped the band as they carried their equipment and packed it into the van, as if he were their longtime roadie. Playing it cool, the band acted as if this was normal.

"When we were done," Morales says, "he asked if he and his entourage could get in the van with us. But at that point, the van was completely full. So we had to call him a cab."

. . .

The hour was late; the city was Oakland, California. Bill Murray got into a taxicab. With a long drive across the bridge to Sausalito ahead of him, he started talking with the cabbie and discovered that his driver was a frustrated saxophone player.

"When do you practice?" Bill asked.

Not very often, the cabbie told him: "I drive fourteen hours a day."

"Well, where's your sax?"

"It's in the trunk."

So Bill told the driver to pull over and to get his sax out of the trunk—the cabbie could play in the backseat while Bill took the wheel. "I know how to drive a car," Bill assured him.

The driver agreed. Sitting on the side of the road, listening to the sound of the trunk opening, Bill started to get excited: "This is going to be a good one," he thought. "We're both going to *dig the shit* out of this."

If the driver had been a lousy player, Bill could have switched places again—but in fact, the guy was great. "He definitely could play," Bill said. "Obviously he needed every day, every hour, to play something." Bill was happy to have a saxophone soundtrack all the way to Sausalito—but then he thought, "Let's go all the way."

"Are you a little hungry?" Bill asked the cabbie in the backseat. Then he drove to "what people would call a sketchy rib place in Oakland at, like, two-fifteen in the morning."

The cabbie was nervous, but Bill told him, "Relax, man, you got the fucking horn—we're cool." So when they arrived, the cabbie played saxophone for the other patrons of late-night BBQ. Bill said, "The crowd's like, 'What the hell, little crazy white dude playing that thing.' "

Bill was right: Both he and the cabbie dug the shit out of their ride together. "It made for a beautiful night," Bill said. "I think we'd all do that. I think anyone, if you saw that moment, you'd make the connection, and you'd do it."

The Tao of Being Yourself
Bill Murray Day

A NEW DAY ON THE CALENDAR, ACCORDING TO the Toronto International Film Festival: "Bill Murray Day," observed on September 5. For the first celebration of that date, in 2014, the festival devoted a sold-out movie theater to screenings of *Stripes* and *Ghostbusters,* followed by a Q&A session with Ivan Reitman (a Toronto native and the director of those two movies), Bill's pal Mitch Glazer, and Bill himself.

Bill came onstage wearing bright red pants, singing along to Prince's "Raspberry Beret." He discussed his history with Reitman and talked about the first time he was up for a movie award (the Genie Award for Best Performance by a Foreign Actor, for *Meatballs;* at the awards ceremony in Canada, he hung out with fellow nominee Will Sampson, the very tall Native American featured in *One Flew Over the Cuckoo's Nest*). He recapped his day, which he said was spent mostly trying to make a specific type of coffee in his hotel room: "People kept coming up, saying things like 'It's really humid out there' . . . maybe seven different people," Bill said. "That's what my day's been like. It's mostly been a weather report."

When a woman asked Bill what movie he would pick if he were to be locked in a room for two years and had to watch one film over and over in a loop, he invited her along into the locked room: "Honey, we can make it work." Then he made two foreign-language choices, François Truffaut's classic *Small Change* ("that's a really funny movie") and Roberto Benigni's *Johnny Stecchino* ("I laughed so hard I thought I was going to come apart").

For the last question, Bill called on somebody dressed in a *Ghostbusters* costume, in the theater's back row: "Who is that full-figured fellow?"

"I'm not a man!" was the response.

"You're backlit, I'm sorry. You're just bringing more to the party as far as I'm concerned." Bill's apology sounded sincere, but he didn't dwell on the faux pas. "What's up? What's your question?"

"What's up, Bill Murray?" she asked. "Don't worry—that's not my question. I actually came all the way from Vancouver for this."

"Is anyone driving back to Vancouver after this?" Bill called out. "Is that the question?"

"There's a million things I could ask you right now," she said. "The only thing that comes to my mind is 'How does it feel to be you?'"

People laughed, but you could see some members of

the crowd roll their eyes—this seemed like exactly the sort of question that would get batted away with a half-assed joke. Bill, however, moved quickly to quell any dissent. "Good question," he said. "It's a great question."

He nodded, collecting his thoughts. A hush fell over the crowd. "I think if I'm going to answer this question, because it is a hard question, I'd like to suggest that we all answer that question right now, while I'm talking. I'll continue—believe me, I won't shut up. I have a microphone. Let's all ask ourselves that question right now. What does it feel like to be you?"

"Awesome!" somebody shouted out.

"Yeah, it feels good to be you, doesn't it?" Bill agreed. "Because there's one thing that you are . . . the only one that's you, right? So you're the only one that's you. And we get confused sometimes and we—or I do, I think everyone does—you try to compete. You think that, dammit, maybe someone else is trying to be me, you know?"

People in the crowd nodded, surprised but not displeased by the turn the conversation had taken. Bill continued, "I don't have to armor myself against those people. I don't have to armor myself against that idea, if I can really just relax and feel content."

He changed tacks: "Just think now how much you weigh. This is a thing I like to do with myself when I get lost, when I get feeling funny. How much do you weigh? Think about how much each person here weighs and try to feel that weight in your seat, in your bottom right now.

Parts in your feet and parts in your bottom. Just try to feel your own weight in your own seat, in your own feet. Okay?" Bill's voice was calm and hypnotic.

"So if you can feel that weight in your body, if you can come back into the most personal identification—which is, *I am, this is me now, here I am right now, this is me now*—then you don't feel like you have to leave and be over there, or look over there. And you don't feel like you have to rush off and be somewhere. There's just a wonderful sense of well-being that begins to circulate up and down, from your top to your bottom, up and down your spine. And you feel something that makes you almost want to smile. It makes you almost want to feel good. It makes you want to feel like you could embrace yourself."

Bill's words hung in the thick silence of the theater. "So what's it like to be me?" he asked. "Ask yourself: 'What's it like to be *me*?' The only way we'll ever know what it's like to be you is if you work your best at being you as often as you can—and keep reminding yourself that's where home is."

Bill smiled. "That's where home is. Thank you."

The Films
of Bill Murray

It's not *that* hard to meet Bill Murray: Go to enough Cubs games and eventually you'll run into the guy. Or if you position yourself in his gallery at Pebble Beach, he might wrestle you in a sand trap. But the easiest way to insert some Bill into your life is to see his movies. Some of them rank among the crowning achievements of cinema; some have landed in the ninety-nine-cent bin (and are overpriced when found there). But almost all of these fifty-nine performances, from 1978 through 2016, have something of his spirit in them: In both comedic and dramatic roles, he brings the ineffable spark of Billness.

If, as Bill says, he is the best version of himself when he's working on a film set, then this body of work is not just the career of a fine actor, it's an alternate map of the Tao of Bill.

All You Need Is Cash (1978, Bill Murray the K.)

"It's Rutles Day! They're going to be here tomorrow, talking
about their trousers—it's a big, big day here in Flushing!
Let's give them a big round of applause—I know I can't hear
you, but I know I can pick up what you're saying, baby!"

The Rutles were a fictional rock band uncannily similar to
the Beatles. *All You Need Is Cash*, six years before *This Is
Spinal Tap*, was a faux documentary that told the story
of the Prefab Four. Eric Idle of Monty Python starred in
it, wrote the screenplay, and co-directed it; Neil Innes of
the Bonzo Dog Doo-Dah Band also starred in it and wrote
the songs (pastiches of Beatles songs, such as "Piggy in the
Middle" for "I Am the Walrus" and "Ouch!" for "Help!").
The result (sometimes retitled *The Rutles*) was more
charming than funny, but it was done with such care and
obvious love for the Beatles that it was a treat for any seri-

ous fan of the group. Adding to the verisimilitude and the star power were cameos from Mick Jagger, Paul Simon, Ron Wood, Gilda Radnér, John Belushi, Dan Aykroyd, and even George Harrison.

The film, originally broadcast on NBC and the BBC, had Lorne Michaels as executive producer, which accounted for the heavy presence of *Saturday Night Live* cast members. Bill Murray, who had joined the Not Ready for Prime Time Players just a few weeks earlier, was enlisted to play Bill Murray the K, a parody of Murray Kaufman, known professionally as Murray the K. The real-life figure was a New York DJ who, at the height of Beatlemania, did some interviews with the band and dubbed himself "the fifth Beatle." Bill Murray's version was a radio broadcaster wearing a Rutles shirt and delivering an overexcited monologue into a microphone; unfortunately, Bill basically shouted his entire performance.

"He just wanted to improvise and improvise. So we have a lot of footage of Bill. He was really funny," Idle said. "And I think he was secretly having an affair with Gilda at this time."

Meatballs (1979, Tripper)

> "Attention, campers! Arts and crafts has been canceled due to bad taste. All junior girls are now junior boys. And Nurse DeMarco says that the raccoon-fever epidemic is officially over."

Meatballs was a low-budget, slapdash comedy, but it worked, mostly because it included a twenty-seven-year-old Bill Murray in his first starring role, as Tripper, an anarchic counselor at an underdog summer camp. Director Ivan Reitman expected that Bill would be the funniest thing in the movie, but he didn't realize that Bill would also give it heart. *Meatballs* was originally conceived as an ensemble summer-camp comedy leaning heavily on the teenage CITs (counselors in training); in the editing room, Reitman saw what worked and what didn't, which meant that most of the CIT material got whittled away. The movie was then bolstered with extra scenes focused on the relationship between Tripper and Rudy (Chris Makepeace), an awkward teen who comes out of his shell when Tripper befriends him.

Bill was reluctant to sign on to *Meatballs*—not only did he want to spend his summer playing baseball, but the script wasn't really finished when shooting started. What convinced him was Reitman telling him that if it was no good, it would never be seen: "They'll show it on military bases in Turkey or someplace."

John Belushi advised Bill to take the role: "I don't care what it is, just take it; you're going to be the star of the movie."

So once Bill showed up to the location in Canada (an actual summer camp), a day after the movie had started shooting, he threw himself into the part, discarding the screenplay for any given scene and improvising his own version of it. Most of the movie's funniest bits, including the "It just doesn't matter" chant and the extended monologue about "Sexual Awareness Week," were done by Bill off the top of his head. (Harold Ramis polished the script and wrote most of Bill's announcements on the public-address system.)

There was one thing Bill wouldn't do for the movie, and that was have makeup applied to him. On his first day, when the makeup artist leaned in to work on him, a cigarette dangling from her mouth, she burned him. Bill remembered, "I looked at her and said, 'You know what? I'm going to get a suntan instead.' "

Mr. Mike's Mondo Video (1979, Ensemble)

"Just clear out that whole rest area, they hit a gasoline truck—boom! Everything goes, you know, and hundreds of people are killed, like over in Spain."

The "Mr. Mike" of the title was Michael O'Donoghue, the legendary firebrand writer at *Saturday Night Live* and *National Lampoon;* this movie is a collection of his sketches, padded out with random clips such as Sid Vicious performing "My Way." A parade of celebrities appear to have given O'Donoghue about fifteen minutes each, including Carrie Fisher, Gilda Radner, Teri Garr, Debbie Harry, and Bill Murray. (Dan Aykroyd actually filmed two whole segments, as the preacher at a church that worships *Hawaii Five-O* star Jack Lord, and as himself, showing off his webbed toes.)

Bill's role doesn't have a name in the credits: He does an interview on a busy New York City sidewalk, answering the question "Should people who are deaf and dumb be allowed to talk with their hands while driving a car?"

"It's a tough question," Bill allows, holding his jaw asymmetrically and using the "honker" voice that would later become synonymous with his groundskeeper character in *Caddyshack.* "Somebody's gotta draw the line somewhere," he decides. "I would not let them drive," he concludes, improvising a scenario where a gesticulating driver kills a crowd of people in a fiery explosion.

Like the rest of *Mr. Mike's Mondo Video,* Bill's segment is pretty tame. The movie begins with a warning—"THE FILM YOU ARE ABOUT TO SEE IS SHOCKING AND REPUGNANT BEYOND BELIEF"—and O'Donoghue repeatedly warns viewers about just how outrageous the material is. Although it was too much for NBC, which declined to air it, these days it seems hard to believe anyone was ever offended by sketches about a swimming school for cats, a French restaurant that insults tourists, or Laser Bra 2000.

Loose Shoes (1980, Lefty Schwartz)

> "You call this quiche? It's slop! And this bouillabaisse?
> Nothing but slop!"

A slipshod collection of crude coming-attraction spoofs— "Invasion of the Penis Snatchers," "The Shaggy Studio

Chief," et cetera—filmed in 1977 but shelved until 1980, when Bill Murray's *Meatballs* stardom made it commercially viable to release. Presumably, Bill shot his scenes just before he got called up to the major leagues (i.e., joined the *Saturday Night Live* cast). He appears in one segment: a prison-movie parody called "Three Chairs for Lefty!" where he plays a man on death row in San Quentin who gives culinary advice to the warden. Bill does his best with weak material and even dons a bald cap, but, like the rest of the movie, his six minutes are profoundly unfunny.

Where the Buffalo Roam
(1980, Dr. Hunter S. Thompson)

> "It still hasn't gotten weird enough for me."

Bill Murray played Hunter Thompson, the famed gonzo journalist, eighteen years before Johnny Depp took a crack at the man in *Fear and Loathing in Las Vegas*. Unfortunately, this movie makes Thompson into a wacky anarchist, with unsatisfying results: It feels like a remake of *Weekend at Bernie's* with Allen Ginsberg trying to stash Jack Kerouac's body. The actor who comes off the best is Bruno Kirby, who plays Jann Wenner, Thompson's editor at *Rolling Stone,* although he's called Marty Lewis and the magazine is renamed *Blast!* He's clearly meant to be a petty boss and an ineffectual authority figure, constantly haggling over hotel expenses. Kirby, however, brings some real emotion to the role, giving insight into how hard it must be to work with a creative loose cannon like Thompson—or Bill.

Bill got to spend time with Thompson, on and off the set, and found a kindred spirit willing to engage in random, excessive, sometimes destructive behavior—Thompson just had a thirteen-year head start. Thompson even tied Bill to a chair after a long night of drinking and threw him into a swimming pool (fishing him out just before he drowned). Bill also went boating with Thompson—who hadn't been out on the water for a little while. "It was hot, and our beer needed quick stashing," Bill remembered. "The starboard cooler, sadly, was found to contain last week's chum, which the tropics had turned into maggots." Recoiling in horror, they instinctively tossed the cooler into the water. But they were still in the harbor, so "the scum of the chum and the maggot spawn flotsam landed and simply stared right back. Like bridesmaids' vomit at a stoplight. It seemed like hours but was probably only twelve seconds before the living school of stench began to move, settling two slips down." When Murray and Thompson heard screams of horror, they gunned the engines and headed for the open water.

Caddyshack (1980, Carl Spackler)

> "So we finish eighteen, and he's going to stiff me. And I say, 'Hey, Lama! Hey! How about a little something, you know,

for the effort, you know?' And he says, 'Oh, there won't be any money, but when you die, on your deathbed you will receive total consciousness.' So I got that going for me, which is nice."

Bill Murray is the heart of *Caddyshack,* one of the most beloved sports comedies ever, and not just because of his performance as the deranged groundskeeper Carl. In many ways, the movie is his life story: His brother Brian Doyle-Murray co-wrote the screenplay and based the teenage protagonist Danny Noonan (Michael O'Keefe) on the caddying experiences of the Murray brothers. Just like an adolescent Bill, Danny wakes up in a house overflowing with kids, is warned by his father that he could end up working at the lumberyard, and then bicycles over to the country club in the rich part of town.

Bill played Carl with the "honker" voice that he had been employing for years, suggesting either drunkenness or brain damage. Carl seems to exist outside the movie's themes of class conflict: He spends most of his time leering at middle-aged women and waging war against a gopher. What was supposed to be a small role kept growing, and the filmmakers repeatedly asked Bill to fly down to Florida to film more scenes. Bill wasn't originally supposed to do the Dalai Lama monologue (quoted above) but stepped in when another actor didn't nail it. And the "Cinderella story" speech, where Bill narrates his victory at the Masters tournament, came when director Harold Ramis asked if he had ever done play-by-play for his own imaginary sports triumphs. Bill knew exactly what he meant and made it up on the spot.

Bill has made a point of praising Harold Ramis for stitching together the disparate comedic styles of himself, Rodney Dangerfield, Ted Knight, and Chevy Chase and making the movie feel like an organic whole. It's particularly impressive that he and Chase were working together, considering the bad blood between them. After Chase left the cast of *Saturday Night Live* at the beginning of 1977, Bill took his place—which meant that when Chase returned to guest-host the show in February, having alienated much of the cast and crew with an advanced case of star syndrome, it fell on Bill, as the new guy, to stand up to him. "It would have been too petty for someone else to do it," Bill said.

The tension came to a head backstage just before Chevy's monologue, with a scuffle that didn't quite turn into a fistfight. Legend has it that Bill won the encounter with a withering insult, dismissing Chase with two words: "Medium talent."

"There's a little bit of bully in Billy," a wounded Chase said decades later. Nevertheless, a year and a half after their showdown, they both signed up for *Caddyshack*. Their characters have only one scene together: a rambling sequence where Ty Webb (Chase) hits a golf ball into the residence of Carl Spackler (Bill) and plays through.

Their other joint scene got cut. In it, Carl, driving an enormous industrial lawnmower, roughly twenty feet wide, pulls up to Ty, jumps off the mower, and gives Ty some tips on how to slow down his backswing. In the course of his demonstration, Carl hits a couple of balls belonging to some other golfers. As the irate golfers run toward them, Carl drives the mower away and Ty hops on to make his escape.

Chase discovered that it was tricky to mount the lawn-mower, because wearing spiked golf shoes, he couldn't get a good grip. He warned Bill not to make any sudden moves behind the wheel, lest he slip and fall into the spinning blades. When they filmed the scene, Chase jumped onto the mower, sliding around and hanging on for his life—and, he said, "Billy makes the fastest right he can make. I had to jump like fifteen feet off the tractor" to avoid getting chewed up.

"That's why he's so great as a humorist—he's dangerous," Chase concluded. "But he's literally dangerous. You never know what he's going to do."

Stripes (1981, John)

> "We're American soldiers! We've been kicking ass for two hundred years! We're ten and one!"

Stripes was originally developed as a vehicle for stoner comics Cheech and Chong, but Bill Murray in the Army also made for a good fish-out-of-water story. As a civilian, Bill's character John Winger was a New York City taxi driver—only five years after Robert De Niro showed just how hostile somebody in that job could be. John Winger has enough free-floating contempt that he would be a thoroughly unlikable guy, except that Bill plays him with insouciant charm.

The relaxed pacing and the topless women mark the movie as an R-rated period piece—the fun of the movie is watching Bill improvise his way through it. A decade after its release, he said, "I'm still a little queasy that I made a movie where I carry a machine gun. But I felt if you were rescuing your friends, it was okay. It wasn't *Reds* or anything, but it captured what it was like on an Army base: It was cold, you had to wear the same green clothes, you had to do a lot of physical stuff, you got treated pretty badly, and had bad coffee."

The *Stripes* cast was full of comedy heavy hitters, including John Candy and Harold Ramis, but the actors regarded Bill with a particular mix of confusion and awe. "You never knew what was real and what was kidding around," said actress P. J. Soles.

John Larroquette, who played the officious Captain Stillman, said, "There's something about his eyes. He's an insane man, and in another century he'd be locked up."

Judge Reinhold would go on to star in major movies like *Fast Times at Ridgemont High* and the *Beverly Hills Cop* series, but his second film role ever was as Elmo Blum, a very green private in *Stripes*. Reinhold's take: "If you expect something from Bill, then that's your downfall. You'll get exactly the opposite." Reinhold learned that early on during the shoot, when he walked up to Bill; he was a twenty-three-year-old actor wanting to express his admiration.

"Hi, Bill," Reinhold said. "My name is Judge and I really enjoy your work." In response, Bill grabbed Judge's cheeks and squeezed them together with one hand. "Does that bother you?" Bill asked. "Does that bother you when I do that?"

Speaking of director Ivan Reitman, Reinhold said, "I watched Ivan control Sherman tanks, helicopters, huge companies of soldiers. The only thing that he could never control in any way would be Bill Murray."

Reitman remembered that Bill didn't officially commit to *Stripes* until two weeks before shooting started—although after the *Meatballs* experience, he wasn't surprised. "I had a secret weapon," Reitman said. That was casting Harold Ramis as Bill's costar. "I think he always felt it was unfair that Harold didn't get selected to be part of that amazing group on *Saturday Night Live*."

The movie's greatest sequence is where Bill and his slovenly squadron, after cramming all night, show off their drill technique while chanting "That's the fact, Jack" and Sly and the Family Stone's "Boom-shaka-laka-laka." Reitman remembered, "I knew we needed to have some spectacular second-act curtain." Reitman commissioned a routine from a military drill specialist and then had the recruits spend weeks practicing it. Bill, however, refused to go to any rehearsal. Reitman implored him, "Bill, you gotta learn this. You're going to be in the front of it—you can't look bad."

"No no no, I'll get it," Bill assured him. He went to one or two practices, putting in maybe five percent of the time the other cast members did. On the day of the shoot, they filmed in front of five hundred people who had never seen the routine before. "As usual, Bill had the routine down perfect," Reitman sighed. "I don't know where the hell that came from."

Tootsie (1982, Jeff)

"That is one nutty hospital."

Tootsie is probably the funniest movie Bill Murray will ever make—and although its success didn't rest on Bill's supporting role as Dustin Hoffman's playwright roommate, he improvised some of its best moments. For example, his monologue about his artistic aspirations, delivered at a party to a dwindling number of listeners: "I don't want a full house at the Winter Garden Theater. I want ninety people who just came out of the worst rainstorm in the city's history. These are people who are alive, on the planet—until they dry off. I wish I had a theater that was only open when it rained. I don't like it when people come up to me after my plays and say, 'I really dug your message, man.' Or 'I really dug your play, man. I cried.' I like it when people come up to me the next day, or a week later, and they say, 'I saw your play. What happened?' "

The part of the roommate was an invention of uncredited screenwriter Elaine May: She reasoned that when Hoffman was busy transforming himself into a woman to get a job on a soap opera, he would need somebody to talk to about it. Hoffman lobbied for Bill to get the part, figuring that he could hold his own against him. With Hoffman acting up a storm, Bill proved to be the perfect deadpan foil. He discovered there was nothing he could do that would overshadow a cross-dressing Hoffman: In one scene, Bill requested a plate of lemon slices, which he ate with no explanation, confident that it would not upstage Hoffman packing a suitcase full of women's clothes.

Although *Tootsie* was a stone-cold classic, its creation was not a happy time, with Dustin Hoffman constantly at loggerheads with director Sydney Pollack. (Hoffman badgered Pollack into taking a role in the movie as his agent, wanting to capture that adversarial relationship onscreen.) According to Hoffman, Bill added to the insanity when he showed up to work: Pollack showed Bill around the apartment that his character shared with Dustin Hoffman's character—they were shooting in an actual loft building. "Wait'll you see how we're doing your room," Pollack told him.

As Hoffman remembered it, "He goes in there, and we hear crashing and things breaking." The cast and crew stood outside the room, in shocked silence, until Pollack emerged from the room, looking as if he had just been mugged. As Hoffman put it, "That was Bill's way of saying he didn't like the way his room was."

And why did Bill object to the bedroom? He thought it was severely underfurnished, with a mattress on the floor. "I said, 'Well, who the fuck lives here? Son of Sam?'"

Bill remembered his introduction to the world of *Tootsie* differently. As he told it, agent Michael Ovitz escorted him on a set visit before he actually started work—they dropped by the studio where the filmmakers were shooting the scenes for the soap opera *Southwest General.* That happened to be the day Hoffman chose to have a massive blowout argument with Pollack. "Staggering, screaming, the veins, the whole thing," Bill said. Ovitz was mortified, but Bill, who had observed plenty of bad actorly behavior before, judged the tantrum to be approximately sixty percent authentic. Still, he saw how the crew members were keeping their distance from the argument and knew that the conflict would kill the camaraderie necessary for a good comedy.

So Bill jumped in and started insulting Pollack: "Give me a fuckin' break with the cowboy boots. You got a crease in your fuckin' jeans and you're wearing boots?"

The crew started watching, assuming that Bill was Hoffman's ally and curious how this was going to play out. "And then I turned on Dustin, I started attacking him," Bill said. "They're like, 'Holy shit, he's Sydney's guy.' Then I started turning on guys in the crew that I knew."

Bill felt like stirring it up worked: "That was when the

crew went, okay, all right, all right, I think we got a movie now."

Ghostbusters (1984, Dr. Peter Venkman)

"Back off, man. I'm a scientist."

The apex of Bill Murray's early career was *Ghostbusters,* where his attitude blended perfectly with ectoplasmic special effects for a smash hit. On paper, his Venkman character doesn't seem particularly appealing: He's lecherous, self-absorbed, and mildly sadistic. But Bill made him seem like the epitome of cool—a wisecracking guy who saved New York City from a vengeful god without breaking a sweat.

When Bill started shooting *Ghostbusters* with director Ivan Reitman and costars Dan Aykroyd and Harold Ramis, he was still dazed and jetlagged from *The Razor's Edge* (see below), which had wrapped only days before. He made an abrupt transition from monasteries in the Himalayas, taking a Concorde to New York City and going straight from the airport to a set on the corner of Madison Avenue and 62nd Street. He had dropped thirty-five pounds while shooting in India, and his first couple of weeks back, he slept as much as possible. The culture shock was severe: "Ten days ago I was up there working with the high lamas in a *gompa,* and here I am removing ghosts from drug-

stores and painting slime on my body," he reflected. "What the hell am I doing here?"

But Bill couldn't help being himself. Ramis remembered the movie's first day shooting on the streets of New York: "Bill and Danny and I were just hanging out on the street, and everyone recognized Bill and Danny from *SNL*. Someone walked by and said, 'Hey, Bill Murray!' And Bill said, in a mock-angry voice, 'You son of a bitch!' And he grabbed the guy and he wrestled him to the ground. Just a passerby. The guy was completely amazed—and laughing all the way to the ground."

Ivan Reitman's son, Jason Reitman (the director of *Juno* and *Up in the Air*), studied the differences between the screenplay and the produced film when he staged a live reading of the script in 2012. "While almost all the dialogue in [the] original screenplay is echoed onscreen, the Venkman character is completely improvised," he reported. "It's as if Bill Murray was given a mumblecore-style essay about each scene and then permitted to say whatever he wanted as long as he got the point across. He's like a jazz musician who knows, 'I have eight measures here and have to hit this note here and as long as I follow those rules everything else is up to me.'"

Ernie Hudson played Winston Zeddemore, the fourth Ghostbuster, a part that Aykroyd said he originally wrote with Eddie Murphy in mind and that got scaled back when Murphy didn't join the cast. (Ivan Reitman disputed this—his memory was that the role was always intended as a secondary part but it got bolstered during filming, when they discovered how good Hudson was.) Hudson said that Bill was directly responsible for making sure that he didn't get squeezed out as the movie got rewritten on the fly, making sure that he got some choice dialogue: "Well, wait a minute, what about Ernie here?"

Hudson also got to see what life was like for Bill Murray: "I saw people driving down the streets and go, 'Oh my God!' and slam on their brakes and jump out of their cars while they're still running. And run over and go, 'Bill Murray! Holy shit, man! Oh fuck, I can't believe it's you!' Bill just never ran from it. He would just wade down the street, like he was the mayor." Bill, Hudson said, never seemed to worry about his personal safety, or the film's schedule. "A guy would say, 'Bill, you know, I got this record collection . . . ' and Bill would take off with him."

At the end of the movie, after the Ghostbusters dispatch the gargantuan Stay Puft Marshmallow Man, white fluff covers Aykroyd, Ramis, and Hudson from head to toe—but not Bill. Why not? "It's one of the mistakes I made as a director," Ivan Reitman confessed. "I thought, 'He's the one who always escapes consequence.' A little bit of a metaphor for what he's really like in his life. But I probably should have done it—covering him in slime was so delicious and became such an iconic moment. Anyway, it was a choice that I've second-guessed myself on ever since."

Nothing Lasts Forever (1984, Ted Breughel)

"You're damn tooting nothing lasts forever!"

Like most film actors, Bill Murray has worked on a bunch of movies that never hit the multiplexes. The most notable of these is *Nothing Lasts Forever*, written and directed by Tom Schiller, who Bill knew from *Saturday Night Live*, where Schiller directed many of the show's short films (including "Perchance to Dream," where Bill plays a homeless drunkard who slips into a dream of being a revered Shakespearean actor). *Nothing Lasts Forever* was a black-and-white science-fiction fantasia in which Bill played the closest thing the movie had to an antagonist: the flight attendant on a bus flying to the moon. It's an odd part in an odd movie, but Bill tuned in to Schiller's imbalanced poetry. While the MGM studio bosses deemed the movie too arty for a proper release, it's made sporadic appearances at film festivals, been screened on TCM, and developed a cult following through the years.

The star of the movie was the teenage Zach Galligan, most famous for his role as Billy Peltzer in *Gremlins*. "There were times when he was very nice to me, very generous and funny," Galligan said. "The Bill Murray that I had always hoped that I would work with. And then there were times that he was sullen and unhappy and kind of moody." Trying to figure out his hero's mood swings left Galligan bewildered, but he treasured the moments of comedy they spent together: Bill even put him in a headlock and gave him noogies, as if he were reprising a nerds sketch from *Saturday Night Live*.

Best of all was the day when Galligan was waiting to film a scene, sitting in his canvas-backed chair, listening to the theme from *Chariots of Fire* on his Walkman. Bill heard the famous piano chords leaking out from the headphones and told Galligan to take the headphones off. He then improvised lyrics to the instrumental theme: "They run by the ocean / They run by the shore / They run almost as fast as a chariot of fire." Bill bowed to the assembled crew. "*Chariots of Fire*, ladies and gentlemen, *Chariots of Fire!*" he announced to general applause.

The Razor's Edge (1984, Larry Darrell)

> "I just want to think . . . and I don't have much experience in that field."

This adaptation of W. Somerset Maugham's 1944 novel (also turned into a 1946 movie starring Tyrone Power) tracks the path of Larry Darrell: a volunteer ambulance driver in World War I who returns home to Illinois and spurns a lucrative job as a stockbroker, instead moving to Paris to read philosophy and work as a fish-packer. After a stint in a coal mine, he goes to India in search of spiritual enlightenment and ends up serving as the cook in a Buddhist monastery. He returns to Paris and then leaves Europe, having learned that there is no reward for a virtuous life, not even love.

The movie has many ham-fisted moments—every revelation is telegraphed—but it also has grace and beauty. Bill Murray's performance, touted as his first dramatic role (whether it actually is depends on how you classify *Where the Buffalo Roam*), is uneven. Sometimes his face is just blank. But there are other times where we can see subtle flashes of suppressed emotion. In a silent scene where Bill is bundled up in the snowy trenches of World War I, he gazes at a photograph of his girl back home, his eyes vulnerable and expressive.

All too often, though, Bill falls back on schtick that feels anachronistic and emotionally off-center. Or considered in a different light: Even as he toiled on a movie that he felt deeply about and hoped would establish him as a capable dramatic actor, he couldn't resist a scene where he got out of a swimming pool and did an impression of a seal. Or telling his love interest: "Your patriotic duty my last night in town is to leave me unable to walk." Or clowning around with oversize vegetables for the benefit of aged Indian women who don't seem to understand English but who crack up anyway, in what appears to be actual footage of Bill transcending the language barrier with extras during the shoot in India.

The film was directed by John Byrum, who was friendly with Margaret "Mickey" Kelly, Bill's first wife. When Mickey was in the hospital after giving birth, Byrum went to visit and left her with a copy of Maugham's novel. "The very next night, around four in the morning, the phone rings," Byrum recalled. It was Bill Murray, but he identified himself as "Larry Darrell."

Once Murray committed to the movie, he and Byrum drove across the country, working on the screenplay as they went. They even included a eulogy for John Belushi, who had recently died. It comes after the death of Piedmont, the leader of Larry Darrell's ambulance unit (played in the movie by Bill's older brother Brian). Murray intones, "He was a slob. Did you ever see him eat? Starving children could fill their bellies on the food that ended up on his beard and clothes. Dogs would gather to watch him eat. I never understood gluttony, but I hate it. I hated that about you. He enjoyed disgusting people, being disgusting, the thrill of offending people and making them uncomfortable. He was despicable. He will not be missed." Even though Murray covers his sentiment in a thick layer of irony, it's an undeniably moving moment.

The film was shot in England, France, and mountainous regions of India such as Srinagar and Ladakh. The Indian locals had prepared cars for the film's principals, labeled "Director," "Producer," and, for Bill, "Hero." They had also built a trailer for Bill, because they had heard that Hollywood stars demanded such things: He described it as being basically a plywood doghouse with no windows, on top of a flatbed truck. "The one time I went in there," Bill said, "all the Indians were sleeping in it, 'cause they got used to me not being there, so I just stretched out on the floor."

Bill grew very close to his polyglot translator and fixer, Chiptan "Tip" Chostock. On his last night in Ladakh, he visited Chostock's family, expecting he would sign a bunch of autographs, but instead he drank vast quantities of buttered tea and had something resembling a religious epiphany in the family's kitchen: "The walls were full of these copper pots covered with carbon, and there was a hole in the ceiling where the smoke went out, and it looked right up to the stars. The stars were very bright; they lit up this room and everybody's faces and all the pots on the wall. And all of a sudden, all the children—there were twelve— sort of materialized out of the walls. The father looked like Fu Manchu—he was the only man I saw over there who was over six feet tall—and I was attacking him and tickling him, and hitting myself on the head with pots, and showing him my stomach, and stuff like that. We were all laughing, and all the sound was going right up through the skylight. There was a perfect exchange of something between the stars and what was happening in the room. I don't think I've ever felt comfortable like that. I felt like if I stayed there longer, something magical would happen, like they'd break down and say, 'Okay, Bill, you passed the test; you're one of us.' I really wanted to stay there. They were so free, so open. They made you feel that you could act like a fool and not feel bad about it, and they made you feel like there was more to it than that, and if you watched yourself, you'd know even more."

Is it any wonder Bill had culture shock when he went straight to the set of *Ghostbusters* in New York City?

In 2014, when I asked Bill to tell me about a mistake he'd made, he cited this movie: "I made this movie called *The Razor's Edge* in 1983. I worked with John Byrum—we had an extraordinary time, we wrote the script together, and I liked everything about it. But the studio tried to talk us out of it—they said, 'Why don't you make it a modern movie?' John wanted to make it in the period, and I was like, I'm with my guy—he's my guy. And that's really the only way I could have done things at that time, was to be with my guy. But I saw later that there was something to what they said. I certainly didn't know people of that era and the fall of the Archduke. But I saw people I knew in the book, people of my time and the Vietnam era, and that's one of the reasons it touched me. For most of my life, that was the coolest job I ever had, shooting in Paris, London, India—it was just crazy. I think I went three decades before I had another job like that."

Little Shop of Horrors (1986, Arthur Denton)

> "I've been saving all month for this. I think I need a root canal. I'm sure I need a long, slow root canal."

In Frank Oz's film version of the off-Broadway musical about a carnivorous plant, Bill Murray makes a cameo as a masochistic dental patient—an updated version of the role played by Jack Nicholson in the 1960 low-budget horror film *The Little Shop of Horrors*. Steve Martin's performance as the blustering, sadistic dentist Orin Scrivello gives the movie an extra jolt—and as his eager partner in pain, Bill has a delightfully sleazy quality. In a shiny suit, Bill crouches on top of the chair in the waiting room, bouncing with anticipation; once the agonizing dental work begins, he sings out, "Thank you!"

The emotional center of the movie is the nasal ingenue Audrey (Ellen Greene)—the killer plant is a distorted version of her, even named Audrey II. But Bill plays another Audrey doppelgänger: While Audrey receives the cruel attentions of Dr. Scrivello unwillingly, Bill seeks them out. For a campy musical about an extraterrestrial plant, *Little Shop of Horrors* has some unsettling material about domestic violence.

Bill arrived in London, rehearsed his scene the night before, and then improvised his way through the actual shoot. According to director Frank Oz, "Johnny Jympson, the editor, deserves a medal, because it was different every single take. Steve also deserves a medal, because he was the comedy stability here. He did the same thing so Billy could riff off him. And Bill deserves a medal just because he's winging it like crazy." By Oz's count, they did no fewer than thirty-two takes of the final moment when Bill leaves the office.

The scene works not so much because of any particular off-the-cuff line but because of the crazy gleam in Bill's eye and his unhinged enthusiasm. The physical comedy and the verbal comedy unite perfectly for one moment, when Bill tells Martin, with a mouth full of cotton and bizarre dental apparatuses: "It's your professionalism that I respect!"

Scrooged (1988, Frank Cross)

> "I get it. You're taking me back in time to show me my
> mother and father, and I'm supposed to get all goosey and
> blubbery. Well, forget it, pal. You got the wrong guy."

Bill Murray is, somewhat unusually for an actor, an astute judge of the quality of his own movies. Talking about *Scrooged* with the late Roger Ebert, and acknowledging that he spent the shoot in constant conflict with director Richard Donner (*Lethal Weapon*), Bill said, "That could have been a really, really great movie. The script was so good. There's maybe one take in the final-cut movie that is mine. We made it so fast, it was like doing a movie live. He kept telling me to do things louder, louder, louder. I think he was deaf."

For his part, Donner said, "Directing Billy is like being a cop at Times Square when all the lights go out."

That conflict explains a lot about *Scrooged*, which has many of the elements of a good movie without actually coming together. It's a retelling of *A Christmas Carol* where Bill plays a heartless TV executive who, after visitations from three ghosts, sees the error of his ways. The cast, which includes rock singer David Johansen, gymnast Mary

Lou Retton, and three of Bill's brothers, is strong; the rapport between Bill and Karen Allen (playing his long-lost love) is excellent. Some of the jokes connect: generally speaking, the broadest ones, like Bill demanding that a production assistant staple tiny antlers onto mice to make them look like reindeer, or the opening sequence where Lee Majors fights alongside Santa Claus to defend the North Pole from a terrorist invasion (an example of the crass programming found on the IBC television network).

Tina Fey has a term for comedy that doesn't work because the people behind it are trying too hard: She calls it "sweaty." *Scrooged* is sweaty. Bill is charismatic enough to hold the center of the movie, and his final, improvised monologue comes off surprisingly well (even though screenwriter Michael O'Donoghue hated that Bill had abandoned the understated script), but for most of the movie, you can see him laboring. A large portion of Bill's appeal comes from the feeling that we're watching him play—if we know he's working, it's not much fun.

Ghostbusters II (1989, Dr. Peter Venkman)

"I have all-new cheap moves."

"I really didn't want to do this movie for the longest time," Bill Murray admitted.

His costar Harold Ramis said diplomatically, "There

are some comedies that satisfy the requirements of art and some that are gratuitous and pandering, and we like to think that we're somewhere in between."

Unfortunately, a paycheck-cashing vibe permeates this sour, unfunny sequel. For a movie that took five years to come to fruition, there's a sloppy quality to the story. For example, Dana (Sigourney Weaver's character), who was an accomplished concert cellist in the first movie, is now an equally accomplished fine-art restorer working on a Gauguin canvas, which makes no sense except as a narrative shortcut. That might be forgivable except that screenwriters Dan Aykroyd and Harold Ramis forgot to write jokes, leaving only the pleasure of familiar faces (hi, Annie Potts!), lightweight horror-movie scares, and reminders of funnier sequences in the original *Ghostbusters*. The climax where the Statue of Liberty comes to life and lumbers through the streets of New York reprises the humongous Stay Puft Marshmallow Man but without any payoff.

Bill hits his marks reliably enough and has a good rapport with his fellow players (including his brother Brian Doyle-Murray, playing a skeptical psychologist). And Bill nails the scene where we see what Peter Venkman has been doing since the Ghostbusters hit hard times: hosting *World of the Psychic,* a third-rate TV show where he cynically interviews rubes about their implausible paranormal experiences. But if he had any spontaneous outbursts of comedy during this shoot, they appear not to have made it onto the screen. One of the movie's few joyful moments is when Venkman dandles a baby, because for a few seconds the artifice drops away and we're watching Bill Murray trying to make a small child laugh.

Given how this movie turned out, it's no wonder Bill spent decades resisting entreaties to take part in another *Ghostbusters* sequel, agreeing to make a cameo in Paul Feig's distaff reboot only when it became clear that it was going to be good without him.

Quick Change (1990, Grimm)

> "He says to Miss Cochrane here, 'Baby, up your butt with a coconut.' I think he was prepared to do it! Except I saw no coconut."

Bill Murray, dressed as a clown, makes his way through an overcrowded subway system and walks down a New York City street, where a hawker for a peep show makes his pitch: "Nude women. Clowns welcome. Clowns welcome." Then, with his girlfriend (Geena Davis) and his doofus best friend (Randy Quaid), he robs a bank. That's the best part of *Quick Change,* but it's over after twenty-two minutes. The rest of the movie, more uneven, shows the trio's getaway journey to the airport. They're trying to get out of town before the police commissioner (Jason Robards) catches up with them, but they're slowed by every urban obstacle possible: construction workers who have removed traffic signs, a taxi driver who speaks no English (Tony Shalhoub, in one of his earliest movie roles), a mugger, a martinet bus driver, and, best of all, a jousting match where bicycles substitute for horses and mops for lances.

Quick Change is the only movie Bill has a directorial credit on: when Jonathan Demme decided not to take the helm, Bill co-directed with screenwriter Howard Franklin. "I don't think directing is particularly for me," he said after the movie wrapped. "Acting is so much more fun— it's so much less work." Nevertheless, with his hands on the steering wheel, Bill made a movie that catered to his attitudes and his self-image. His urban-planner character is burned out on New York City; at that point in his life, Bill had not only relocated from the city to upstate New York, he had spent long stretches of time living in France. His character disguises himself as a clown; Bill considered the term "clown" to be a badge of honor, not an insult, and liked to compare himself to the corpulent French clown Coluche, telling French people that he was a Coluche with cheekbones. ("They used to think that was pretty good, except they didn't quite get what the 'with cheekbones' thing meant," he confided.)

Crucially, Bill puts his alter ego in situations where only loudmouthed spur-of-the-moment invention can save the day: demanding a monster truck during a hostage situation, disarming an angry yuppie played by Phil Hartman by spinning a fantasy of a farm upstate, bluffing his way out of a Mafia warehouse by pretending he's the new bagman. *Quick Change* is both a showcase for Bill's talents and a way to frame his gifts as having applications in the real world.

His love interest and co-conspirator (played appealingly by Davis) is impressed by his improvisational skills but worries that they might form the totality of his personality—a concern that feels drawn from Bill's own life and relationships.

While working on *Quick Change,* Davis went through her usual thespian process, meeting with an acting coach, analyzing every line, and densely marking up her script with a thicket of annotations. This got the attention of Murray—especially the notes. "Bill would always be looking at my script—'What does that say? What does that say?'—and I didn't want him to see it!" she confessed. But he finally snuck a look at her script, and then the next day he ostentatiously waved around his own copy of the script, waiting for Davis to ask him what he had done. Finally she succumbed and said, "What you got there?" The answer: He had marked up a bunch of pages with parodies of her notes, resulting in marginalia such as "Mad?! I'm *furious!* What gives?" Davis said, "It was so funny, I practically couldn't work that day."

What About Bob? (1991, Bob Wiley)

> "Gimme, gimme, gimme! I need, I need, I need, I need!"

The tone of *What About Bob?* is uncertain. At the beginning, the movie feels like a character study, but somewhere along the line it turns into a live-action Road Runner cartoon, climaxing when one character tries to kill another with an excessive amount of explosives. The viewer has to make some large leaps to accept the movie's premise; the biggest of all is probably the idea that the uptight psychiatrist played by Richard Dreyfuss would let any patient, no matter how persistent, ingratiate himself into his family's personal life. Bill Murray plays that patient: the anxiety-ridden Bob, who shows up at his doctor's vacation home, teaches the family various life lessons, and ends up driving Dr. Leo Marvin utterly insane.

"Terribly unpleasant experience. We didn't get along, me and Bill Murray," Dreyfuss said years later.

"Anything that I could think of to annoy someone in a scene, particularly if it was Dreyfuss, I went with it," Bill said.

Their antipathy wasn't as big a problem as it might have been, considering the contempt that Dreyfuss's character feels for Bill's, but it does remove any sense of joy in scenes with the two of them. So they both overact in different fashions: Dreyfuss gets more tightly wound, while Bill plays a walking collection of tics and neuroses.

The needy, wheedling, obtuse Bob isn't a fun character to watch. In some ways, he's a cautionary tale for those seeking to emulate Bill's gate-crashing approach to life. If you do it right, you become a ringleader of good times; if you do it wrong, you're the biggest jerk at the party. "It's not so much what you do, but the way in which you do it. I can slap you on the back and it can be a wonderful thing, if it's done with joy," Bill has said. "But if I slap you on the back just as you're coming out of the elevator, and I've had too much to drink, it's a completely different thing."

Groundhog Day (1993, Phil Connors)

> "This is one time where television really fails to capture the true excitement of a large squirrel predicting the weather."

Standing alongside *Pulp Fiction* and *Memento* as hit movies that were formally radical, *Groundhog Day* not only brilliantly plays with structure, it's also incredibly funny in ways large and small—and it's the rare movie that makes the people who see it want to be better human beings.

Bill Murray plays Phil Connors, a Pittsburgh TV weatherman who sourly goes to Punxsutawney to cover the annual Groundhog Day festivities and finds himself trapped in the same day, living February 2 over and over again—for years, or maybe even millennia. Phil then recapitulates the stages of human development, or of grief as defined by Elisabeth Kübler-Ross—and isn't it fascinating that those two progressions dovetail so well? Childlike denial gives way to adolescent rebellion, where Phil indulges every whim, seemingly without consequence, and matures into depression, where he realizes that the sybaritic life is a trap and even death is no escape, before he comes to accept his fate and seeks only to improve the small, snowbound world around himself.

Huge credit goes to director (and co-writer) Harold Ramis, doing the best work of his career, and the original screenwriter Danny Rubin, who made his Buddhist philosophy work in a narrative format. But the movie doesn't work without an actor who can handle both the broad comedy of stuffing his face with angel-food cake—Bill worked without a spit bucket—and a romance with Andie MacDowell that grows from infatuation into something true. Bill grounds the movie, even when the days spin around him like a washing machine. Off camera, he was in the middle of a traumatic divorce, and his personal relationship with Ramis was shattered by this movie. But inside the skin of Phil Connors, he found his fundamental humanity.

"There is a nasty side of Bill that he wasn't afraid to reveal in this film," Ramis said. "And there's a tremendously generous and wise side that he comes to later, which is as genuine."

In a scene late in the movie, Phil encounters, for the umpteenth time, Ned Ryerson (Stephen Tobolowsky), an obnoxious high school classmate who has become an insurance salesman. But this time, instead of dodging him or punching him, he gives him a hug and says, "I have missed you so much." When the cameras rolled, Bill added the line "I don't know where you're headed, but can you call in sick?" and held the hug for longer than anyone expected, making a simple act of human contact into an effort to embrace the entire world.

Mad Dog and Glory (1993, Frank Milo)

> "Don't ever ever fuck with me. Don't ever lie to me, disrespect me, underestimate me. If you do, your life becomes a raging sea. But come to me like a man, come to me eyes open, head up, hand out, then I become more than a friend, more than a shoulder. I become the expediter of your dreams."

The role of Frank Milo, a small-time Chicago gangster with dreams of show-biz fame, was originally offered to Robert De Niro—who chose to play the other male lead in this film, a nebbish cop (Wayne, ironically nicknamed "Mad Dog") who hasn't fired his gun in fifteen years but manages to save the life of Frank during a convenience-store robbery. Uma Thurman played the third lead: Glory, a woman indebted to Frank, who sends her to his new friend Mad Dog for one week of "personal services." When Wayne falls in love with Glory, Frank doesn't want to let her go.

The movie, more drama than romance, was produced by Martin Scorsese and directed by John McNaughton (*Henry: Portrait of a Serial Killer*)—but its voice belongs to screenwriter and crime novelist Richard Price (*Clockers*), who savors the language and the battles for pecking order among both the police and the criminals. Aside from Cypress Hill on the soundtrack in the opening sequence, it feels as if it could have been made anytime in the preceding fifty years.

Playing "Frank the Money Store," Bill Murray excels, filling the role with steely menace. It wasn't generally hailed in 1993 as his best dramatic performance to date, but it should have been. (Frank has a therapist coaching him on his anger issues—beating *The Sopranos* by six years.) Even when Frank gets onstage to do a stand-up set at the comedy club he owns, Bill doesn't revert to his own schtick: He lets us see Frank's insecurities and tough-guy charisma. His performance shows us that it's possible to be funny *and* cruel: It's a blurry picture of who Bill might be if he lacked his sense of perpetual joy.

Ed Wood (1994, Bunny Breckinridge)

> "What about glitter? When I was a headliner in Paris, audiences always liked it when I sparkled."

Ed Wood, the sixth (and possibly best) feature film directed by Tim Burton, is like many of Burton's other movies an affectionate portrait of a misfit played by Johnny Depp. In this case, Depp played Wood, generally considered one of the worst movie directors ever. The movie has the triumphant tone of a rise-to-glory biopic but applies it to a low-budget director with amateurish working methods and a penchant for transvestism.

The movie surrounds Depp with a gang of social outcasts, including a pro wrestler, a psychic, the aging star Bela Lugosi (a role that earned Martin Landau an Oscar), and Bill Murray's part: Bunny Breckinridge, the gay scion of an upper-crust California family. Bill commands the screen in a small role, and not just because he's so powdered that he glows in the black-and-white footage. He gives an indelible, inscrutable performance as Bunny, who yearns for a sex-change operation and always seems to be gliding through the demimonde. Bill said that he agreed to make the movie before he had read the script, just because Burton was directing it. "And then I saw the script and went, Oh, damn. This part is written nelly. . . . The last thing I want is to be obvious, direct, and offensive."

Bill, however, brings nuance and commitment to every moment as Bunny. His best scene comes when Wood convinces all his friends to get baptized so that a Baptist congregation will finance the movie *Plan 9 from Outer Space*. When Bunny dips a toe into the swimming pool that's serving as a baptismal font, that toe is covered by a suede shoe, and when he's asked if he rejects Satan and all his works, his reply is "Sure."

Burton said, "I don't always assume I know best, particularly when I'm working with a talent like Bill Murray, who was just great in *Ed Wood*. I love people I don't understand, and there's something deeply puzzling about Bill.

Prior to shooting, he prepared for his character by having all the hair on his body waxed, and believe me, it looked extremely painful. I love him and that performance so much that I still daydream about doing a music video of the scene of Bill with the mariachis."

Kingpin (1996, Ernie McCracken)

"You're on a gravy train with biscuit wheels."

This bowling comedy, directed by the brothers Bobby and Peter Farrelly, has their trademark approach: a well-constructed script with a sentimental heart, covered with dollops of bodily fluids. The movie tells the slapstick redemption story of Roy Munson (Woody Harrelson), a once-promising professional bowler who ended up with a hook for a hand and became a drunken wastrel—until he met an Amish bowling prodigy (Randy Quaid).

Bookending the movie is Bill Murray, playing the villainous bowling champion "Big Ern" McCracken, who engineers Munson's downfall in 1979 and then plays against him at the Silver Legacy Reno Open in the movie's climax. The Farrelly brothers asked Bill if he wanted to take bowling lessons before they started filming; he demurred, saying, "Ah, give me the ball and let's see," not letting on that he was a sufficiently accomplished bowler that he could fall out of bed and score 160 or 170.

The payoff for his sandbagging came when the movie had one day at the National Bowling Center in Reno, Nevada, to shoot the climactic face-off between McCracken and Munson. The National Bowling Center, "the Taj Mahal of tenpins," has a thousand-seat theater that was packed with extras that day. Peter Farrelly explained to the crowd that for the movie's plot, McCracken was going to bowl three strikes in a row, but that Bill, not being a professional bowler, would likely need multiple takes so they could get three strikes that would later be edited together: "I told them I'd announce what strike we're shooting and they'd build the applause for each one."

Murray walked up to the line and, with his first ball, bowled a perfect strike. "We don't cut," Peter remembered. "The ball comes back and he rolls again. Strike. The place is going crazy. Then the third one is a strike—and not only that, but the last pin wobbles a little before it goes down. You've never heard a more realistic crowd scene in a movie. We had to hold people back from storming the court."

"Big Ern" is a marvelous comic invention: an unctuous, arrogant star, every inch the scoundrel, whose bowling ball has a rose embedded in Lucite. In the championship match, he plays to the crowd, strutting, winking, cupping his ear, thrusting his pelvis. When a diner waitress brings him the "Tanqueray and Tab" that he ordered, he tells her, "Keep 'em coming, sweets—I've got a long drive." When he's mobbed by reporters after winning a million-dollar purse, he shouts out, "I finally got enough money that I can buy my way out of anything!" followed by "Finally, Big Ern is above the law!"

Bill improvised those lines—as he did most of his dialogue. The Farrellys spoke of his performance in awe: how every day Bill came to the set, would find out the point of the scene, throw out the pages, and proceed to invent something much funnier than what was in the screenplay. He even conceived two distinctive hairstyles: a perm for the 1970s and an awe-inspiring, gravity-defying comb-over for the 1990s. The Farrellys' conclusion: "When Bill runs with it, you gotta run with him."

Larger Than Life (1996, Jack Corcoran)

> "There's two types of animals in this world—ones you can hitch with and ones you can't hitch with."

Larger Than Life is remembered as an elephant-size bomb: the movie where Bill Murray sold out his dignity with depressing, unprofitable results. He plays a motivational speaker scrabbling for bigger gigs, who inherits an elephant and then has to take it across the country to get rid of it. By the end, the film is reaching for unearned sentiment, with Bill intoning, "You know, they say an elephant never forgets. But what they don't tell you is that you never forget an elephant."

Throughout its ninety-three minutes, the movie keeps squandering its comic opportunities: Scenes where Murray is trying to climb onto the elephant or coax it into moving, which seem like they could be tour de forces of physical comedy, consistently end prematurely. Janeane Garofalo, who plays a brusque zookeeper, is given literally no funny lines. Matthew McConaughey, appearing as a manic, paranoid trucker, gives the movie a jolt of energy, but his performance feels desperate and off-putting. With a firmer hand on the steering wheel, the movie might have worked as a solid commercial comedy, but the director was Howard Franklin (Bill's co-director on *Quick Change*), who seems to have been overwhelmed by the whole enterprise.

For all its problems, the movie is gently entertaining, and that's because of Bill. He kicks off the movie with a strong scene where he delivers a motivational speech to a crowd at the American Motion Upholstery Conference, psyching himself up behind a curtain and then getting members of the audience to form a human pyramid. And although his scenes with the elephant are woefully underwritten, they are satisfying on a fundamental level—it's always fun to watch Bill interact with a costar he can't predict. *Larger Than Life* is probably less enjoyable than an hour of outtakes of Bill and the pachyderm would be, but he makes it watchable.

Bill did what he could to enliven the production: When they were shooting in L.A. and Bill saw a great country band one night, he hired them to come play for the cast and crew during the next day's lunch break. He wanted to make sure that making the movie didn't feel like a clock-punching routine: "Otherwise, you might as well be washing cars in Manitoba."

However, when the production stopped in a remote western locale to film a scene by the Colorado River, there wasn't much available in the way of distractions. "It was kind of an impoverished situation—no restaurants or places to hang out," Bill said. "But it was this crazy place that was so incredibly beautiful." So Bill chartered a river-rafting company to take groups of the filmmakers down the Colorado all day long.

"But no one wanted to go first, because it was one of those productions where everyone was determined to be much more professional than the guy next to him—because no one wanted to be less professional than the elephant," Bill said. So Bill forced the head of every department, including director Howard Franklin and cinematographer Elliot Davis, to go on the first ride with him. After twenty-five minutes on the river, invigorated and soaking wet, they all rushed back to work. "By having the key person in every department go first, that made it cool for everyone else to relax and take their turn," Bill explained. "To me, it was like this: I shot a movie on the Colorado River, and if I didn't experience it, just walk to work every day, it's like it never happened. You might as well fly over it."

Space Jam (1996, Himself)

> "Larry, I'm going to give us both twos back there. We weren't in any kind of emotional state to putt."

Space Jam isn't, by any conventional standard, a good movie. It's a weird corporate mishmash of the NBA, the Looney Tunes characters, and Michael Jordan, Inc. And yet, powered by Jordan's charisma, it somehow works—it became the most popular basketball movie of all time and, two decades later, still entertains small children. (Win trivia contests by naming the five basketball players who had their talent stolen by extraterrestrials: Charles Barkley, Patrick Ewing, Larry Johnson, Shawn Bradley, and Muggsy Bogues.) Wandering into this movie as if he's stopping by on his way to the concession stands for a beer: Mr. Bill Murray. He plays golf with Jordan and Larry Bird, pestering them about whether he has the skills to compete in the NBA, and then teams up with Jordan and Bugs Bunny for the basketball game against the extraterrestrial Monstars.

The movie was directed by Joe Pytka, but producer Ivan Reitman says he took over as an uncredited director for Bill's scenes. "It was a delightful five days of work with him," Reitman reports. Bill seems loose in his extended cameo, equally happy to be sharing the screen with Larry Bird and Tweety Bird, and he plays himself as a slightly deluded sports fan who enjoys every moment of his life—not so far from the truth.

The Man Who Knew Too Little
(1997, Wallace Ritchie)

> "Why do you always have to go out the window? It's more
> dramatic, I guess. But it's kind of a *Starsky & Hutch* thing,
> isn't it?"

A commercial failure, largely ignored then and now, this farce is a small gem. The premise: Wallace Ritchie, played by Bill Murray, is a nebbish clerk at a Blockbuster video store in Des Moines, Iowa. For his birthday, he flies to London and pays a surprise visit to his yuppie banker brother, James (Peter Gallagher). While fond of his hapless brother, James is hosting an important dinner party that evening, so he sends Wallace off to the "Theatre of Life," an interactive play where audience members are forced to improvise with actors playing criminals and policemen. Through a series of escalating misunderstandings, Wallace is mistaken for a ruthless hitman and pulled into a scheme to sabotage an Anglo-Russian friendship pact. Even when he's being chased by the police or being shot at by criminals, Wallace believes that they all are paid thespians giving him a first-class theatrical adventure.

A movie like this is a delicate soufflé—one misstep and the whole enterprise collapses. But director Jon Amiel (*The Singing Detective*) gets the tone just right, as does Bill, who is completely believable as a sweet but confused Midwesterner. When Wallace tries "acting," he is awkward and overwhelmed but just believable enough that the people around him assume he is sincere. And when he gets to smash through a door, or fake his way through an epic sequence of Russian dancing, or kiss a character played by the beautiful Joanne Whalley, his innocent pleasure at these new adventures is infectious. Bill largely had to adhere to the script, given how precisely engineered its misunderstandings are, but there are a few scenes where he got to improvise, including his interview with an immigration officer at Heathrow, where he names all the things he wants to do in England. Amiel said he had to edit down an endless, hilarious list to a few highlights: "I want to see the Queen ride on a horse," "I want to get a suit made," "I want to try that pudding that's made of meat."

The result feels like a lost Cary Grant movie, maybe a follow-up to the screwball thriller *Charade* (directed by Stanley Donen in 1963). Actor Hugh Laurie once quoted critic Pauline Kael as saying that Cary Grant was the greatest of all film stars. "The reason she gave was that he always looked aware of the fact that he was in a film. He was amused by his predicament: not the predicament of his character but the predicament of Cary Grant in a film. And I could never decide whether that was a great thing, or whether actually James Stewart was the greater film star because he never gave that away." (This is sufficiently far away from what Kael wrote about Grant that we have to conclude that it's actually Laurie's theory, not hers.) Judged by this yardstick, Bill Murray is the modern actor most like Grant: He is often inside and outside his role at the same time. But Bill doesn't use the premise of *The Man*

Who Knew Too Little to deliver a winking *Austin Powers*–style send-up of cinematic secret agents. He throws himself into the video-clerk role and lets the plot deliver the goods like a well-engineered piece of clockwork.

Wild Things (1998, Kenneth Bowden)

> "We have got a knockdown airtight motherfucker lawsuit against Sandra Van Ryan."

Wild Things was a big-screen version of a late-night Cinemax soft-core movie or an episode of the *Red Shoe Diaries* (even hiring that show's composer, George S. Clinton—not to be confused with the Parliament/Funkadelic leader). Unfortunately, even with a multitude of plot twists, it's only intermittently thrilling, and, despite nudity from both Denise Richards and Kevin Bacon, it's not especially sexy.

In a supporting role, Bill Murray plays the low-rent lawyer hired by a high school guidance counselor (Matt Dillon) when one of his students (Richards) accuses him of rape. He isn't given much to do, but he makes the most of his meager material. He initially sports a neck brace—"I don't have to wear it all the time. There was an insurance guy around earlier," he explains—but when he has a legal triumph and it becomes clear that he is about to become a very rich man, he removes the brace in the courtroom with a flourish.

Bill doesn't embarrass himself here, but he also doesn't look like anything other than an actor cashing a check. The filmmakers said that they cut together his performance three times: first in a serious mode, then in an antic mode, and then somewhere in between. That they could do that indicates both that Bill was professionally giving them options and that the movie wasn't very certain of its own tone. But the DVD contains a compilation of Bill's various responses to Matt Dillon when he delivers the line "I don't fuck my students!" They show off his willingness to switch from sarcastic to sincere to smarmy at a moment's notice, proving that improvisational skills can improve even an overripe erotic thriller. Six different takes:

"Hip hip hooray, Sam."

"Whoop-de-doo."

"Forgive me."

"That's wonderful [sniffs]. That's great."

"Oh, you are so tender. So precious."

"And I don't jerk off [winks]."

With Friends Like These . . .
(1998, Maurice Melnick)

> "This is an elephant's graveyard of faces you cannot name."

This tepid Hollywood satire was centered on character actors, all allegedly friends, trying to outmaneuver each other for the plum role of Al Capone in a Martin Scorsese movie. Also known as *Mom's on the Roof,* it went straight to video in 1998 (probably because it felt like a watered-down version of *The Player* or *Swimming with Sharks*); unusually, it got a brief theatrical release years later, in 2005 (maybe because of the rising fortunes of stars Adam Arkin and David Strathairn).

Cameos (mandatory for the genre) include Scorsese as himself, Garry Marshall as a Toyota salesman, and Bill Murray as a Hollywood power player. With a cream suit, a light-pink shirt, and a supercilious air, Bill shows up at a party thrown by one of the actors. He loads up a plate at the buffet, makes no attempt to conceal his boredom, and leaves with a bag full of expensive cheese. Thirteen minutes into the movie, he drives off in his black BMW, never to be seen again. Dripping insincerity, he's the behind-the-scenes counterpart to Bill characters such as Nick the Lounge Singer. It's the sort of role Bill can do in his sleep, and here he almost does.

Rushmore (1998, Mr. Blume)

> "Yeah, I was in the shit."

At age forty-eight, Bill Murray kicked off the second half of his film career. *Rushmore* showcased how his comic timing could blend perfectly with a heartfelt dramatic performance; how the flip side of his youthful irony was jaded middle age; how a know-it-all could mature into somebody

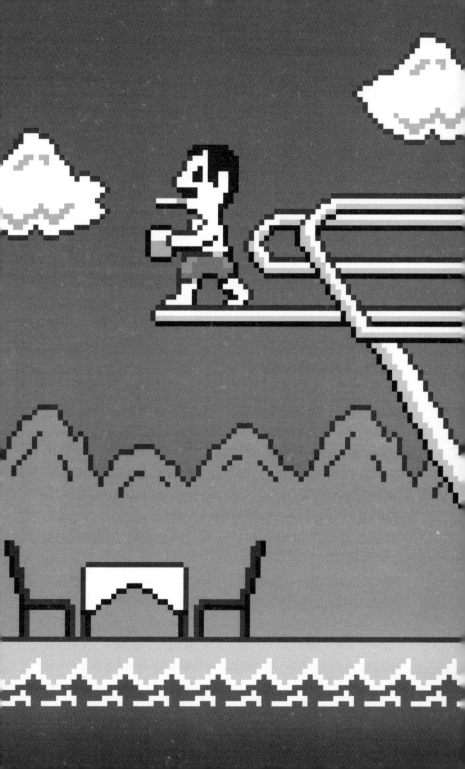

who was sure of very little. It also marked the beginning of Bill's most extensive collaboration with any filmmaker— he's been in every movie director Wes Anderson has made from *Rushmore* onward (seven and counting).

Anderson was a Bill Murray fan from childhood: one Halloween, he dressed up as Peter Venkman, Bill's *Ghostbusters* character. He had wanted Bill to be in his first feature film (*Bottle Rocket*), in the part ultimately played by James Caan, but hadn't been able to track Bill down. Hoping to cast Bill in a major role in *Rushmore,* he enlisted Bill's agent, who sent him multiple copies of *Bottle Rocket* on videocassette. In addition, Anderson personally mailed Bill four VHS tapes of the movie. "I've got them all over my house like people have catalogs from Pottery Barn," Bill said.

When Bill read the script for *Rushmore,* he quickly agreed to take the part. To everyone's surprise, he said he didn't need to meet with Anderson in person before they made the movie. He didn't even need to watch any of his vast collection of *Bottle Rocket* videotapes. Bill explained, "I figured the writing was so specific that whoever wrote it knew exactly what they were going to shoot. I never have a problem with guys who make a movie that misses as long as they make the movie they want to make."

He did call Anderson for an hour-long phone conversation. They spent most of that time talking about Akira Kurosawa's 1965 movie *Red Beard:* the director's last collaboration with actor Toshirô Mifune, about a doctor in nineteenth-century Japan. Anderson had never seen the movie, so the conversation was actually Bill walking him through the story and its nuances. Anderson was bewildered by the conversational topic—and watching the movie later didn't prove any more enlightening for him— but the call went well enough that Bill signed up for the movie, working for scale.

In the movie that Anderson and Owen Wilson co-wrote—with Bill in mind, although casting him had seemed like a dream—Bill plays Herman Blume, an industrial tycoon worth over $10 million, who has gotten rich manufacturing steel pipes, is stuck in an unhappy marriage, and has two teenage sons who are lunkhead jocks for whom he feels no affinity whatsoever. He visits their expensive private school, Rushmore Academy, and gives a speech at chapel encouraging the poor students at the school to take down the rich ones. That begins Blume's relationship with the movie's lead, Max Fischer (Jason Schwartzman), a high-school student with more enthusiasm than aptitude, who is flunking all his classes but engaging in an extraordinary number of extracurriculars (president of the calligraphy club, captain of the fencing team, founder of the bombardment society). They become unlikely friends and then unlikely rivals when both fall in love with the same first-grade teacher (Olivia Williams) and start a campaign of dirty tricks against each other (Max puts bees in Blume's hotel room; Blume drives over Max's bicycle; et cetera). "You know, you and Herman deserve each other," that teacher ultimately tells Max. And they do, for good and ill—something they both figure out by the movie's end.

In Bill's best scene, he has no dialogue. He watches his sons' backyard birthday party with antipathy, idly throwing golf balls into his swimming pool. Then he climbs onto the diving board, a cigarette in his mouth, a glass of Scotch in his hand, and a pair of Budweiser swimming trunks on his ass. He does a cannonball into the pool, splashing the party guests, and stays underwater for as long as possible—in a shot on interlibrary loan from *The Graduate*—because it's the only place where he can find some peace.

"*Rushmore* is the first movie I've done in a while that's completely whole," Bill said. "It was great to be able to serve the story without waving a flag over my head, which you often have to do when you're the lead and have to carry the film. So I enjoyed playing Blume, because I really believe an actor's job is to serve."

Cradle Will Rock (1999, Tommy Crickshaw)

> "Vaudeville will be around long after you and your communists are."

Bill Murray once told David Letterman that he would win an Oscar the same year he won the Heisman Trophy. A few days later, Tim Robbins sent him the script for *Cradle Will*

Rock with a handwritten note: "Bill, this is your Heisman." So Bill signed up for Robbins's third movie as a director: a sprawling, passionate film about art, commerce, and politics in 1930s New York City, with war and Fascism brewing in Europe and Orson Welles trying to mount a musical under the auspices of the Federal Theater Project. While Robbins's ambitions may have slightly exceeded his reach, he kept a complicated narrative hurtling forward and was bolstered by an insanely star-studded ensemble, with actors including Vanessa Redgrave, John Cusack, Susan Sarandon, Hank Azaria, Paul Giamatti, John Turturro, and Emily Watson. The movie was a flop, and it ended Robbins's career as a director, but for all its flaws and didacticism, it was often magnificent.

"I live to go down with those guys who have no fuckin' chance," Bill said. When he first read the screenplay, he told Robbins, "It doesn't have a *chance. It doesn't have a chance in hell, Tim!* But you know what? I gotta like you for trying."

Bill played most of his scenes with Joan Cusack, Jack Black, and Kyle Gass (Black's partner in the band Tenacious D)—and a dummy named Red. His character, Tommy Crickshaw, is an old-time ventriloquist, sour and scared by the world changing around him. He resents having to teach his secrets to eager young pupils; he awkwardly courts a younger woman by denouncing Communists with her and finally acknowledges his radical past in a riveting scene where he self-destructs onstage and his dummy sings

"The Internationale." The *Cradle Will Rock* team didn't end the season in a bowl game, but Bill's melancholy, nuanced performance deserved a Heisman.

For one scene, the production needed Bill on a particular day that was the only time they could shoot in an old Jersey vaudeville house. Robbins thought (incorrectly, Bill said) that he was unavailable because it was game one of the Chicago Bulls playing the Utah Jazz in the 1998 NBA Finals (which turned out to be Michael Jordan's final championship run). So Robbins offered to bring a TV set into the theater—a decision he would regret. "Any mother with dinner on the table knows how long the last five minutes of an NBA game can last," Bill said.

Then the game went to overtime—and Bill kept drifting away from the movie set to the TV set. Robbins, who was having difficulty filming a complicated shot in a mirrored dressing room, clenched his jaw tighter and tighter. Finally, with two minutes left in OT, a stressed Robbins marched over to the television like an angry father and snapped it off. Bill told him, "Oh, Tim, you were doing so well."

After the shoot ended, Bill felt he should make a peace offering, so he took Robbins out for golf and cigars. "The guy has a frightening golf swing, but ice hockey taught him the concept of shots on goal," Bill reported.

Charlie's Angels (2000, John Bosley)

"A buddy of mine took a fighting muffin in the chest. They sent him home in four Ziploc bags."

The *Charlie's Angels* movie was big-budget, semi-coherent froth: Drew Barrymore, Cameron Diaz, and Lucy Liu dressed up in costumes that were both sexy and absurd, did wire-assisted martial arts (at a point when that was new to American audiences), and generally looked like they were having a blast. John Forsythe reprised his role from the 1970s TV show as the voice of their boss, Charlie, while Bill Murray played John Bosley, the older male sidekick to the Angels (the part originated by the late David Doyle).

A lot of Bill's job was playing dress-up alongside the Angels: in a pit-crew jumpsuit as a grease monkey at a race-track, with a walrus mustache and a tuba when the women deliver a yodeling telegram in lederhosen, with a toupee and a smoking jacket when he infiltrates a party as a self-help guru. Best of all might have been Bill in a sumo-wrestler body suit, banging against Tim Curry in another suit: Those suits were provided by Bill himself, who borrowed them from one of his minor-league baseball teams. They provide entertainment for fans of the St. Paul Saints between innings when fans (or even ejected managers) dress up and fight each other.

With an air of not taking any of the proceedings seriously, Bill fit right in with the tone of the movie (maybe too well, since that attitude is funnier when you have something to react against). Kelly Lynch, who played a romantic scene opposite Bill (both of them committed to the picture when Mitch Glazer, her husband and Bill's pal, came on as an uncredited screenwriter), said that many takes were lost because the crew was laughing too hard at something unexpected: for example, Bill setting his head on fire and sticking his head in an ice bucket. The best sustained bit of improvisation from Bill came when he was taken prisoner and locked in a cell. Director McG kept multiple cameras rolling as Bill threw his body against the door, had a conversation with a bird, and described his cell as looking like Cher's bedroom.

Famously, Bill had a blowout argument on the set with Lucy Liu (while filming the scene where he first appears in the movie, briefing the Angels on their new case). Depending on who tells the story, either they had a heated disagreement about the quality of the screenplay or Bill said that Liu couldn't act and she then took a swing at him. "Look, I will dismiss you completely if you are unprofessional and working with me," Bill said later. "When our relationship is professional and you're not getting that done, forget it."

McG acknowledged that he had his own conflicts with Bill. A decade after *Charlie's Angels* wrapped, he said, "I don't think there's been a film I've made where there hasn't been some sort of physical fight. I mean, I've been headbutted by an A-list star. Square in the head. An inch later and my nose would have been obliterated." Asked who the star was, the director said, "I probably shouldn't. But it was Bill Murray."

Bill vehemently denied that the incident happened: "That's bullshit! That's complete crap! I don't know why he made that story up," Bill said. "He deserves to die," Bill said of McG. "He should be pierced with a lance, not head-butted."

Whatever the reason, Bill declined to sign on for the *Charlie's Angels* sequel and was replaced by Bernie Mac.

Hamlet (2000, Polonius)

> "Since brevity is the soul of wit and tediousness the limbs and outward flourishes, I will be brief. Your noble son is mad."

Director Michael Almereyda set this version of *Hamlet* in the modern day (well, the year 2000—these days, functional pay phones and Blockbuster video stores both seem like period touches), with the Denmark Corporation and the Hotel Elsinore. Ethan Hawke does a good job in the title role, sulking around in a knit ski cap and editing his student films; Hamlet's character makes a lot of sense if you think of him as an overwrought undergraduate. The all-American cast is uneven, but standouts include Julia Stiles (Ophelia), Liev Schreiber (Laertes), and Sam Shepard (the ghost of Hamlet's father). And, somewhat surprisingly, Bill Murray.

"The guy's a great actor," Hawke said. "He should do Beckett, he should do Shakespeare. He should do whatever he pleases."

Bill often improvises his dialogue—in this movie, he was locked into what Shakespeare had written four hundred years earlier, but he nimbly played the role of Polonius, embodying a fatuous corporate vice president who loves to hear the sound of his own voice. In Bill's performance, Shakespeare's iambic pentameter became a conversational flow, and he gave the measure of the man inside the expensive suit. He hasn't done Shakespeare since, but it's not too late: maybe Prospero?

Osmosis Jones (2001, Frank Detorre)

"Is beer a fluid?"

An utterly mediocre kids' movie, featuring both animation and live-action segments. The Farrelly brothers are credited as directors of the whole shebang, although they did just the live-action parts, which star Bill Murray as Frank, a slovenly zookeeper with extremely poor dietary habits. The majority of the movie's running time is filled with the animated adventures of what's going on inside Frank's body—directed by Tom Sito and Piet Kroon—where a white-blood-cell policeman (Chris Rock) and an over-the-counter cold remedy (David Hyde Pierce) are fighting a deadly virus.

The Farrelly brothers deliver a PG version of their humor: farts, boogers, exploding zits. Bill gamely delivers the least-glamorous version possible of himself: pasty complexion, unshaven face, gut bulging like a Macy's Thanksgiving Day Parade balloon. Grimacing and mugging more than acting, he rehashes his performance style from two decades earlier in movies such as *Stripes* and *Meatballs*. The difference is that in those movies his apathetic attitude was a direct rebuke to the people with power over him, whether that was a summer-camp administrator or the chain of command of the entire United States Army. It's not as much fun when the voice of authority he's rebelling against is his ten-year-old daughter, who'd like him to eat healthier food.

The Royal Tenenbaums (2001, Raleigh St. Clair)

"You've made a cuckold of me."

Wes Anderson's third movie, hilarious and sad, is filled with longing for what's been lost: love, family, the New York City of an earlier era. It's centered on the Tenenbaums, an eccentric family of child geniuses who grew up into deeply unhappy adults; Bill Murray plays Raleigh St. Clair, the long-suffering husband of Margot Tenenbaum (Gwyneth Paltrow). His character, based on Oliver Sacks, is a writer and a neurologist (the author, we learn, of *The Peculiar Neurodegenerative Inhabitants of the Kazawa Atoll*). Like most of the characters in the movie, he always wears the same clothes: in his case, a brown corduroy jacket. In a movie with a huge, impressive cast (Anjelica Huston, Ben Stiller, Danny Glover, Luke Wilson, Owen Wilson), Bill's role feels almost vestigial: He's playing maybe the tenth-most-prominent character in the film. But he settles into a melancholy groove, giving Raleigh St. Clair a wounded dignity. When he's conducting cognitive experiments on his patient Dudley (Stephen Lea Sheppard), it feels like a sad gloss on Venkman, his character in *Ghostbusters:* What would he be like if all his smart-ass defenses were stripped away?

Just by showing up, Bill demonstrated his commitment to being part of the Wes Anderson repertory company. The movie's lead, playing the family patriarch, was Gene Hackman, who was brilliant and curmudgeonly. Wes Anderson was sufficiently abused by Hackman that he asked Bill to visit the set on his days off to run interference, because Bill was the only member of the cast or crew who wasn't intimidated by Hackman.

"I'll stick up for Gene," Bill said ten years later. "The word 'cocksucker' gets thrown around a lot. . . . I'd hear these stories, like, 'Gene threatened to kill me today.' *Kill* you? You're in the union, he can't *kill* you. 'Gene threatened to take all of us and set fire to us.' It's a union shoot, it's New York, there are Teamsters, he can't set fire to you."

Speaking of Sex (2001, Ezri Stovall)

"This is serious goddamn business. Salacious, yes. Scandalous, of course. Titillating, possibly."

Working with director John McNaughton in the nineties, Bill Murray made one good movie (*Mad Dog and Glory*) and one bad one (*Wild Things*). Apparently McNaughton laid out a great craft-services table, because he got Bill to sign up for another project, with the weakest script of the three. *Speaking of Sex* is a broad sex farce, in which James Spader plays a psychiatrist accused of unethical behavior with a patient (Melora Walters). (We know he had sex with her in an elevator—the question is whether she was actually a patient of his.) Bill plays the lawyer defending the psychiatrist—making it two movies in a row where McNaughton cast him as a scheming lawyer with a sex-crimes case. This time, Bill's attorney opens the movie with more trappings of mid-level success—unrumpled suits, cigars, and a toupee—and has the arrogant attitude to go along with it.

The action is busy, with car chases, sex scenes, and shoot-outs, and the general tone is light and engaging—unfortunately, punch lines are in short supply. Bill is just one member of an all-star group of comedians working hard without much of a payoff: also giving their best efforts are Jay Mohr, Lara Flynn Boyle, Nick Offerman, Megan Mullally, and especially Catherine O'Hara, who plays opposing counsel to Bill. The chemistry between O'Hara and Bill is the best thing about the movie. (O'Hara, like Bill, was in the Second City comedy troupe in the early seventies—but she was in the Toronto company, while he was in the Chicago group.) They end up together in an enormous bubble bath—and they leave viewers wishing that they would work together again, in a better movie.

Lost in Translation (2003, Bob Harris)

> "Taking a break from my wife, forgetting my son's birthday, and getting paid two million dollars to endorse a whisky when I could be doing a play somewhere. But the good news is, the whisky works."

Lost in Translation is a beautiful fever dream of a movie, with the woozy quality of both jet lag and the first flush of love. Bill Murray has described *Lost in Translation* as "my favorite movie that I've made." Admittedly, director Sofia Coppola was standing next to him at the time, but he's never been shy about razzing and abusing his directors, especially when they are in close proximity.

Bill plays Bob Harris: an aging action star, a Harrison Ford type, who has come to Japan to film a commercial for Suntory whisky. Scarlett Johansson, just seventeen at the time the movie was made, plays Charlotte, a young college graduate who is in Tokyo with her husband (Giovanni Ribisi), a celebrity photographer. Bob and Charlotte are both staying in the same luxury hotel, the Park Hyatt Tokyo. They notice each other in the elevator and then in the bar. A flirtation becomes a friendship, which becomes a deep connection full of unconsummated desire, like a relationship in an Edith Wharton novel.

The characters have both been smothered by unhappy marriages and confusion over where life has landed them. Together, they explore Tokyo and the longing in their hearts. Bill has often gotten the girl in movies, but *Lost in Translation* was the first time he made an out-and-out romance (give or take *Groundhog Day*). He explained why he had avoided the genre: "The romantic figure has to behave romantically even after acting like a total swine. It's, 'I'm so gorgeous, you're going to have to go through all kinds of hell for me,' and that isn't interesting to me. Romance, like comedy, is very particular."

There are a few sight gags in the movie (Bill in mortal combat with an exercise machine, Bill towering over Japanese people in an elevator) and a few funny scenes that got cut (an extended sequence of Bill doing water aerobics). But Bill seemed only incidentally concerned with dialing up the comedy in this movie: He was content to look within himself and give the most heartfelt performance of his career.

In 2003, the year *Lost in Translation* came out, I asked Sofia Coppola what her wish for the following year was. She looked startled. "My wish came true," she told me. "Bill Murray did my movie."

Coffee and Cigarettes (2003, Bill Murray)

> "Yeah, I'm Bill Murray, but let's keep that just between us,
> all right?"

Coffee and Cigarettes is a black-and-white anthology film made by Jim Jarmusch over a couple of decades: actors and musicians, many playing versions of themselves, sitting around and talking. In one segment, Tom Waits and Iggy Pop verbally joust; in another, Jack White shows off a Tesla coil to Meg White; in another, Cate Blanchett plays both halves of the scene, starring as a glamorous movie star and as a sullen, jealous cousin visiting her in a hotel lobby.

Bill Murray appears in a segment starring GZA and RZA of the Wu-Tang Clan; late at night, they sit in a café, drinking herbal tea and discussing alternative medicine. Then Bill appears as their waiter, wearing an apron and a paper hat, and is recognized by the rappers as "Bill Groundhog Day Ghostbustin'-ass Murray." Bill sits down with them, drinks coffee straight from the glass coffeepot, and gets advice from RZA on how to treat his smoker's cough (gargle with diluted hydrogen peroxide or with oven cleaner). He never explains why he's working as a waiter, and the hip-hoppers consistently refer to him by his full name (e.g., "So, Bill Murray, you hiding out or something?" or "Don't swallow, Bill Murray."). At the end, Bill goes off to gargle in the kitchen and RZA and GZA leave (after a brief conversation about whether you need to tip your waiter when he's Bill Murray).

The scene is charming and surprising, and the Wu-Tang members have a good rapport with Bill. In many ways, this vignette feels like the urtext of Bill Murray anecdotes: Bill shows up somewhere unexpected, acknowledges that he is who you think he is, and throws himself into the moment, before leaving abruptly and without explanation. In 2003, most people didn't know that this was something he did—but it still felt right and true.

Garfield: The Movie (2004, Garfield)

> "Hey, what do you say we play brain surgeon? Would you
>   go get my power tools?"

Garfield is a minor entertainment, made without much ambition other than keeping young children distracted for an hour and a half. If you don't mind it not being very funny, it's pleasant enough to watch because of a likable cast: Breckin Meyer, Jennifer Love Hewitt, and Stephen Tobolowsky are all live-action actors. Bill Murray provides the voice of the CGI-rendered Garfield, America's favorite gluttonous, slothful cat.

Bill's presence mystified many people—he appeared to have finally taken a job just for the paycheck. Years after the movie's release, he denied it: "I didn't make it for the dough!

Well, not completely." As he told the story, he thought it might be challenging to do a cartoon voice-over—plus he had glanced at the cover page of the script, by Joel Cohen and Alec Sokolow, and thought that Joel Cohen was actually Joel Coen, one half of the brilliant Coen brothers, responsible for films such as *Fargo* and *The Big Lebowski*. So once his payment had been raised from fifty thousand dollars ("I don't even leave the fuckin' driveway for that kind of money") to a much higher number ("That's more befitting of the work I expect to do!"), Bill signed on.

As usual, Bill showed up to work—in this case, a Los Angeles recording studio—without having actually read the script. The plan was that he would watch each scene—with live actors and a gray blob of rudimentary animation where Garfield was going to be—and then record his dialogue. But presented with page after page of a mediocre screenplay, Bill would respond, "That's the line? Well, I can't say that." He kept trying to improve the dialogue on the fly, and the exercise kept getting more complicated as he got penned in by his various decisions. On the second day of recording, with only twenty minutes or so of the movie completed, Bill was "soaked in perspiration. I had drunk as much coffee as any Colombian ever drank, and I said, 'You better just show me the rest of the movie.'"

He watched it, bewildered that Coen was making such terrible choices. When it was done, he sat for two minutes in stunned silence. Then he announced, "I can fix this, but I can't fix this today. Or this week. Who wrote this stuff?" The answer, of course, was Joel Cohen, one of the screenwriters on *Toy Story* and *Cheaper by the Dozen*—not Oscar winner Joel Coen.

With some cursing, Bill ended up doing multiple sessions in California and Italy to finish the film. "It was sort of like *Fantastic Mr. Fox* without the joy or the fun," he said. So it was an object lesson, if Bill wanted to learn it—you can spend life flying by the seat of your pants, but now and then you'll land without a parachute.

"We managed to fix it, sort of," Bill said. "It was a big financial success." The film is basically true to the Garfield brand, but it's bland and without much of Bill's comedic spark. (Exception: the three songs he sings, especially the version of James Brown's "I Feel Good," where the movie lets him cut loose as Garfield the Lounge Singer.) Bill fans who watch it hoping for a bravura voice-over performance that subverts the whole enterprise, or even just provokes laughter, will be disappointed. They may even wonder just how incoherent the movie could possibly have been before Bill showed up.

"Do you have any regrets?" Bill (playing himself) was asked in *Zombieland,* just before he died.

His answer: "*Garfield,* maybe."

The Life Aquatic with Steve Zissou

(2004, Steve Zissou)

> "Well, if you'll excuse me, I'm going to go on an overnight drunk, and in ten days I'm going to set out to find the

shark that ate my friend and destroy it. Anyone who
would care to join me is more than welcome."

A movie unlike any other—if you've never seen a Wes Anderson movie. In this film, Anderson employed many of
his favorite devices—sets seen in cross-section, lavish refer-
ences to Jacques Cousteau, oil paintings of Bill Murray—
but this trip on the SS *Whimsy* felt like a slow cruise to
nowhere.

The cast is almost uniformly excellent: Bill plays Steve
Zissou, a world-weary oceanographer; Owen Wilson is an
Air Kentucky pilot who believes that Zissou is his father;
they are joined by Cate Blanchett, Anjelica Huston, Jeff
Goldblum, and Willem Dafoe. And it's stuffed full of
charming touches, from the matching uniforms of Team
Zissou to the David Bowie songs sung in Portuguese to Bill
rocking a Speedo. ("I made the acting choice to have a
little bit of a belly," Bill claimed, saying that he didn't think
Zissou would be buff. "I could have gotten in shape. I actually had to get a little bit out of shape. Which is not hard
for me.") So why didn't the movie work?

According to Bill, "Every single scene of that movie was
funny, but when Wes assembled it, he streamlined and ex-
cised the detonation point of the laughter. The idea is you
keep it bouncing and never skim the energy off of it. You
keep it building in the name of a big emotional payoff—
which comes when they're all in the submarine together
and they see the jaguar shark."

That's a generous reading of the problem, especially

considering how arduous the shoot was for Bill: Five months on location, in a movie where he was in almost every scene, made him think about quitting acting altogether. "The movie better be the greatest movie ever made," Bill said before it came out. "If it's not, I'm gonna kill Anderson. He's a dead man. If it's not the greatest movie ever made, or in the top ten, he may as well just move to China and change his name to Chin, and he better get himself a small room in a small town—and even then, I'll hunt him down."

Fortunately, Bill spared Wes Anderson's life.

Broken Flowers (2005, Don Johnston)

"I'm a stalker in a Taurus."

Jim Jarmusch, who like Bill Murray spent a formative six-month period of his life attending movies at the Cinémathèque Française, made an art film with Bill: a road movie without a clear destination, a movie where the silences weigh as heavily as the words, a color movie with a black-and-white soul. Bill plays Don Johnston (similarity to the *Miami Vice* actor's name very much intentional), an aging lothario who has cashed out of his business (something to do with computers). As the movie begins, his latest girlfriend (Julie Delpy) breaks up with him, leaving him to face life alone, which he does with a blank face that might denote depression or just Zen acceptance.

Don receives an unsigned letter from an ex telling him that he has a son, not quite nineteen years old, who may be coming to look for him. Hectored by his next-door neighbor Winston (Jeffrey Wright), who is as industrious as Don is passive, Don makes a list of five women who could be the mother of such a child. One, it turns out, has died, but he goes to visit the other four (Sharon Stone, Frances Conroy, Jessica Lange, Tilda Swinton—all giving powerhouse performances) to see what he can figure out about his son (if he actually exists) and his place in the universe.

"Just the very thought of someone my age going to visit old girlfriends had instant appeal," Murray said. "Even women think, 'That would be interesting.' Not comfortable, but interesting. It is not a comfortable film at any point." (It's the mirror version of *Mamma Mia!* If the title of *Broken Flowers* ended with a punctuation mark, it wouldn't be an exclamation point, but a colon with nothing after it but the unknown.) Bill agreed to make the movie on the condition that all the locations be within an hour's drive of his house in the Hudson Valley. Also helping with the close-to-home feeling: a cameo in the movie's final minutes by Bill's eldest son, Homer.

One morning, while shooting in the house they were using as the home of his character, Bill went on an unannounced excursion. Without explaining what he was doing, he left the set and walked across the street to another house: a home not rented by the film production or otherwise involved with it. Bill didn't knock on the door: He just opened it and walked in. "What do you do?" Jarmusch asked rhetorically. "Well, it's Bill; I'm not going to do anything."

Ten minutes later, Bill emerged with a plate of cookies that the neighbors had given him; he walked around and shared them with the crew. Jarmusch said, "What I would have liked to see was the people inside eating breakfast when Bill Murray walks in."

Bill's performance is a minor-key symphony: Handled wrong, the role could be flat or affectless, but he's expressive and nuanced as Don Johnston gradually opens himself up to a larger set of possibilities. "I never had a job like this one before," Bill said. "Usually, if you get the lead in a show, you're sort of driving the boat. But here, I never knew ahead of time how any of the actresses were going to play their scenes. So I had to be completely open and just react to them." Bill was so satisfied with his performance, he thought of retiring from acting altogether, reasoning that there was no way he would ever do better. "It was a perfectly written film, I acted as well as I've acted, it was edited perfectly, and I thought it was just a beautiful film," he said.

After six months or a year, Bill realized that while he had hoped another way to spend his life—"like organic gardening"—would turn up, it hadn't, so he might as well go back to work. But during those months that he was secretly retired, he went out on top.

The Lost City (2005, The Writer)

"I'm a stand-up comedian who prefers to remain seated."

Andy Garcia's sole feature film as a director was a passion project sixteen years in the making, telling the story of a Cuban nightclub owner buffeted by the 1950s revolution that brought Fidel Castro to power. It's sumptuously filmed and features some top-notch musical performances. It's also burdened with a clunky, ponderous screenplay; it takes two and a half hours to tell a story that was much more effectively rendered as a subplot in *The Godfather: Part II.*

Bill Murray knew Garcia from the Pebble Beach golf tournament. "He's a gent," Bill said, "though he's one of the slowest golfers on God's green earth." But that wasn't enough for Bill to commit to the part, he said. "What made the Andy movie happen is, my wife likes Andy: 'That's okay. Go work with him. He's a gentleman.' "

So Bill landed in this mess, playing a character known only as the Writer, a figure with no relevance to the plot, presumably meant to be an allegorical commentator, like a Shakespearean fool or the Stage Manager in *Our Town.* Bill doesn't have much to work with, but he does his best to hang some meat on those bones, and it's fun to see him dressed for the tropics in a tie, suit jacket, and shorts. He clowns around with a handheld fan, improvises wisecracks about a contortionist ("So just about any clothes fit you?"), and makes the most of his scenes with Dustin Hoffman (playing gangster Meyer Lansky) in a *Tootsie* roommate reunion. It's not clear whether Garcia cast Bill because he thought Bill was perfect for the role or because he knew the film shoot would be more fun with Bill there.

Garfield: A Tale of Two Kitties
(2006, Garfield)

> "When history speaks of me, and she will, I want to be remembered as the party prince."

The second *Garfield* movie was about as good as the first, and maybe even a little better. It helped, frankly, that there was less of Garfield: The movie, which involved a trip to England and a case of feline mistaken identity, was dominated by Scottish comedian Billy Connolly. In a constant state of high dudgeon, Connolly was a worthy successor to John Cleese.

Not learning his lesson after the first *Garfield* movie and/or cashing an extremely large check, Bill Murray returned to voice the sluggard cat. Once again, his work was professional but unremarkable, but this time Bill had an even unhappier experience recording his dialogue. "The second one was beyond rescue; there were too many crazy people involved with it," Bill said. He had asked the producers to let him vet the screenplay before they shot it and was indignant that they hadn't complied—although it's hard to imagine him reading the script if they had managed to get a copy to him. "They sort of shot themselves in the foot, the kidneys, the liver, and the pancreas on the second one," Bill said. "The girl, Jennifer Love Hewitt, she was sweet. In the second movie, they dressed her like a homeless person. You knew it wasn't going to go well."

The Darjeeling Limited
(2007, The Businessman)

"That's my train!"

By the time Wes Anderson made his fifth feature film, his tics had become familiar to moviegoers. But this story of three brothers (Owen Wilson, Jason Schwartzman, Adrien Brody) traveling on a train through India was more than the sum of his trademark mannerisms. The movie is extremely funny in Anderson's dry way—but it's also a deeply felt meditation on grief and its consequences. The three Whitman brothers are mourning the absence of their mother and the death of their father: For most of the movie, they're literally carrying his baggage around. Wilson's character is the one whose emotional damage is most readily visible; his face is scarred and bandaged after a motorcycle accident that was probably a suicide attempt.

Bill Murray's role in all this? He provides a fake-out in the movie's opening minutes, playing an agitated Western businessman in India, late for his train. Wearing a suit, tie, and hat, he leans forward in a speeding taxicab, checking his watch. When he finally makes it to the station and runs for the Darjeeling Limited as it pulls out of the station, he is overtaken by Brody. Bill misses the train and stands defeated on the platform: This movie's narrative is headed elsewhere. Bill was scheduled for three days of filming, which got completed in a day and a half—but since he was in India, he stayed for a full month.

Some people believe that Bill's character is meant to represent the father of the three brothers, but Anderson claims that as originally conceived, he was meant to symbolize American interests abroad, like Karl Malden in the old American Express commercials or maybe a CIA agent. How'd he convince Bill to take the role? "I ran into him in New York and he was asking me what I was going to do next," Anderson explained. "I told him that we had this cameo part that he probably wouldn't be able to do because he'd have to go to India and it wasn't even a cameo, more a symbol. But he replied, 'A symbol? I could do that.'"

Get Smart (2008, Agent 13)

"I get it. Who wants to talk to a guy in a tree?"

Hollywood took *Get Smart,* the 1960s spy-spoof TV show created by Mel Brooks and Buck Henry, and unwisely up-

dated it by adding lots of action set pieces and deempha-
sizing the comedy, making it feel like a minor-league
Mission: Impossible. The leads, Steve Carell and Anne
Hathaway, are both appealing, and the movie takes a
novel (okay, bizarre) approach toward their twenty-year
age gap, attempting to reduce the squick factor when they
become a couple: The plot claims that Hathaway's Agent
99 is actually substantially older but has had massive plastic surgery.

Bill Murray appears in a cameo role: Agent 13, who on
the show was played by Dave Ketchum and was always sta-
tioned in uncomfortable locations, such as the inside of a
cigarette machine. Here, he is assigned to duty inside a
tree with the explanation "Communications got knocked
out, so they put me in a tree." We see just Bill's face: He's
funny and needy and bitter in a scene lasting less than one
minute, and then he's gone.

The production wanted to cast somebody famous for
the role. Their first thought was Bill, but not having any
way to get in touch with him, they were going to explore
other possibilities—until costume designer Deborah Scott
(who had worked with Bill on *The Lost City*) overheard the
conversation, said Bill was a friend of hers, and volunteered to ask. Much to the surprise of everyone making
the movie, Bill agreed. On the set, he made it clear he had
no interest in doing the scene as written—he and Carell,
both veterans of Second City, improvised a dozen takes instead. Director Peter Segal remembers Bill asking of the

THE FILMS OF BILL MURRAY   283

scripted pages, "Do you want to do this scene? Or do you want it to actually be funny?"

City of Ember (2008, Mayor Cole)

"I love my city and everyone in it."

Before *The Hunger Games* and *The Maze Runner,* the state of the art of American teenage dystopia was *City of Ember:* first a hit YA novel, and then this flop movie. It was set in a city deep underground, which provided shelter from an unspecified disaster many generations earlier. Two centuries later, the subterranean dwellers are running out of food, but they've forgotten that they're supposed to return to the surface; the young heroes played by Saoirse Ronan and Harry Treadaway have to navigate a rickety plot and find the way.

The filmmakers got the script into Bill's hands, and he was intrigued when he saw that the screenwriter was Caroline Thompson, most famous for *Edward Scissorhands.* Many years earlier, when Bill's agent was encouraging him to take meetings with Hollywood screenwriters, Bill met Thompson—at a Mexican bar where a full orchestra was playing. "The temperature was about 130 degrees, and all people did was drink rum straight and dance," Bill remembered. "I thought, I could work with this writer." After receiving the screenplay, Bill called her up—she was riding a horse in the San Fernando Valley—and she vouched for the director, Gil Kenan. Bill watched Kenan's animated feature *Monster House* and "figured this guy's good enough to work with by my rigid standard."

Bill's mayoral character embodies corruption: In a city full of starving people, he's the only one with a potbelly. Bill is definitely the villain, and he plays that part with gusto. "It's so much easier to be a bad guy. It's a piece of cake," Bill said. "I keep saying, 'Why do they give Oscars to guys who play bad guys?' . . . Play a really decent, good person. *That's* hard." Bill doesn't just sneer and chew the scenery, though: He has moments where you see flashes of unexpected thought. For example, when he's about to walk onto his balcony to address the citizens of the city, you can see a split second where he turns a scowl into a beaming expression, putting on his public face. And when Lina (Ronan's character) escapes his clutches, just for a moment, a smile plays on Bill's lips. The quick grin is either because the mayor relishes the hunt for a young girl or because Bill enjoys being the antagonist.

Bill said he was influenced by knowing that his sons had read the book, and that led him to emphasize the mayor's hypocrisy: "I think a mayor can be a father figure who can disappoint you. I'm a father figure and I've probably disappointed on occasion," he said.

The Limits of Control (2009, American)

"What is your fucking agenda here? You people don't understand a fucking thing about how the world really works."

Just as *Ghost Dog* was Jim Jarmusch's version of a samurai movie and *Dead Man* was his version of a western, *The Limits of Control* was his version of a James Bond movie. A solitary assassin (Isaach de Bankolé) in an expensive suit makes his way through a colorful foreign landscape (Spain), on a mission to kill somebody he doesn't know; a beautiful naked woman (Paz de la Huerta) shows up in his bed, ready to kill him or screw him. The pace is languorous; the mood is philosophical; the relationship between reality and fiction is flexible. Jarmusch said that he was making an action film with no action.

There are a series of encounters where an eccentric character played by a famous actor (Tilda Swinton, John Hurt, Gael García Bernal) shows up and passes the killer a matchbox with coded instructions inside—after ritualistically checking that he doesn't speak Spanish, they then deliver monologues on hallucinations, or film, or bohemians. Bill Murray doesn't deliver a matchbox: He plays the assassin's target, a powerful American sequestered in a well-guarded fortress in rural Spain. Facing death in a soundproofed bunker, Bill is defiant and arrogant, lecturing his killer on how his worldview has been poisoned by fantasy and delusion. Bill's appearance is brief but memorable; when he takes off his hairpiece, he rests it on a human skull.

Jarmusch, who made two other movies with Bill (*Coffee and Cigarettes, Broken Flowers*), described how one motivates the actor: "Bill Murray has a valuable childlike part of him. Somebody asked, while we were shooting, 'How do you get Bill's attention?' I said, 'Well, if you sit down with some crayons and a coloring book and say, 'Look, Bill, I'm coloring. Isn't it fun?', he's not interested. But if you sit down and ignore him and you're coloring and he comes over and says, 'What are you doing?' And you say, 'Ehhh, I'm coloring.' He's like, 'Oh, can I color?' 'Yeah, let's color.' "

Fantastic Mr. Fox (2009, Badger)

> "Well, I guess we should probably split into a certain number of groups and start doing something, right?"

Wes Anderson adapted a Roald Dahl book: The resulting movie, made with stop-motion animation, was a total delight. The cast included George Clooney in the title role, Meryl Streep as his wife, Jason Schwartzman as their son, and Bill Murray as the family lawyer, a badger.

Anderson wanted the voice actors to interact, so rather than record them separately in a professional studio, he taped them on location: outside, underground, in a stable. That gives extra life to scenes, like the one where Bill's

Badger and Clooney's Mr. Fox circle each other, snarling and saying, "If you're going to cuss with somebody, you're not going to cuss with me, you little cuss!" ("Cuss," charmingly, is the movie's all-purpose curse word.)

For a minor supporting role, Bill put a lot of work into his performance, inspired by the fact that Wisconsin is known as the Badger State and using impressionist skills that hadn't gotten a heavy workout since his *SNL* days: "I first performed the Badger with a Wisconsin accent. I thought that was pretty appropriate. And it was a really, really strong Wisconsin accent. It was very good. Chris Farley would have been very proud of my accent. I listened to NPR, public radio of Wisconsin, for weeks. And I could bore you to death in that accent. But [Anderson] said, 'No, I just think that's a little bit too much.' But he was wrong."

Zombieland (2009, Himself)

> "I do it to blend in. You know. Zombies don't mess with other zombies. Buddy of mine, makeup guy, he showed me how to do this. Cornstarch. You know, some berries, a little licorice for the ladies. Suits my lifestyle. I like to get out and do stuff. Just played nine holes on the Riviera."

The second-funniest zombie comedy ever (after the unimpeachable *Shaun of the Dead*) stars Jesse Eisenberg, Emma Stone, Abigail Breslin, and Woody Harrelson as an unlikely crew making their way across a post-apocalyptic America in search of Twinkies and an amusement park. Halfway through, they break into a Beverly Hills mansion with "BM" on the gates: not Bob Marley, or Barry Manilow, but "the tippy-top of the A-list," Bill Murray.

Bill, it turns out, has survived the zombie onslaught, wearing zombie makeup so that the walking dead will leave him alone. He gets stoned with his gate-crashers, re-creates a *Ghostbusters* sequence with them (with Harrelson wearing an original jumpsuit and proton pack, and with Bill deploying a vacuum cleaner instead of a proton pack), and graciously accepts the praise of Harrelson, who plays an overexcited fan: "Six people left in the world—one of them is Bill Fucking Murray! I know that's not your middle name." Asked if his performance in that scene was a way of doing schtick about encounters with his own overwhelmed fans, Harrelson said no, his enthusiasm for Bill was sincere. Even international film stars can be reduced to gibbering fanboys in the presence of Bill Murray.

Bill wasn't the first choice for the scene: Originally, it was going to be Patrick Swayze, but he fell ill and had to pass. A parade of other actors declined, including Sylvester Stallone, Matthew McConaughey, Jean-Claude Van Damme, Joe Pesci, and Mark Hamill. With the scene about to get cut from the movie, Harrelson made the Hail Mary play of asking Bill: He had costarred with him in *Kingpin* but had no way of getting in touch with him other than calling his 1-800 number. But Bill called back right away, asking for pages to be faxed to a Kinko's in New York. Director Ruben Fleischer recalled, "We were saying that the person with the most important job in Hollywood that day was the kid working at Kinko's."

Bill said, "*Zombieland* came out of nowhere. It was like putting on an old coat and finding a couple hundred dollars in it." His appearance was an unexpected windfall for him and audiences alike, just like his appearance as himself in *Coffee and Cigarettes* six years earlier. Both movies suggest that even in the most bizarre circumstances, you might run into Bill Murray doing something improbable.

Get Low (2010, Frank Quinn)

> "I sold twenty-six of the ugliest cars ever made one December in Chicago with the wind blowing so hard up my ass, I was farting snowflakes in July."

"How does one get into the Bill Murray business?" producer Dean Zanuck asked Bill's attorney.

The discouraging reply: "Well, they don't."

Nevertheless, the makers of *Get Low* pursued Bill for their movie. They got him a synopsis, which led to Bill leaving an answering-machine message requesting that a screenplay be sent to a PO box, and then after several weeks of hearing nothing, director Aaron Schneider sent Bill a heartfelt letter. Bill says three things convinced him to make the movie: that letter, the making-of featurettes on the DVD of Schneider's Oscar-winning short film, *Two Soldiers* ("This really should be kept secret, but you can learn a lot by watching the making-of DVDs"), and the film's lead actor, Robert Duvall. Bill reasoned, "Well, no one's ever asked me to work with Robert Duvall before."

In *Get Low,* Duvall plays a bearded hermit who emerges from the backwoods of America sometime in the 1930s with a wad of cash, looking to pay for his funeral. The catch: He wants it to happen while he's alive, so he can attend. He ends up hiring a small-town funeral parlor. Bill is that funeral parlor's director, a man with loud socks and a hole in his shoes. His glib patter barely covers up the desperation he feels from running a failing business. "People are dying in bunches, everywhere but here," he complains. "One thing about Chicago, people know how to die."

Get Low has a central mystery (what's the hermit's secret?) and a redemptive character arc, but those elements feel rote. What makes the movie work is top-notch actors at work (the cast also includes Sissy Spacek), listening to each other and playing off each other's rhythms. Bill brought his A game to the role, with a perfect blend of despair and comic timing; in return, an admiring Duvall called him "a smart-ass with talent."

Passion Play (2011, Happy Shannon)

"I suppose you have another picture of a jackalope that
could be available for the right price."

It's the eyes. Even framed by tinted prescription glasses,
they communicate steely malice. Bill Murray's performance as crime boss Happy Shannon is understated and
menacing, but although everything else about his de-
meanor says "mild-mannered accountant," his eyes let
people know that this is not a man to be trifled with.

Passion Play, written and directed by Bill's longtime
friend Mitch Glazer, aimed for romantic poetry but ended
up as a soggy pile of pretension. Mickey Rourke played a
shattered trumpeter (but couldn't be bothered to learn
how to play the trumpet, or even how to mime it), while
Megan Fox played his love interest, a beautiful young
woman with wings who might just be a bona fide angel. Bill,
as the antagonist, gave the film a welcome jolt but couldn't
salvage it.

Bill was an emergency replacement. Three days into
the shoot, actor Toby Kebbell quit the movie (Glazer says it
was because he got cold feet about acting opposite Rourke,
his idol). Bill was chatting on the phone with Glazer, asking him how the movie was going; when Glazer explained
his predicament, Bill volunteered to play the part.

Glazer found himself balancing the preferences of his
two male stars: Rourke liked to do one or two takes, to
keep everything spontaneous, while Bill was just getting

warmed up after two takes, getting ready to play around and try some of his own ideas. "He scared Mickey to death, just how odd a villain he was," Glazer said. And those tinted glasses he wore in every scene? They were Glazer's own, with a prescription completely opposite Bill's own, which meant that Bill literally did the movie in a blur.

Moonrise Kingdom (2012, Mr. Bishop)

> "I'm sorry, can we get back to the rescue now?"

This Wes Anderson movie is a love story between two twelve-year-olds, Sam and Suzy, who run away together on a small New England island. The young couple treks through the wilderness and makes an idyll for themselves, but they can't escape from the authorities, a hurricane bearing down on the island, or a dogged troop of Khaki Scouts. It's funny, poignant, and altogether enchanting.

Bill Murray plays a supporting role, as Suzy's father, Walt. He's a lawyer married to another lawyer (Frances McDormand) who's not doing a very good job of concealing her affair with the island's police officer (Bruce Willis). Bill and McDormand have a great rapport: Their characters snark at each other, call each other "Counselor," and portray a marriage where familiarity replaced passion long ago.

Otherwise, Bill's job is to wander through the background in loud plaid pants (shirt optional) and become the image of enraged fatherhood when his daughter runs away with a boy. In his best moment, he does both at once, holding a bottle in one hand and an ax in the other and interrupting three young children playing Parcheesi with the announcement "I'll be out back. I'm going to find a tree to chop down."

Although the adult actors in the movie include Ed Norton, Tilda Swinton, and Harvey Keitel, Bill spent much of his time on the shoot hanging out with the younger performers, who included his son Cooper. Kara Hayward, the young actress who played Suzy, remembered a time when Bill posed for a photo with a tuba on his head—and then started to play the tuba. "He was actually very good," she said.

Bill filmed several promo videos for *Moonrise Kingdom,* including a tour of the sets that began with him looking into the camera and saying, "Oh, hello. I'm Bill Murray." Going through Wes Anderson's filmography, he got to *Bottle Rocket,* Anderson's feature debut—the only full-length movie the director has made without Bill—and admitted, "I still haven't seen that one." Bill observed that Anderson wears his pants very short: "So he likes everyone in the film to wear their pants really short, to look just a little bit like the kind of person you might want to mug." Bill concluded, "Here I am in a cardigan sweater, sitting here in Newport, Rhode Island, living la vida loca."

"I had wanted to have Bill Murray and Fran McDormand together," Anderson said. "I always have such a good time with him, and I've always loved what he did for my movies. I'm just lucky enough that so far, he doesn't pass on them."

A Glimpse Inside the Mind of Charles Swan III (2012, Saul)

> "Samurai helmet, fifteen thousand dollars. You can't afford that. I'm gonna return it."

Bill Murray's worst movie in over three decades was directed by Roman Coppola, who had co-written the screenplay for *Moonrise Kingdom* (and who is the brother of Sofia Coppola, who directed one of Bill's best movies, *Lost in Translation*). Starring Charlie Sheen as Charlie Swan—playing another variation on his caddish bachelor persona, in this case a graphic designer whose girlfriend recently walked out on him—the movie careens between Charlie's reality and his overactive fantasy life. Typical sequences: Charlie accepting an award from the Academy of Sexy Women or being pursued by an elite female military force of "ball busters." The production values are high, and Coppola convinced cool people like Jason Schwartzman, Patricia Arquette, and Aubrey Plaza to join the cast, but the whole thing is aimless, vaguely misogynistic, and plays like a fifth-rate *All That Jazz*.

Playing Charlie's accountant Saul, Bill's job was to look dour, wear brown, and warn Charlie of impending financial disaster. Bill hits his marks when he has dramatic material (Saul's marriage is on the rocks, we learn), and he brings energy to flagging comic bits, applying the hard-won experience that comes from being in dud *SNL* sketches that aired at 12:50 A.M.

Hyde Park on Hudson (2012, FDR)

"I'd say I'm sorry, but that wouldn't do any good right now, would it?"

Bill Murray plays Franklin Delano Roosevelt, the thirty-second president of the United States. In this film, set largely in 1939, he tries (1) to broker a closer relationship between England and the United States, with the King and Queen on a groundbreaking state visit to the U.S.A. and (2) to get a hand job from his cousin Daisy Suckley. He succeeds on both counts. The movie is narrated by Daisy (a fine performance from Laura Linney), who became one of FDR's mistresses, which gives it a point of view and circumscribes its ambition. The movie is well made but feels determinedly modest, like a low-key sequel to *The King's Speech* (the Oscar-winning movie from two years earlier, also featuring King George VI). Bill gives an engaging performance as Roosevelt, for example, but the character remains as distant and enigmatic at the end of the movie as he was at the beginning. Yet there are images that linger, such as an assistant carrying Roosevelt's polio-wracked body from one room to the next, while everyone pretends they don't notice the disability of the leader of the free world.

Many people were skeptical of director Roger Michell wanting to cast Bill as FDR—including Bill himself. Michell said that he cast Bill not as a stunt but because Bill possessed a "lethal combination of mischief and charm and forgivability." That personality fuels Bill, onscreen and offscreen, but it was also the source of FDR's political power: On a basic level, the American people found him likable.

Michell got a script to Bill via the "props girl" on the director's previous movie, *Morning Glory*. Then he waited a long time for Bill to call: a "deafening silence" that went on for several months. When the phone finally rang, "It was a bit like Howard Hughes calling you out of the blue." They had a good conversation, but Bill didn't commit for quite a while. Then one day, Michell got a text: "Dear Rog, I'm in!" Bill wrote, saying that he was in a van on the way to the Masters golf tournament in Augusta, Georgia, immersing himself in books on FDR. The movie's financiers, aware of Bill's habit of not signing contracts, were willing to accept a screen capture of that text as evidence that he would show up and make the movie.

Bill is a talented vocal impressionist—although unlike,

say, Meryl Streep, he doesn't often need to show off those capabilities for his film work. But he does excellent work here capturing FDR's clenched vowels and patrician accent, and he's always approached the impressionist part of his job with a technician's precision. Consider his analysis of newscaster Walter Cronkite's voice (whom he impersonated for an *SNL* bit): "He's projecting in the back of his throat, and he's not projecting high, so it's bouncing off the front of his throat and then back up and out."

For this movie, Bill learned to get around with crutches, calipers, and his upper body, just as FDR did after polio denied him the use of his legs. That aspect of his performance had personal resonance: His younger sister, Laura, contracted polio at a very young age, in an era when treatments included medieval methods such as immersing patients in scalding water. (As an adult, she still walks with a limp and has had to cope with some late-blooming symptoms.) In the 1980s, Bill described the experience of watching home movies with Laura when she could be seen walking with braces at age two as "like there was a jack on the inside of my brain that was spreading my skull apart." But although he always felt compassion for Laura, he gained a new, visceral understanding of what she had gone through once he spent a couple of days wearing braces: Both Laura and FDR were unendingly stoic while dealing with terrible physical pain. A couple of days into the production, Bill called his sister and told her, "I'm sorry. I'm sorry. I'm sorry. I never had any idea."

The Monuments Men (2014, Richard Campbell)

"Right now, you wish that German had shot you."

You know what you're getting with a movie directed by George Clooney: a cast full of his A-list pals; a brisk, light-on-its-feet narrative; and the inescapable sense that the people in the movie had a better time making it than you are having watching it. *The Monuments Men* is the Hollywoodified story of the U.S. military program in World War II to protect and recover the art treasures of Europe from the Nazis. Its heart is in the right place: The movie firmly believes that art and cultural heritage are worth fighting for (although it's not as certain on whether they're worth dying for).

The movie gets by on the strength of its cast (Cate Blanchett, John Goodman, Clooney himself) and some exquisite scenery. But it's severely underwritten; most of the characters are interchangeable, all art experts who are quick with a quip but too old to be going through basic training. Bill plays an architect from Chicago who's a grandfather. That's nice, but it's about all we learn about him or his temperament. That doesn't give him much to work with or do much to distinguish him from, say, Matt Damon's museum curator from New York who's a father of two. Bill does have a good rapport with Bob Balaban, who plays his partner in most scenes, and he gets an emotionally arresting moment when he hears a home recording of his grandchildren singing "Have Yourself a Merry Little Christmas."

Bill and Clooney became friends when they worked together on *Fantastic Mr. Fox* and then spent a couple of months hanging out together; making this movie together cemented the relationship. Bill was invited to Clooney's wedding to Amal Alamuddin in Venice in September 2014, and even gave a toast. "They were so beautiful," Bill said after. "She's a real beautiful girl and a real huge heart and she's a great humanitarian, and funny too. She's the funniest Lebanese since Danny Thomas."

The Grand Budapest Hotel
(2014, Monsieur Ivan)

> "Your train departs in four and a half minutes. Here's your tickets."

By the time of Wes Anderson's eighth feature film, it was a given that there'd be a part for Bill Murray. This time, it was a small supporting role as a concierge at the Excelsior Palace hotel, also a member of the elite concierge society known as the Society of the Crossed Keys. Bill imbued the part with an old-world charm and a bruised dignity, echoing Ralph Fiennes's magnificent performance as the concierge Gustave, who treats the Grand Budapest Hotel as a sacred responsibility.

The movie was an epic Anderson caper, with a prison break and a chase scene on a ski slope, but it was also filled with melancholy at the passing of a more elegant world and the ravages of war and time. The star-studded cast included F. Murray Abraham, Adrien Brody, Willem Dafoe, Harvey Keitel, Jude Law, Edward Norton, Jason Schwartzman, Tilda Swinton, and Owen Wilson; asked why all those people wanted to work with Anderson, Bill said, "It's long hours and little pay."

Bill said that, like most actors, he didn't want Anderson to give him line readings—"I have a problem with obedience, probably"—but he had come to understand that he had to say his dialogue with a certain "bounce."

"Usually people want to gravel it up, but it's not that way," Bill explained. "It's got to pop along because the script's really moving." He compared acting in Anderson's movies to playing guitar: "A young player can play it, and if he wants to play, like, a high note or a fast rhythm, it has a certain desperate quality to it. But when you get a really sophisticated player playing those notes, he can play those same notes in a tempo, but there's space in between it."

St. Vincent (2014, Vincent)

> "I'm showing him how the world works. You work, you get paid, you drink."

Bill Murray's bottom line on what needed to happen with *St. Vincent* for it to be a great film: "I just thought if we could avoid being schmaltzy." His verdict: "We almost did."

Bill, always an astute judge of his own work, was right:

St. Vincent is a good movie that, without some mawkish moments, might have been an excellent one. Bill is superb in a role originally offered to Jack Nicholson: Vincent MacKenna is a crusty, hostile Vietnam vet with a working-class New York Irish accent and weaknesses for booze, betting on horses, and Russian prostitutes (well, at least the one played by Naomi Watts). Inevitably, the movie humanizes him (he befriends the young boy next door) and reveals his secret sorrows (he has a wife with Alzheimer's), but felling Vincent with a stroke and putting him through recovery seems like a bit much.

Even when the plot gets sentimental, Bill's performance is cranky and idiosyncratic. An unexpected highlight is in the closing credits: Bill with a Walkman on, singing along to "Shelter from the Storm," from Bob Dylan's *Blood on the Tracks*. Bill drifts in and out of the lyrics while smoking a cigarette, reclining on an old lounge chair, and spraying a backyard patch of dirt aimlessly with a garden hose—and you can't look away.

On the last day of shooting *St. Vincent,* Melissa McCarthy was supposed to leave slightly early—she was scheduled to depart at 5:00 P.M. so she could catch a plane to L.A. and get back to work on the sitcom *Mike & Molly.* Murray didn't just rib her for cutting out: He presented her with a large cake, inscribed: "To Melissa, thanks for staying as long as you did." McCarthy appreciated the joke—and when she stayed on the set longer than expected and missed her plane, the cake tasted even sweeter.

The day after *St. Vincent* had its world premiere in Toronto, Bill told me, "When I looked at it, I saw the whole family lineage—the way everyone moves. I saw my brother, my father, my grandpa." Bill remembered the way his grandfather used to scare small children, by removing his dental work: "He used to pop his choppers out."

Bill got emotional while watching the movie; even when you know its every twist and turn, it has some wallop. He found himself starting to cry, and he knew something in the core of his being: When the lights came up at the end of the movie, he did not want everyone to see that his own performance had moved him to tears. "I really had to pull it together," he confided. "I'd rather start stabbing myself in the stomach with a pen than cry."

Olive Kitteridge (2014, Jack Kennison)

> "You can't throw that bleeding-heart crap at me. You're just as intolerant as I am."

At first, this four-hour miniseries seems as if it's going to be the sort of domestic drama where a husband and wife glare at each other across the kitchen table the whole time. But while there's plenty of frost in the air between Frances McDormand (playing the prickly title role) and Richard Jenkins (as her genial pharmacist husband), there's also humor, surrealism, and some deeply moving sequences centered on mortality and suicide.

Bill Murray becomes a significant player in the final

half hour of *Olive Kitteridge:* His character, Jack, is a Republican widower with a silver Porsche. His lifestyle and worldview are totally at odds with Olive's austere Maine outlook. But when Olive finds him lying on the ground by a bicycle path—he's fallen off a park bench and is unsure if it's worth the effort to ever stand up again—they forge a tentative friendship, with nothing in common except for the fundamental fact that they are still alive.

We see Jack at a very specific moment in his life, not long after the death of his wife. He's wallowing in familiar pleasures, from wine to Rush Limbaugh's radio show, but he has no appetite. He's proud—too proud to reconcile with his estranged daughter—and confused and devastated by grief. And sometimes, because his life is absurd and he can't help himself, he is funny. Reunited with McDormand, his *Moonrise Kingdom* costar, Bill takes a small role and turns it into a tone poem of sorrow.

Director Lisa Cholodenko (*The Kids Are All Right*) was excited to be working with Bill but worried that he would run roughshod over her, so she handled him carefully on the set. "I was very diplomatic, warm, and didn't give him too much fodder to tease me in public or in front of my crew."

Olive Kitteridge ended up winning eight Emmys, including a best-supporting-actor statue for Bill—who didn't show up at the ceremony because he was in Philadelphia for the wedding of his son Luke. That weekend, Bill was spotted not just at the formal wedding events but also at many of Philadelphia's finest dive bars.

Dumb and Dumber To (2014, Ice Pick)

"Best day ever. Greatest day of my life, really."

For better and for worse, Bobby and Peter Farrelly craft their movies as delivery systems for outrageous gags. When one of their movies works, it provides belly laughs; when it doesn't, it's just a belly flop. While Jim Carrey and Jeff Daniels reprising their moron characters twenty years after the original *Dumb and Dumber* had box-office appeal, way too many jokes in this sequel (i.e., almost all of them) were misfires.

Bill Murray made a cameo, working with the Farrelly brothers for the third time. And he was fine with his scene appearing in the final cut, unlike Jennifer Lawrence, who reportedly also filmed a scene for the movie but then asked for it to be removed (possibly because she saw the movie and realized how bad it was). The joke: Ice Pick (Bill's character) is living with Harry (Jeff Daniels's character) and has turned their kitchen into a meth lab, but dim-witted Harry thinks that Ice Pick is just cooking up cappuccino and rock candy. The meta-joke: Bill is costumed like Walter White in *Breaking Bad,* with a full-body hazmat suit and a gas mask, rendering him almost completely anonymous. It's one of the least recognizable uses of a major Hollywood star since George Clooney appeared on an early episode of *South Park* as the gay dog Sparky, with no dialogue beyond barking.

Peter Farrelly explained how they cast Bill: "Since you never see Ice Pick, we were thinking, 'Hey, we should get someone who's iconic to do it.' And who's more iconic than Bill Murray?" The idea was just perverse enough to appeal to Bill, and casting him had fringe benefits: "Anytime you have Bill Murray on the set, everybody on the crew is happy. So we wanted to bring Bill in just so we could hang around him."

When Bill's day of shooting was done, the Farrelly brothers asked him how much he wanted to be paid. He looked around the set and spotted some furniture used in a scene at the "Blue Crab Motel": beds with crustacean headboards. "Where do you get those crab beds?" he asked. Informed that they had been custom-made for the movie, he said, "Just give me those." So when the shoot was done, he received a special delivery: crab beds.

Aloha (2015, Carson Welch)

"Speak to me in subservient English."

Aloha, Cameron Crowe's best movie since *Almost Famous* in 2000, has a lot going on: a romantic triangle, issues of native Hawaiian culture and appropriation, a teenage daughter whose parentage has long been concealed, communication satellites as boons and banes. The result is excessive but well intentioned, much like the foot of Bradley

Cooper's character, which had an extra big toe grafted onto it after he got caught in the crossfire of a gunfight in Afghanistan.

In an all-star cast including Rachel McAdams, John Krasinski, Danny McBride, and Emma Stone (excellent but utterly miscast as Allison Ng, a woman of one-quarter Hawaiian, one-quarter Chinese ethnicity), the standout cameo belongs to Alec Baldwin as a perpetually furious Air Force general. Bill Murray was encouraged to join the cast by Stone (who had remained friendly with him after *Zombieland*); he plays the movie's villain, an unshaven tech billionaire who has a biographer following him around and is given to fatuous pronouncements such as "The future isn't just something that happens." Bill is fully believable in the role, which requires him to be charismatic, erratic, and inscrutable. But his best scene is at the holiday mixer at the military base where he shows off his dance moves to Daryl Hall & John Oates's "I Can't Go for That (No Can Do)."

By the end of the movie, Bill has turned into a Bond-style super-villain, which is approximately where the movie goes off the rails. Offscreen, however, he was looking after Stone, who was suffering from sleep problems and an acne condition during the shoot. He would bring her gifts to cheer her up: a key chain, a visor, some slippers, Maui Onion potato chips.

Rock the Kasbah (2015, Richie Lanz)

"I am not a loser. I am a quitter."

Mitch Glazer saw his friend Bill Murray in a dramatic role—he thinks it was *Broken Flowers*—and left the movie thinking that "his acting was so powerful and minimal, but it wasn't every arrow in his quiver." He wanted to see Bill in a big, outrageous comedic role again, so he wrote *Rock the Kasbah,* where Bill starred as Richie Lanz, a washed-up rock promoter who gets stranded in Afghanistan when his client flees a USO tour. "It was everything I've ever wanted to see him do, including sing 'Smoke on the Water' to Pashtun tribesmen," Glazer said.

It took seven years for the movie to get made: movie-studio executives were nervous about a comedy set in Afghanistan, even before ISIS started beheading people. But eventually they got a green light for the minimal budget of $15 million. Director Barry Levinson signed on, as did Zooey Deschanel (as the client who goes AWOL), Kate Hudson (as a "hooker with an ass of gold," as Glazer's script described her), Danny McBride (as a low-level arms dealer), and, in the crucial role of a young Afghan woman with a dream of appearing on *Afghan Star,* her nation's version of *American Idol,* Leem Lubany. Bruce Willis played a tough-as-nails American mercenary with dreams of writing a bestselling memoir; he and Bill have a great rapport, especially when they're improvising dialogue about Richie's romantic history with Danielle Steel.

Shareef don't like it, the Clash informed us in "Rock the Casbah," and neither did many film critics, who found the movie both slapdash and trivializing of the Afghan conflict. But the movie's flaws are worth overlooking because there's a hugely entertaining Bill performance at the center. He tells bullshit stories about Stevie Nicks and Eddie Money; he rocks a denim shirt and turquoise beads; he talks his way out of impossible situations. The most Bill-ish moment might be an extended sequence that runs during the closing credits: Negotiating the purchase of souvenirs with a merchant who doesn't speak English, Bill dithers and ends up buying multiple balls of string. The actor playing the merchant really didn't speak English— off the top of his head, Bill improvised a monologue and gradually filled his hands with string, creating a scene that could be in a Buster Keaton movie.

"It was great working in Morocco, where my phone didn't work," Murray said. "That was living. There was no Internet service in the desert. And so I had a very good time just focusing on the job, and I think we did unbeliev-able work."

Bill Murray being Bill Murray, he didn't just work, of course. One day during the shoot, while the lighting crew was setting up a shot, Levinson joined Bill on one of his walkabout expeditions: strolling through crowds, wander-ing into bars, exploring a new city. Levinson mentioned living in L.A., and Bill said, "No, it's not for me." When Levinson asked why, Bill told him, "I need to be some-where where I can just bump into things."

On weekends, Bill would gather a crowd (including Glazer and his wife, Kelly Lynch, and two of Bill's six sons) and head out on Moroccan road trips, in a "party bus" with blue disco lights installed. One favorite destination: the beach town of Essaouira. "It's apparently where Jimi Hendrix wrote 'Castles Made of Sand,' or that's the legend," Glazer said. "And it's beautiful: camels on the beach. We'd all be singing on the bus, and it was like summer vacation." They also visited the Medina in Fez, a dizzyingly crowded bazaar. "He would just dive into the middle of it as if he knew where the hell he was," Glazer reported. "There are locals still wandering around looking for ways to get out of the Medina. You want to turn around and retrace your steps, and that's when Bill goes deeper. Saying he made the most of it is putting it too mildly."

Glazer continued, "Bill doesn't use celebrity as his backstage pass. He connects with people even if they don't recognize him." In Morocco, Bill visited a local business: a tannery, where skins are rendered into leather. "It smells like a slaughterhouse," Glazer said. "They give you sprigs of mint to hold up under your nose because the smell is so brutal." Bill zeroed in on the woman sitting behind the counter at reception: a middle-aged Muslim woman. To entertain her, he stuck the mint up his nose and then sat on her lap. She had no idea who this strange American man was, but she laughed so hard, she started to cry.

A Very Murray Christmas (2015, Himself)

> "You look like you'd like to have your photograph taken with me. I notice that that seems to really cheer people up."

"Bill is so full of fun, it brightens up the holiday," said Sofia Coppola, who directed *A Very Murray Christmas*. "Everyone is happy when they see him, and he knows how to bring joy." The subtext: Bill Murray is our twenty-first-century Santa Claus, showing up everywhere and spreading good cheer to all, regardless of whether they're naughty or nice.

Or as Bill puts it at the end of a production number with George Clooney and a troupe of dancers (dubbed "the Murray-ettes" by Coppola), "I am the *king* of Christmas!"

The plot of this hour-long special: Bill is supposed to star in a live Christmas special, singing seasonal songs at the Carlyle hotel in New York City, but a huge snowstorm means that none of his celebrity-friend guests, such as Clooney, can make it. Initially mired in a sour mood, he ends up befriending (and singing songs) with other people stranded in the hotel, like Rashida Jones and Jason Schwartzman, who play a couple who have had to cancel their wedding because none of the guests could make it. (Other guest stars include Chris Rock, Amy Poehler, and Miley Cyrus.)

"It's a Rat Pack view of the saddest Christmas turning into the happiest Christmas ever," said Paul Shaffer, the special's musical director.

Coppola worked with Bill for the first time since 2003's *Lost in Translation* (also set in a hotel!); the spark was Coppola's desire to see Bill sing torch songs for a week at the Carlyle. When she started working with Bill and Mitch Glazer, the original idea was to do a Valentine's Day special, which turned into a Christmas special.

They filmed it on location in New York City in just four days, which accentuated the spontaneity in Bill's performance. Many of the musical numbers were done for the first time live on the set: When Maya Rudolph sings a killer version of Darlene Love's anthem "Christmas (Baby, Please Come Home)," you can actually hear Bill laughing with delight and surprise in the background, witnessing it for the first time.

Having traded in irony for so long, Bill gives unexpected weight to Christmas sentiment here (in a way that he didn't in *Scrooged*); at the end, when he delivers an understated line reading of "Merry Christmas, everyone," Bill seems sincere, and he finds the emotion behind the cliché.

"The show is really sincere, but then we're being playful with it," Coppola said. "I think it has a lot of heart, because Bill has a lot of heart."

The Jungle Book (2016, Baloo)

"You have never been a more endangered species than you
are at this moment."

Jon Favreau's just so-so version of *The Jungle Book* triangu-
lates the cinematic territory between Rudyard Kipling's
stories (published between 1893 and 1895), the Walt Disney animated film from 1967, and a twenty-first-century
blockbuster. The movie looks like live action in a lush jungle, but except for Neel Sethi, the young actor playing
Mowgli, it's all computer animation.

The animals that help and hinder Mowgli are voiced by
stars like Christopher Walken, Ben Kingsley, and Idris
Elba—and as Baloo the bear, Bill Murray. Bill's a natural at
playing a slothful, gluttonous grifter with a heart of gold,
and he does a fine job with Baloo's trademark song, "The
Bare Necessities." His performance is hampered, however,
by his CGI-rendered bear looking much faker than the
rest of the jungle's featured creatures. Whenever Baloo
speaks, it feels like we're hearing Bill Murray in a recording studio, not a bear in the Indian jungle. Bill's personality is bigger than the movie.

Director Jon Favreau had unsuccessfully pursued Bill
for a part before—he wanted him to play the bad guy in
the first *Iron Man* movie, a role that Jeff Bridges ended up
with. This time, Favreau joked, "I put the note in the hollow log in the forest," and Bill signed on. "I get it now,"

he said of Bill's methods after working with him. "He's completely available when you're in direct contact. He's an incredibly authentic, generous person who understands who he is, what he represents to everybody. He embraces it."

Acknowledgments

I am lucky enough to have many excellent people to thank.

Thank you to Caitlin McKenna, a gold-medal editor who has been granted more than her fair share of diligence, patience, and publishing acumen. Her eye has made this book better in hundreds of ways. And many thanks to all her excellent colleagues at Random House, especially Christine Mykityshyn, Sally Marvin, Tom Perry, Andy Ward, Avideh Bashirrad, Leigh Marchant, Alaina Waagner, Katie Rice, Joelle Dieu, Denise Cronin, Toby Ernst, Rachel Kind, Robbin Schiff, and Vincent La Scala.

Thanks also to Liz Cosgrove for her sparkling design, to Derek Eads for his delightful cover art, and to Kathy Lord for her diligent copyediting.

My agent Daniel Greenberg is a mensch and a wizard—this book wouldn't exist without him and his sage advice. I am grateful to him and everyone at the Levine-Greenberg-Rostan Agency, especially Tim Wojcik, Miek Coccia, and Melissa Rowland.

I have been a fan of Robert Sikoryak for a quarter of a century, ever since I read "Good Ol' Gregor Brown," his brilliant mash-up of Charles Schulz and Franz Kafka in the pages of *Raw*. I am honored that he contributed to this book, delighted by how much fun he was to work with, and awed by the genius illustrations that resulted. (He, in turn, would like to thank his wife, Kriota Willberg.)

A huge salute to everyone who spoke to me about the time they had spent with Bill Murray (years for some people, minutes for others): Michael K. Allio, Lee Briccetti, Kyra Bromley, Peter Chatzky, Sofia Coppola, Jordan Dann, Joseph Davenport, David Gault, Mitch Glazer, Diana Green, Andrew Groothuis, John Knizeski, Barry Levinson, Joe Levy, Ayoka Lucas, Trine Licht, Lyle Lovett, Melissa McCarthy, Dan McLaughlin, Brett McKee, Ted Melfi, Massie Minor, Becca Daniel Noyes, Joe Printz, Ivan Reitman, Danny Rubin, E. J. Rumpke, Paul Shaffer, Carol Sharks, David W. Smith, Pam Tietze, Tyler Van Aken, and Naomi Watts. And thanks to Tina Fey and Hugh Laurie for sharing their insights on the careers of Lorne Michaels and Cary Grant (respectively) with me.

Many people helped me with my research, either by pointing me in the right direction or by politely letting me know when I had taken a wrong turn. An equally huge thank-you to René Auberjonois, Jon Carroll, Alex Cox, Denise Cronin, Deirdre Dod, Meryl Emmerton, Andy Fischer, Joe Fritsch, Joe Gross, David Handelman, Marjorie Ingall, Megan Kashner, Ben McGrath, Emily Nussbaum, Jennifer O'Connor, Kira Pace, Abby Royle, Alan Schwarz, Hillary Seitz, Morgan Sorne, Jimi Turco, and Bumble Ward. And my special thanks to Jessica Jernigan for generously granting permission to quote from her interview with Bill Murray where he told the story of Elvis Presley's funeral.

I should thank librarians in general, but I would especially like to single out the staffs of the Margaret Herrick Library (of the Academy of Motion Picture Arts and Sciences), the central branch of the Los Angeles Public Library, the special collections of the UCLA Library, and the central branch of the Brooklyn Public Library. Their help was invaluable.

Before I had any inkling that I would be writing this book, I interviewed Bill Murray for *Rolling Stone* and got a taste of what it's like tracking him down for a movie: Months of waiting ended when I got a phone call telling me to get on a plane to Toronto the following day. Thanks to Sean Woods, who edited that article; Caryn Ganz and David Fear, who edited subsequent pieces I wrote about Bill for the *Rolling Stone* website; and many other excellent *Rolling Stone* editors and staffers, past and present, including Jason Fine, Nathan Brackett, Will Dana, Gus Wenner, Brandon Geist, Coco McPherson, Christian Hoard, Simon Vozick-Levinson, Andy Greene, Chris Weingarten, Hank Schteamer, Jason Newman, Alison Weinflash, and especially Jann S. Wenner.

Thanks to Kim Barrett of the Weinstein Company, who is in show business—without her, that original interview wouldn't have happened.

Rob Sheffield is John Winger to my Russell Ziskey, and Egon Spengler to my Peter Venkman. He provided invaluable feedback on the manuscript of this book, as did Bill Tipper, who is overflowing with insight, wit, and seltzer. Armed with surrealism and bravery, James Hannaham has long been my ally in a strange world. It devastates me that I no longer live five minutes away from Steve Crystal, who is a kindred spirit and a perpetual inspiration. Robert Rossney has a generous soul, an astonishing mind, and the rare ability to shuffle stacks of board-game tiles. I am honored and humbled by their friendship.

I will long remember the kindness and hospitality of Rita Kashner and the late Howard Kashner, who graciously hosted me when I was doing research for this book in the Hudson Valley. Thank you.

I don't have enough words for my awe-inspiring wife, Jen Sudul Edwards, but I am eternally grateful for the joy and love she brings into my life. All my love to her, our sons, Strummer and Dashiell, and the rest of my family, especially my parents; Nick; Julian and Sharon; Miranda and Will; Aunt Lis; Tim, James, and Chris; Megan, Trina, Zane, and Tessa; and Alex and Cynthia and Big Al.

When I was halfway done with this book, we moved across the country from Los Angeles to Charlotte, North Carolina—I drove thousands of miles in a car with Rob Sheffield, a chinchilla, and a didgeridoo. I am grateful for so many people who have helped make Charlotte into a new home, including Massoud and Sherrill Shiraz, Jeff Jackson, Gillian and Mike Allen, Beth Troutman Whaley and Craig Whaley, Mike Corressell, Philip and Jody Lomac, Michael Solender, Cherie and J. D. DuPuy, Lea Harkins,

Rob and Erin Janezic, Donald White, Andy Smith, Alan Michael Parker and Felicia van Bork, Jerald and Mary Melberg, Murray and Kathleen Whisnant, Ena Swansea, Jim McGuire, Kevin Lamp, and the Pepper family. Also: the entire staff of the Bechtler Museum of Modern Art, particularly John Boyer, Shannon White, and Christopher Lawing.

In the past year, when I was surrounded by unpacked boxes and piles of manuscript pages, I was especially grateful for the following people all over the world, who made life better in many ways, sometimes just by being their badass selves: Luke Bailey-Wong, Melissa Bailey-Wong, Lily Burana, Shayne Bushfield, Terry Castle, Tom Castle, Nick Catucci, May Chen, Theresa Claire, Shannah Clarke, John Collins, Scraps de Selby, Steve Doberstein, Philip Farha, Julie Farman, Shary Flenniken, Ted Friedman, Karl Gajdusek, Joe Greene, Christine Street Gregg, David Gregg, Matthew Hawn, Molly Ker Hawn, Joanne Heyman, Katie Hollander, Xandra Kayden, Jason Lehmbeck, Leah Lehmbeck, Kate Lewis, Colin Lingle, Moby, Chris Molanphy, Brendan Moroney, Tom Nawrocki, Morgan Neville, Nettie Neville, Susan Schnur, Ally Sheffield, Syd Sidner, Ben Smith, Brian Smith-Sweeney, Sabrina Smith-Sweeney, Clive Thompson, Pam Thurschwell, and Marc Weidenbaum.

Thanks to everybody who is making the world into a more Bill Murray place. If you've made it this far in the acknowledgments, that probably includes you. It certainly includes the big toe himself, Mr. Bill Murray. He's set up his life so that he doesn't have to be bothered by projects like this book, so I thank him for the time he spent talking with me, sharing secrets and explaining himself. Beyond that, I am profoundly grateful that Bill has lived his life the way that he has. Writing this book was a constant joy, both because I kept finding one wonderful story after another and because those stories have served as an inspiration to me not to live my own life on autopilot. Thank you, Bill Murray.

Sources

If you want to know where I got my information, you're in the right place. And if you have a true Bill Murray story of your own that you want to share, send it to me at gavin42@gmail.com.

Author's Note

Cohen, Richard, *Monsters: The 1985 Chicago Bears and the Wild Heart of Football,* Farrar, Straus and Giroux, New York, 2013.

Raab, Scott, "Good Luck," scottraab.com, April 25, 2016.

Young, Alex, "Bill Murray Is Not Legally Allowed to Steal Back Wu-Tang's Album, But He Should Anyways," consequenceofsound .net, December 10, 2015.

"Yeronisos Island Expedition," www.yeronisos.org/Yeronisos_Field _Expedition/ExecU-Dig_Program.html.

Introduction

PAGES 3-7

Interview with Melissa McCarthy.

Interview with Dan McLaughlin.

Fierman, Dan, "Bill Murray Is Ready to See You Now," *GQ*, August 2010.

Hyde, Lewis, *Trickster Makes This World: Mischief, Myth, and Art,* Farrar, Straus and Giroux, New York, 1998.

PAGES 7-24

Interview with Tina Fey.

Interview with Bill Murray.

Interview with Ivan Reitman.

Borrelli, Christopher, "Sister Act," *Chicago Tribune,* April 23, 2009.

Connelly, Christopher, "The Man You Are Looking for Is Not Here," *Premiere,* August 1990.

Crouse, Timothy, "The Rolling Stone Interview: Bill Murray," *Rolling Stone* 428, August 16, 1984.

Davis, Robert, "News Briefs," *Chicago Tribune,* September 22, 1970.

Ebert, Roger, "Bill Murray, 'Quick Change' Artist," *Chicago Sun-Times,* July 13, 1990.

English, T. J., "The King of Comedy," *Irish America,* November 1988.

Felton, David, "Bill Murray: Maniac for All Seasons," *Rolling Stone* 263, April 20, 1978.

Fierman, Dan, "Bill Murray Is Ready to See You Now," *GQ,* August 2010.

Grossberger, Lewis, "Bill Murray: Making It Up as He Goes," *Rolling Stone* 350, August 20, 1981.

Hill, Doug, and Jeff Weingrad, *Saturday Night: A Backstage History of Saturday Night Live,* Beach Tree Books/William Morrow, New York, 1986.

Hirschberg, Lynn, "Bill Murray, in All Seriousness," *The New York Times,* January 31, 1999.

Martin, Brett, "Harold Ramis Gets the Last Laugh," *GQ,* July 2009.

Murray, Bill, with George Peper, *Cinderella Story: My Life in Golf,* Doubleday, New York, 1999.

"One More Reason to Love Bill Murray," thesmokinggun.com, September 20, 2010.

Perrin, Dennis, *Mr. Mike: The Life and Work of Michael O'Donoghue,* Avon Books, New York, 1998.

Puskar, Susan, "Murray's 'Scrooge' Role That of a Creep," *Toledo Blade,* December 18, 1988.

Raab, Scott, "Bill Murray: The ESQ+A," esquire.com, May 22, 2012.

Rader, Dotson, "Life Is Easier If You Can Share the Burdens," *Parade,* February 21, 1999.

Rashad, Ahmad, "Behind the Scenes with Bill Murray," back9network .com, October 8, 2014.

Schnakenberg, Robert, *The Big Bad Book of Bill Murray: A Critical Appreciation of the World's Finest Actor,* Quirk, Philadelphia, 2015.

Thomas, Mike, *The Second City Unscripted: Revolution and Revelation*

at the World-Famous Comedy Theater, Northwestern University
Press, Evanston IL, 2009.

"Times London Encounters Bill Murray," rushmoreacademy.com,
October 22, 2009.

Fantastic Four episodes: https://archive.org/details/Fantastic
Four-10Episodes.

PAGES 24-32

Interview with Bill Murray.

"Bill Murray Accused of Drug, Spouse Abuse," thesmokinggun.com,
May 29, 2008.

Coyle, Jake, "Bill Murray: Divorce Was 'Devastating,'" Associated
Press, November 7, 2008.

Hirschberg, Lynn, "Bill Murray, in All Seriousness," *The New York
Times,* January 31, 1999.

Labrecque, Jeff, "Bill Murray: Curious Case of Hollywood's White
Whale," ew.com, August 27, 2013.

Martin, Brett, "This Guy Could Be President," *GQ,* January 2013.

Murray, Bill, with George Peper, *Cinderella Story: My Life in Golf,*
Doubleday, New York, 1999.

Pearce, Garth, "Old Stone Face Cracks," *The Guardian* (UK), October 21, 2005.

Raab, Scott, "The Master: Bill Murray," *Esquire,* December 2004.

Seitz, Matt Zoller, *The Wes Anderson Collection,* Abrams, New York,
2013.

Charlie Rose, January 29, 1999, archived on *Rushmore* DVD, Criterion, 2000.

PAGES 32-36

Interview with Joe Levy.

Interview with Ayoka Lucas.

Interview with Brett McKee.

Interview with Bill Murray.

Interview with Ivan Reitman.

Correspondence with Danny Rubin.

Bill Murray at "Bill Murray Day" in Toronto, September 5, 2014.

Rosenbaum, Ron, "Bill Murray, Secret Zen Master," *New York Ob-
server,* August 12, 1996.

Commentary track on *Groundhog Day* DVD, Sony Pictures, 2002.

The Ten Principles of Bill

Hochberg, Mina, "Bill Murray on *Get Low, Ghostbusters 3,* and That Time He Washed a Guy's Dishes," vulture.com, July 30, 2010.

THE FIRST PRINCIPLE: OBJECTS ARE OPPORTUNITIES.

Stockholm:

Associated Press, "Bill Murray Cruises Through Stockholm in Golf Cart," August 22, 2007.

Collett-White, Mike, "Bill Murray Explains That Golf Cart Incident," reuters.com, September 3, 2007.

Late Show with David Letterman, November 2, 2007.

Wabash College:

Thomas, Mike, *The Second City Unscripted: Revolution and Revelation at the World-Famous Comedy Theater,* Northwestern University Press, Evanston, IL, 2009.

Pub crawl:

Late Night with Seth Meyers, November 27, 2014.

VW Super Beetle:

Hirschberg, Lynn, "Bill Murray, in All Seriousness," *The New York Times,* January 31, 1999.

Shales, Tom, and James Andrew Miller, *Live from New York: An Uncensored History of Saturday Night Live,* Little, Brown, Boston, 2002.

Bill Murray Meets the Youth of America:

Interview with Keith M. Jones.

Popcorn:

Interview with Trine Licht.

Charleston cigarette:

Interview with Joseph Davenport.

THE SECOND PRINCIPLE: SURPRISE IS GOLDEN. RANDOMNESS IS LOBSTER.

Lobster on the loose:

Interview with Ivan Reitman.

Slow-motion walk:

Interview with David W. Smith.

Tales from the Grape D'Vine:

Interview with Joe Printz.

Murray Christmas:
  twitter.com/r_roddy_piper/status/412632248454631424.

Wrong numbers:
  Miller, Prairie, "The Life Aquatic: Bill Murray Interview," rotten
    tomatoes.com, March 26, 2007.

Sergio Leone:
  Hornaday, Ann, "Bill Murray Talks About FDR, Ambition, and the
    Power of Saying 'No,'" *The Washington Post,* December 6, 2012.
  Streeter, Michael, *Nothing Lost Forever: The Films of Tom Schiller,*
    BearManor Media, Boalsburg, PA, 2006.

On the Dark Side:
  Conrad, Harold, "At Large with Bill Murray," *Smart,* July/August
    1989.
  White, Timothy, "The Rumpled Anarchy of Bill Murray," *The New
    York Times,* November 20, 1988.

Making Out in Japanese:
  "Bill Murray Teaches Japanese": www.youtube.com/watch?v=2ttJ-c
    _A9zE.
  Geers, Todd & Erika, *Making Out in Japanese,* Yenbooks, Tokyo,
    1988.
  Murray, Bill, "Bill Murray Here: OK, I'll Talk! I'll Talk!," AMA ("Ask
    Me Anything") on reddit.com, January 17, 2014.
  The Graham Norton Show, "Episode 213," BBC One (UK), Febru-
    ary 14, 2014.

Banana peels:
  Interview with Melissa McCarthy.

Wrigley Field 1990:
  Richmond, Peter, "The Sports Fan," *The National,* August 30, 1990.

INTERLUDE: VOICE OF HAROLD
  Interview with Ivan Reitman.
  Apatow, Judd, *Sick in the Head: Conversations About Life and Comedy,*
    Random House, New York, 2015.
  Friend, Tad, "Comedy First," *The New Yorker,* April 19, 2004.
  Labrecque, Jeff, "Groundhog Day: My Favorite Bill Murray Story,"
    ew.com, February 2, 2012.
  Martin, Brett, "Harold Ramis Gets the Last Laugh," *GQ,* July 2009.

Martin, Brett, "This Guy Could Be President," *GQ,* January 2013.

Meyers, Kate, "Wild Man Bill Murray," ew.com, March 19, 1993.

Murray, Bill, "Bill Murray Here: OK, I'll Talk! I'll Talk!," AMA ("Ask Me Anything") on reddit.com, January 17, 2014.

Ramis, Harold, "We Are Stardust, We Are Frozen," *Premiere,* February 1993.

Thomas, Mike, *The Second City Unscripted: Revolution and Revelation at the World-Famous Comedy Theater,* Northwestern University Press, Evanston, IL, 2009.

THE THIRD PRINCIPLE: INVITE YOURSELF TO THE PARTY.

Elvis Presley funeral:

Jernigan, Jessica Lee, "Archival Interview: Bill Murray," jessica leejernigan.typepad.com, August 9, 2004 (originally published May 1999).

MC Hammer:

Mitchell, Elvis, "Being Bill Murray," *Cigar Aficionado,* November/December 2004.

Harvard-Cornell game:

Finocchiaro, Peter, "Uh, What Was Bill Murray Doing at Cornell This Weekend?," ivygateblog.com, October 10, 2011.

McLaughlin, Claire M., "Bill Murray Conducts the Harvard Band (In Pink Shorts!)," thecrimson.com, October 9, 2011.

Williamsburg party:

Huddleston, Tom, "Bill Murray Talks FDR, Cheese, and the Meaning of Life," *Time Out London,* January 29, 2013.

"Is Bill Murray New York City's New Party Boy?" *Page Six Magazine (New York Post),* December 9, 2008.

Wedding photos:

Interview with Ashley Donald.

Bobby Vinton:

Time Out, episode 135, October 5, 1984, archived at mediaburn.org.

Bill Murray Meets the Youth of America:

Interview with E. J. Rumpke.

Texas City Stars:

Neyer, Rob, "Bill Murray's Baseball Summer: An Oral History," Just a Bit Outside, foxsports.com, February 16, 2015.

Kickball:

> Cockenberg, Marina, "Interview: Bill Murray Crashed Our Kickball
> Game," collegehumor.com, October 15, 2012.
> Martin, Brett, "This Guy Could Be President," *GQ*, January 2013.
> "Playing Kickball on Roosevelt Island," billmurraystory.com, October 2012.

THE FOURTH PRINCIPLE: MAKE SURE EVERYBODY ELSE IS INVITED TO
THE PARTY.

Moonrise Kingdom party:

> Yuan, Jada, "Vulture Dances with Bill Murray at Cannes," vulture
> .com, May 17, 2012.

Garry Trudeau:

> Buxton, Ryan, "Garry Trudeau Explains the Complicated Process of
> Casting Bill Murray," huffingtonpost.com, October 27, 2014.

Tales from the Grape D'Vine:

> Interview with Joe Printz.

Jimmy Buffett in Aspen:

> Interview with Kyra Bromley.

Martha's Vineyard engine trouble:

> Interview with Massie Minor.

Bill Murray Meets the Youth of America:

> Harris, Will, "Random Roles: Jami Gertz," The A.V. Club, November
> 7, 2012.

Sister Nancy:

> Borrelli, Christopher, "Sister Act," *Chicago Tribune*, April 23, 2009.

Gilda's farewell party:

> Schindehette, Susan, and Jeannie Park, Victoria Balfour, Alan
> Carter, Leslie Strauss, Mark Zwonitzer, Michael Alexander, Tom
> Cunneff, and Vicki Sheff, "Saturday Night Live!" *People*, September 25, 1989.
> Shales, Tom, and James Andrew Miller, *Live from New York: An Uncensored History of Saturday Night Live*, Little, Brown, Boston, 2002.

INTERLUDE: IT'S HARD TO BE A SAINT IN THE CITY
Interview with Ted Melfi.

D'Allesandro, Pete, "St. Vincent Writer/Director Ted Melfi Talks About His New Dramedy Starring Bill Murray," finaldraft.com, 2014.

Mandell, Andrea, "Read What It's Like Casting Bill Murray in a Movie," *USA Today,* September 5, 2014.

Shoard, Catherine, "The Gospel According to Bill Murray," *The Guardian* (UK), November 20, 2014.

Steinberg, Don, "How Bill Murray Was Wooed by a Hollywood No-Name," *The Wall Street Journal,* September 30, 2014.

Whipp, Glenn, "How to Hire Bill Murray," *Los Angeles Times,* September 5, 2014.

THE FIFTH PRINCIPLE: MUSIC MAKES THE PEOPLE COME TOGETHER.

Karaoke:

John, "What If Bill Murray Just Showed Up in Your Karaoke Room?" thechive.com, January 5, 2011.

Letterman's first show:

Interview with Paul Shaffer.

Abrams, Brian, *And Now . . . An Oral History of "Late Night with David Letterman," 1982–1993,* Amazon Digital Services, 2014.

Merrill, Sam, "The Playboy Interview: David Letterman," *Playboy,* October 1984.

Clint Eastwood:

"Bill Murray & Clint Eastwood rock out!": www.youtube.com/watch?v=FClSLcHutDs.

Elvis Mitchell: Under the Influence, "Bill Murray" episode, broadcast on TCM, 2008.

On the Dark Side:

Interview with Ivan Reitman.

"Duck" Dunn:

Huddleston, Tom, "Bill Murray Talks FDR, Cheese, and the Meaning of Life," *Time Out London,* January 29, 2013.

Newport hotel piano:

Interview with Andrew Groothuis.

INTERLUDE: THE FRIENDLY CONFINES

Charney, Noah, "Bill Murray on Drinking, the Red Sox, and Making Men Weep," esquire.com, October 24, 2013.

Downey, Mike, "Nothing Was Sacred During Murray's Stint as Cubs' Harry for Day," *Los Angeles Times,* April 20, 1987.

Reiter, Bill, "As Rick Sutcliffe Fights Cancer, He Treasures the Connection with His Hometown the Most," *The Kansas City Star,* May 27, 2008.

Sutcliffe, Rick, "What Will You Remember Most About Shea Stadium?" espn.com, September 26, 2008.

"Expos vs. Cubs Highlights," www.youtube.com/watch?v=H3TtEx2 WOOg.

THE SIXTH PRINCIPLE: DROP COIN ON THE WORLD.

Sturgeon:

Brozan, Nadine, "Chronicle," *The New York Times,* July 30, 1994.

Crouse, Timothy, "The Rolling Stone Interview: Bill Murray," *Rolling Stone* 428, August 16, 1984.

Bill Murray Meets the Youth of America:

www.youtube.com/watch?v=FkAI2isftgM.

Groundhog Day Danish:

The Tobolowsky Files, episode 29, at slashfilm.com, May 28, 2010.

Blind golfer:

Murray, Bill, with George Peper, *Cinderella Story: My Life in Golf,* Doubleday, New York, 1999.

Tales from the Grape D'Vine:

Interview with Joe Printz.

Barbecue sandwiches:

Rahman, Ray, "Tours Gone Wild: Backstage Tales," *Entertainment Weekly,* May 30, 2014.

THE SEVENTH PRINCIPLE: BE PERSISTENT, BE PERSISTENT, BE PERSISTENT.

Road House:

Harris, Will, "Random Roles: Kelly Lynch," The A.V. Club, October 15, 2012.

Martin, Brett, "This Guy Could Be President," *GQ,* January 2013.

Sign Your Name:

Interview with Peter Chatzky.

Interview with Becca Daniel Noyes.

Conrad, Harold, "At Large with Bill Murray," *Smart,* July/August 1989.

Pereira, Alyssa, "Bill Murray Autographs 'Miley Cyrus' on Fan's Head, Calls St. Louis Cardinals 'Satan's Messengers,'" live105 .cbslocal.com, July 9, 2015.

Garrison Golf Club:

Earl, David, "Bill Murray," *Golf,* August 1990.

Questlove:

Rosenthal, Jeff, "The Roots Perform Cereal-Themed Set, Tell Weird Bill Murray Story," rollingstone.com, June 26, 2014.

Sands, Darren, "Q&A: Questlove on Winning Three Grammys, the Glory of Esperanza Spalding, and Having His Parties Closed Out by Bill Murray," villagevoice.com, February 16, 2011.

On the Dark Side:

Hirschberg, Lynn, "Bill Murray, in All Seriousness," *The New York Times,* January 31, 1999.

Cubs in Florida:

Keller, Tom, "Murray Visits with Cubs Prior to Finale," mlb.com, September 27, 2007.

INTERLUDE: POETRY IN MOTION

Interview with Lee Briccetti.

Akbar, Kaveh, "Gerald Stern," divedapper.com, July 13, 2015.

Collins, Billy, *Billy Collins Live: A Performance at the Peter Norton Performance Space, April 20, 2005,* Books on Tape, 2007.

Haber, Leigh, "That Time Bill Murray Read Us His Favorite Poems," *O,* April 2016.

Mercogliano, Ann, "Poets and Bill Murray Walk Across Brooklyn Bridge," pix11.com, June 8, 2015.

Stern, Gerald, *Stealing History,* Trinity University Press, San Antonio, 2012.

Vanmetre, Elizabeth, "Bill Murray Leads Hundreds of Poets Across Brooklyn Bridge for Annual Walk," New York *Daily News,* June 9, 2015.

Jimmy Kimmel Live!, March 31, 2016.

"Gathering Paradise": www.poetshouse.org/watch-listen-and-discuss/watch/gathering-paradise-bill-murray.

THE EIGHTH PRINCIPLE: KNOW YOUR PLEASURES AND THEIR PARAMETERS.

Grays Harbor Loggers:

Interview with Ivan Reitman.

Grossberger, Lewis, "Bill Murray: Making It up as He Goes," *Rolling Stone* 350, August 20, 1981.

Neyer, Rob, "Bill Murray's Baseball Summer: An Oral History," Just a Bit Outside, foxsports.com, February 16, 2015.

Acid in Telluride:

Interview with David Gault.

Bill Murray Meets the Youth of America:

Interview with Jordan Dann.

Greater Milwaukee Open Pro-Am:

Murray, Bill, with George Peper, *Cinderella Story: My Life in Golf,* Doubleday, New York, 1999.

Fact Checkers Unit:

Miller, Liz Shannon, " 'Premature' Director Dan Beers on Wooing Bill Murray, Lessons Learned from Wes Anderson and Finding Heart in Hard-On Jokes," indiewire.com, July 2, 2014.

St. Paul Saints:

Karlen, Neal, *Slouching Toward Fargo: A Two-Year Saga of Sinners and St. Paul Saints at the Bottom of the Bush Leagues with Bill Murray, Darryl Strawberry, Dakota Sadie, and Me,* Avon, New York, 1999.

Tales from the Grape D'Vine:

Interview with Joe Printz.

Making out with Bill Murray:

Interview with Pam Tietze.

INTERLUDE: EVERY GRAIN OF SAND

Acquisto, Charles, *Tap Room Tales: A Clambake Collection from Golf's Greatest Pro-Am,* Amazon Digital Services, 2011.

Diaz, Jaime, "Send in the Clowns," *Sports Illustrated,* February 13, 1995.

Dusek, David, "Bill Murray Ready to Defend Title at Pebble Beach Pro-Am," golf.com, February 7, 2012.

Garner, James, and Jon Winokur, *The Garner Files: A Memoir,* Simon & Schuster, New York, 2012.

Malcolm, Chris, "Putter Nonsense: Anything Can Happen When Bill Murray Hits Pebble Beach," *Chicago Tribune,* February 10, 2005.

Murray, Bill, with George Peper, *Cinderella Story: My Life in Golf,* Doubleday, New York, 1999.

Newman, Bruce, "Pebble Beach Celebrities," *San Jose Mercury News,* February 12, 2015.

Purdy, Mark, "It's a Cinderella Story for Actor Bill Murray at the AT&T Pebble Beach National Pro-Am," *San Jose Mercury News,* February 13, 2011.

Stewart, Jerry, "Tales from Those Who Are Lucky Enough to Play a Part in Murray's Act," *Monterey Herald,* February 8, 2012.

Stewart, Jerry, "A Timeline of Bill Murray's Best Moments at the AT&T Pebble Beach National Pro-Am," ncga.org, December 16, 2014.

Van Sickle, Gary, "Back in Business," *Sports Illustrated,* February 10, 1997.

Van Sickle, Gary, "Top Banana at the Pebble Beach Pro-Am," *Sports Illustrated,* February 17, 2003.

Verdi, Bob, "Murray Laughs Off Pebble Beach," *Chicago Tribune,* January 30, 1992.

THE NINTH PRINCIPLE: YOUR SPIRIT WILL FOLLOW YOUR BODY.

Leaping for the check:

Felton, David, "Bill Murray: Maniac for All Seasons," *Rolling Stone* 263, April 20, 1978.

Hasty Pudding Society:

Interview with Michael K. Allio.

Associated Press, "Bill Murray Honored by Hasty Pudding Club," February 20, 1985.

Tales from the Grape D'Vine:

Interview with Joe Printz.

The Finger Lakes:

Abrams, Brian, *And Now . . . An Oral History of "Late Night with David Letterman," 1982–1993,* Amazon Digital Services, 2014.

Walking the dog:

Interview with John Knizeski.

Sex scene:

Interview with Naomi Watts.

Hendrickson, John, "Bill Murray Made Naomi Watts Crack Up During a Sex Scene, Of Course," esquire.com, March 5, 2015.

Bill Murray Meets the Youth of America:

Interview with Diana Green.

Sigourney Weaver:

Conrad, Harold, "At Large with Bill Murray," *Smart,* July/August 1989.

Labrecque, Jeff, "Bill Murray: Curious Case of Hollywood's White Whale," ew.com, August 27, 2013.

Skydiving:

Coyle, Jake, "Bill Murray: Divorce Was 'Devastating,'" Associated Press, November 7, 2008.

Elder, Robert K., "Bill Murray on Sky Diving, Movie, Politics," *Chicago Tribune,* October 9, 2008.

THE TENTH PRINCIPLE: WHILE THE EARTH SPINS, MAKE YOURSELF USEFUL.

Washing dishes in Scotland:

Hochberg, Mina, "Bill Murray on *Get Low, Ghostbusters 3,* and That Time He Washed a Guy's Dishes," vulture.com, July 30, 2010.

Wynne-Jones, Jonathan, "Bill Murray Turns Fiction into Fact," *The Telegraph* (UK), October 15, 2006.

Traffic jams:

English, T. J., "The King of Comedy," *Irish America,* November 1988.

On the Dark Side:

Grieve, Cayte, "Bill Murray Pushes Green Bay Fan at Playoff Game, Calls Ray Nitschke a Pussy," *BlackBook* (bbook.com), January 28, 2011.

Grateful Dead show:

Mohr, Ian, "Bill Murray Helps Cleaning Crew After Grateful Dead Show," *New York Post,* July 7, 2015.

Tending bar at the Shangri-La:

Interview with Tyler Van Aken.

Paine, Jake, "GZA: Drunken Master," hiphopdx.com, March 22, 2010.

"Bill Murray Bartending at SXSW 2010": vimeo.com/33287283.

Michael Ovitz:

Hirschberg, Lynn, "Bill Murray, in All Seriousness," *The New York Times,* January 31, 1999.

Steakhouse bet:

Granger, David, and Scott Raab, "We Gave Bill Murray a Ride in From the Airport," *Esquire,* May 2016.

Bill Murray Meets the Youth of America:

Interview with Keith M. Jones.

Tia Carrera:

Gross, Joe, "Bill Murray Makes Local Band's Night," austin360.com, March 17, 2012.

Taxicab saxophonist:

Interview with Bill Murray.

Bill Murray at "Bill Murray Day" in Toronto, September 5, 2014.

THE TAO OF BEING YOURSELF: BILL MURRAY DAY

Bill Murray at "Bill Murray Day" in Toronto, September 5, 2014.

The Films of Bill Murray

A note for completists and sticklers: This book covers all of Bill Murray's significant movie roles but excludes some blink-and-you'll-miss-them uncredited appearances (*Next Stop, Greenwich Village* and *She's Having a Baby*) and some early voice work for cartoons (*The Missing Link* and *Tarzoon: Shame of the Jungle*). It includes one-shot projects that were released on television, such as *The Rutles, Olive Kitteridge,* and *A Very Murray Christmas,* but not Bill's work with ongoing TV series (for example, his appearances as the dead mayor in *Parks and Recreation,* as a substitute teacher in *Square Pegs,* as an indicted senator in *Alpha House,* as a grocery clerk in *Angie Tribeca,* and in a wide variety of roles on four seasons of *Saturday Night Live*). Bill's characters' names are rendered here as they appear in the films' credits. The dialogue quoted at the beginning of each entry was all spoken by Bill.

All You Need Is Cash:

Commentary track on *The Rutles: All You Need Is Cash* DVD, Rhino Theatrical, 2001.

Meatballs:

Interview with Ivan Reitman.

Bill Murray and Mitch Glazer at "Bill Murray Day" in Toronto, September 5, 2014.

Where the Buffalo Roam:

Murray, Bill, with George Peper, *Cinderella Story: My Life in Golf,* Doubleday, New York, 1999.

Caddyshack:

"19th Hole" documentary on *Caddyshack* DVD, Warner Home Video, 2010.

Martin, Scott, *The Book of Caddyshack: Everything You Ever Wanted to Know About the Greatest Movie Ever Made,* Taylor Trade, Lanham, MD, 2007.

Shales, Tom, and James Andrew Miller, *Live from New York: An Uncensored History of Saturday Night Live,* Little, Brown, Boston, 2002.

Stripes:

Interview with Ivan Reitman.

Meyers, Kate, "A Bill Murray Filmography," ew.com, March 19, 1993.

"Stars & Stripes," a short film on the *Stripes (Extended Cut)* DVD, Sony Pictures Home Entertainment, 2005.

Tootsie:

Schruers, Fred, "Isn't He Romantic?," *Premiere,* October 2003.

"A Better Man," on the *Tootsie 25th Anniversary Edition* DVD, Sony Pictures Home Entertainment, 2008.

Ghostbusters:

Interview with Ivan Reitman.

Breznican, Anthony, " 'Ghostbusters' Live-Read Grabs Seth Rogen, Jack Black, and Rainn Wilson," ew.com, December 11, 2012.

Labrecque, Jeff, "Ghostbusters: An Oral History," ew.com, November 14, 2014.

Nothing Lasts Forever:

Streeter, Michael, *Nothing Lost Forever: The Films of Tom Schiller,* BearManor Media, Boalsburg, PA, 2006.

The Razor's Edge:

Interview with Bill Murray.

Crouse, Timothy, "The Rolling Stone Interview: Bill Murray," *Rolling Stone* 428, August 16, 1984.

Tighe, K., "Found in Translation," *San Francisco Bay Guardian*, August 8, 2006.

Little Shop of Horrors:

Commentary track on *Little Shop of Horrors* DVD, Warner Home Video, 2000.

Scrooged:

Interview with Tina Fey.

Christie, James, *You're the Director . . . You Figure It Out: The Life and Films of Richard Donner*, BearManor Media, Boalsburg, PA, 2010.

Ebert, Roger, "Bill Murray, 'Quick Change' Artist," *Chicago Sun-Times*, July 13, 1990.

Ghostbusters II:

Goldstein, Patrick, "Return of the Money-Making Slime," *Rolling Stone* 553, June 1, 1989.

Quick Change:

Connelly, Christopher, "The Man You Are Looking for Is Not Here," *Premiere*, August 1990.

Jernigan, Jessica Lee, "Archival Interview: Bill Murray," jessicaleejernigan.typepad.com, August 9, 2004 (originally published May 1999).

What About Bob?:

Koltnow, Barry, "Murray Became the Annoying Man," *Deseret News*, May 21, 1991.

Martin, Brett, "This Guy Could Be President," *GQ*, January 2013.

Rabin, Nathan, "Random Roles: Richard Dreyfuss," The A.V. Club, October 8, 2009.

Shales, Tom, and James Andrew Miller, *Live from New York: An Uncensored History of Saturday Night Live*, Little, Brown, Boston, 2002.

Groundhog Day:

Ramis, Harold, "We Are Stardust, We Are Frozen," *Premiere*, February 1993.

Commentary track on *Groundhog Day* DVD, Sony Pictures, 2002.

Ed Wood:

Hirschberg, Lynn, "Bill Murray, in All Seriousness," *The New York Times*, January 31, 1999.

McKenna, Kristine, "The Playboy Interview: Tim Burton," *Playboy*, August 2001.

Kingpin:

Guerrasio, Jason, "The Farrelly Brothers on Their 7 Most Memorable Scenes," esquire.com, March 3, 2015.
Commentary track on *Kingpin* DVD, MGM, 1999.

Larger Than Life:

Mitchell, Elvis, "Being Bill Murray," *Cigar Aficionado*, November/December 2004.
Pearce, Garth, "Old Stone Face Cracks," *The Guardian* (UK), October 21, 2005.

Space Jam:

Interview with Ivan Reitman.

The Man Who Knew Too Little:

Interview with Hugh Laurie.
Commentary track on *The Man Who Knew Too Little* DVD, Warner Home Video, 1998.

Wild Things:

"An Understanding Lawyer" on *Wild Things* DVD, Sony Pictures Home Entertainment, 2002.
Commentary track on *Wild Things* DVD, Sony Pictures Home Entertainment, 2002.

Rushmore:

Murray, Bill, and Wes Anderson, "Funny Men," *Interview*, February 1999.
Charlie Rose, January 29, 1999, archived on *Rushmore* DVD, Criterion, 2000.

Cradle Will Rock:

Murray, Bill, with George Peper, *Cinderella Story: My Life in Golf*, Doubleday, New York, 1999.

Charlie's Angels:

Maher, Kevin, "Bill Murray: Do Not Disrespect the Oddball," *The Times* (UK), October 16, 2009.
Silverman, Stephen M., " 'Charlie's' Bedeviled," *People*, October 1, 1998.

Smith, Adam, "I Was Headbutted by Bill Murray," *The Guardian* (UK), May 29, 2009.

Hamlet:

Anderson, Jeffrey M., "Interview with Ethan Hawke & Michael Almereyda," *Combustible Celluloid,* May 4, 2000.

The Royal Tenenbaums:

Everett, Cory, "NYFF: Wes Anderson & Cast of 'Royal Tenenbaums' Talk the Challenges of Working with Gene Hackman," The Playlist, indiewire.com, October 15, 2011.

Lost in Translation:

Interview with Sofia Coppola.

Hirschberg, Lynn, "Bill Murray, in All Seriousness," *The New York Times,* January 31, 1999.

"A Conversation with Bill Murray and Sofia Coppola," *Lost in Translation* DVD, Focus Features, 2004.

Garfield: The Movie:

Fierman, Dan, "Bill Murray Is Ready to See You Now," *GQ,* August 2010.

Murray, Bill, "Bill Murray Here: OK, I'll Talk! I'll Talk!," AMA ("Ask Me Anything") on reddit.com, January 17, 2014.

The Life Aquatic with Steve Zissou:

Martin, Brett, "This Guy Could Be President," *GQ,* January 2013.

Raab, Scott, "The Master: Bill Murray," *Esquire,* December 2004.

Broken Flowers:

Douglas, Edward, "Interview: Bill Murray Checks Into the Grand Budapest Hotel," comingsoon.net, February 14, 2014.

Pearce, Garth, "Old Stone Face Cracks," *The Guardian* (UK), October 21, 2005.

Winters, Laura, " 'Flowers' Arranger," *The Washington Post,* July 31, 2005.

The Lost City:

Mitchell, Elvis, "Being Bill Murray," *Cigar Aficionado,* November/December 2004.

Garfield: A Tale of Two Kitties:

Murray, Bill, "Bill Murray Here: OK, I'll Talk! I'll Talk!," AMA ("Ask Me Anything") on reddit.com, January 17, 2014.

The Darjeeling Limited:

"The Darjeeling Limited—Wes Anderson Interview," IndieLondon, 2007.

Get Smart:

Billington, Alex, "Follow-Up Interview: *Get Smart*'s Director Pete Segal," firstshowing.net, June 20, 2008.

City of Ember:

"Talking to City of Ember Mayor Bill Murray," comingsoon.net, October 9, 2008.

The Limits of Control:

"Broken Flowers: The Writer/Director: Q&A with Jim Jarmusch," cinema.com, 2009.

Fantastic Mr. Fox:

Bill Murray at "Bill Murray Day" in Toronto, September 5, 2014.

Zombieland:

Carroll, Larry, " 'Zombieland' Writers Tell the Hilarious Story Behind Bill Murray's Bizarre Cameo," mtv.com, February 5, 2010.

Raab, Scott, "Bill Murray: The ESQ+A," esquire.com, May 22, 2012.

Commentary track on *Zombieland* DVD, Sony Pictures Home Entertainment, 2010.

Get Low:

Douglas, Edward, "Robert Duvall, Bill Murray and Sissy Spacek Get Low," comingsoon.net, July 28, 2010.

Fierman, Dan, "Bill Murray Is Ready to See You Now," *GQ*, August 2010.

Commentary track on *Get Low* DVD, Sony Pictures Home Entertainment, 2012.

Passion Play:

Smith, Krista, "Q&A: Mitch Glazer on Megan Fox, Mickey Rourke, and His New Miami Gangster Series," vanityfair.com, May 6, 2011.

Moonrise Kingdom:

Goodsell, Luke, "Interview: Kara Hayward on *Moonrise Kingdom*," rottentomatoes.com, June 15, 2012.

Lemunyon, Kristin Joy, "Wes Anderson on 'Moonrise Kingdom': 'Why Bill Murray Agreed to Do It, I Don't Know,' " hypable.com, May 15, 2012.

"Bill Murray Hosted Tour of Moonrise Kingdom": www.youtube
.com/watch?v=m-8OOvf1NPY.

Hyde Park on Hudson:

Felton, David, "Bill Murray: Maniac for All Seasons," *Rolling Stone*
263, April 20, 1978.

Phillips, Michael, "Bill Murray Scoffs at Doubt," *Chicago Tribune*, December 13, 2012.

White, Timothy, "The Rumpled Anarchy of Bill Murray," *The New
York Times*, November 20, 1988.

Commentary track on *Hyde Park on Hudson* DVD, Focus Features,
2013.

The Monuments Men:

Maresca, Rachel, "Bill Murray Reveals He Spoke at George Clooney,
Amal Alamuddin's Wedding," New York *Daily News*, October 7,
2014.

The Grand Budapest Hotel:

Douglas, Edward, "Interview: Bill Murray Checks Into the Grand
Budapest Hotel," comingsoon.net, February 14, 2014.

St. Vincent:

Interview with Melissa McCarthy.

Interview with Bill Murray.

Q&A with cast after world premiere of *St. Vincent*, Toronto, September 5, 2014.

Olive Kitteridge:

Middleton, Josh, "Bill Murray Misses Emmys to Party in Philly All
Weekend," phillymag.com, September 21, 2015.

Miller, Liz Shannon, "Lisa Cholodenko on Getting Under the Skin
of Frances McDormand's 'Olive Kitteridge,'" indiewire.com, November 2, 2014.

Dumb and Dumber To:

Fox, Jesse David, "Watch Bill Murray Do His Best Walter White Impression," vulture.com, November 13, 2014.

Smith, Patrick, "Peter Farrelly Interview: 'Jon Stewart Was Nearly
the Lead in There's Something About Mary,'" *The Telegraph*
(UK), December 18, 2014.

Aloha:

Miller, Julie, "How Bill Murray Cheered Up Emma Stone on the Set of *Aloha*," vanityfair.com, May 28, 2015.

Rock the Kasbah:

Interview with Mitch Glazer.

Interview with Barry Levinson.

Interview with Bill Murray.

A Very Murray Christmas:

Interview with Sofia Coppola.

Interview with Paul Shaffer.

The Jungle Book:

Raab, Scott, "Good Luck," scottraab.com, April 25, 2016.

Sperling, Nicole, "Jon Favreau on 'The Jungle Book,' His Lead Actor, and Tracking Down Bill Murray," ew.com, April 15, 2016.

The Tonight Show with Jimmy Fallon, April 6, 2016.

Index

About the Author

GAVIN EDWARDS is the *New York Times* bestselling author of eight books, including *Last Night at the Viper Room, Can I Say* (written with Travis Barker), *VJ* (written with the original MTV VJs), and *'Scuse Me While I Kiss This Guy*. As a longtime contributing editor for *Rolling Stone*, he has written a dozen cover stories for the magazine, traveled the world from Bahrain to New Zealand, and taken a city bus to the Grammys. He lives in Charlotte, North Carolina, with his wife and their two sons.

rulefortytwo.com

@mrgavinedwards